The Complete
Book of Dreams

The Complete Book of Dreams

Edwin Raphael

foulsham
LONDON • NEW YORK • TORONTO • SYDNEY

foulsham

The Publishing House, Bennetts Close
Cippenham, Berkshire, SL1 5AP, England.

ISBN 0-572-01714-6

Copyright © 1992 and 1996 W. Foulsham & Co. Ltd.

Phototypeset in Great Britain by Typesetting Solutions, Slough, Berks.
Printed by St Edmundsbury Press Ltd, Bury St Edmunds, Suffolk.

Introduction

For thousands of years, man has been fascinated by the world of dreams. Confusing and unnerving or starkly clear, even those who profess to be sceptics are intrigued to find the meaning of a recurring or particularly vivid dream. And although occasionally we come across people who can truthfully tell us that they cannot remember a dream, this does not mean that they do not dream. We all dream.

Throughout history, dreams have always been held to have the greatest significance, although people in the past had as much disagreement on their actual meaning as they do today. It used to be thought that the mind departed to strange and wonderful worlds during sleep, where the dreamer found new discoveries and gleaned new knowledge. Often, the dream is seen as a method of communication – bringing a message from God, as in so many famous dreams in the Bible, or foretelling the future. Psychologists value the interpretation of dreams as indicative of the mental state of their patients, believing that dreams are the re-sorting of information, facts, fears and stresses absorbed by the conscious mind.

But before we begin to look at this fascinating subject of dreams and their interpretation in more detail, it is important to realise that these curious mental experiences belong to two very distinct classes. There are dreams which are merely the result of physical discomfort, and there are dreams which might be better described as visions.

Any mental disturbance that is due to a purely physical cause cannot possibly carry a meaning, and must be ignored by those who wish to learn how to deal with real meanings.

First among the physical dreams we can place those horrible experiences known as nightmares, which are almost always due to digestive trouble. This causes an irregular supply of blood to the brain and also, no doubt, an impure supply. Either or both of these troubles will prove sufficient to cause a nightmare, which can always be distinguished by the extravagance and impossibility of the happenings through which the dreamer appears to pass.

There is, however, a great difference between impossible happenings and improbable events. The improbable dreams deserve investigation, for they are often of the nature of visions, whereas the really impossible can be ignored as due to some physical cause.

Sometimes, however, a perfectly possible event will figure as a dream, yet it may be due to a simple physical cause. A man who was a strong believer in dreams had a vivid experience one night, when he believed that he was out in the desert, pursued by a lion, who was so close to him all the time that the animal was constantly biting him in the thigh, though never able to overtake him.

When he awoke, he was sweating profusely and was deeply impressed by what he took to be a dream of warning. However, when he got up he found that his false teeth had somehow slipped into the bed, so that in reality he had been biting himself all the time, thus inducing this particular dream.

Many people believe that a persistent dream in which the same incident is repeated, though the details may vary considerably, must be a warning of great importance. This is doubtful, however, if the dream recurs more than a few times and is really persistent, the cause is most likely to be a traumatic event in the past. An example of this is a lady who regularly suffered the same ghastly dream. Her husband knew when this was the case because of her terrified screams. In this case, however, it turned out that as a girl the woman had been involved in an unpleasant incident which resulted in two girls being expelled from her school, although she herself escaped this fate. She had been so terrified at the thought of what her parents would have done if she had also been expelled that the dream had haunted her sleep ever since.

The majority of dreams come to us while we are asleep at night. But many people who are highly sensitive receive these mental impressions quite easily when awake. Such dreams are obviously visions, or mental impressions received from some intimate friend or relation.

An actual experience will illustrate this type of dream. A musician had spent the weekend with some old friends in the country, but on arriving home had had a vivid daydream that he saw a doctor standing by a bedside. He wrote to his host that evening asking if anything unexpected had happened, but a letter crossed with his telling him that the youngest daughter had been taken ill just after his departure. This child was very fond of him and this was clearly a case of thought transference.

As a guide, it is safe to assume that any perfectly natural action or event, when the dreamer merely looks but does not take any active part, as seen in a dream, is a warning or a mirage from some outside source. On the other hand, where the dreamer visualises himself or herself as one of the actors in the drama, the message comes from within and should be interpreted as affecting the dreamer personally.

But in both cases the action or event must be a reasonable one, something that could happen in everyday life, even though it may be extremely improbable as far as the dreamer is concerned. For example, if you are flying on wings, this cannot be a vision, but if you are flying an aeroplane – however unlikely this may be – it could happen and therefore must be investigated.

These points are very important because all impossible actions and events should be traced to some physical cause first of all, and should only be treated as dreams worth considerable investigation when no other explanation appears possible.

There are many cases of people who have received perfectly accurate visions in their sleep of actual places – a town or a house, for example – that they had never seen, although every detail has later proved to be correct.

An author had a vivid dream of a visit to Eastbourne, a popular resort about which he knew nothing whatsoever. He saw himself driven from the railway station to a hotel on the front, then he watched the incoming tide for some time before turning down a street off the front in order to have a cup of coffee at a café where he knew they made excellent coffee.

The dream was so vivid that he even saw the name of the street – Queen Street or some such common name. Yet he had never been to Eastbourne in his life. So impressed was he by the reality of this dream that he determined to 'make it come true'.

He made the journey at the first opportunity, went straight to the hotel, which he recognised immediately, and then turned down Queen Street, where he found the identical café at the first corner on the left.

This type of dream is by no means uncommon, and it is very difficult to find an explanation. Obviously it is not a warning – either of good or evil. It is merely a peculiar experience and raises the question whether in very deep sleep the spirit or psyche can ignore physical space. Some casual reference to Eastbourne, perhaps in a newspaper paragraph, may have raised a subconscious thought that he had never been there and then, in sleep, he visited the town mentally.

A somewhat similar experience, though not a dream, happened to a man who was an enthusiastic gardener. One day he spent the whole day building a rockery in a shady corner of his garden, and worked until it was too dark to see. When he was tidying up he found that he had lost the glass from his watch. It was too dark to go out again, so all he could do was to go to bed as usual and wait. But as soon as he was dressed next morning, he felt sure he knew where he could find the glass. He went straight to a certain spot on the rockery and there he saw the glass lying on the surface of the soil. How did he know where the glass would be (for he went straight to the point without hesitation)?. Many investigators would say that his psyche had been searching the rockery while his body was asleep, and probably they would be right.

It may be asked why certain interpretations are attached to certain dreams, but this point is really a simple one once explained. It is impossible to conceive a thought without some article, action or quality associated with it. You cannot actually dream a warning of danger, but you can and do dream some mental picture that is associated in your mind with a sense of danger. Dreams, therefore, are mental pictures of some thought of your own, or a message from some other person, conveyed to you in the form of a pictured incident.

Many people believe that dreams go by contrary, but this is only true in certain instances. The important point is that the picture provided in the dream gives the clearest message to the dreamer.

Many people have considered and investigated dreams, and it is only natural that their interpretations differ. Much of our knowledge concerning dreams comes to us from the East and from sources that are many centuries old. But it would not be accurate for the modern Westerner to accept all these interpretations, as certain articles, situations and actions will have quite different associations.

For example, in the East, the peacock used to be a sacred bird and it meant death for anyone other than a priest to possess even a feather – hence the popular and very prevalent association of ill-luck with a peacock feather. But in the West we have never run any risk of losing our lives in this way, so the old interpretation is not relevant.

In this book, we have brought together a range of research covering over 20,000 dream subjects, each one often containing a range of interpretations depending on the details of the dream. Multiply that by the combination of subjects which so often appears in a dream, and you will appreciate the scope and depth of this project. Whatever your dream, you should find help here to unravel the mysteries of the dream world.

Note from the Publisher
The dreams in this book are based on traditional interpretations. Please be aware that any specific predictions of death or disaster would be considered by a modern dream interpreter as exaggerated and misconstrued. Traditional interpretations of misfortune are now more commonly explained as the end of a phase in the life or perhaps at worst, a general run of bad luck. It is wise to remember that dream imagery is open to analysis of many different kinds, and thus all interpretations should be approached with an open mind.

ABACUS An abacus in a dream is an indication of financial improvement through careful work.

ABALONE To eat abalone in a dream indicates an unusual occurrence. To see the shell is a sign to guard against jealous friends.

ABANDONMENT This is an unfavourable dream, and indicates the loss of friends, or the failure of some fortunate expectation. Trouble is indicated, whether you abandon some other person, or whether they abandon you.

ABBESS To dream that you meet an abbess is a favourable sign, showing restored peace and comfort after some distress or illness.

ABBEY To dream of going into an abbey means that your present situation in life will not change. To the lover it indicates that there will be constancy, faithfulness and devotion in all his/her love affairs. The more important

the structure, the better are the prospects.

ABBOT This indicates danger to you and your affairs. If the abbot is old you will lose your money, and if he is a man disguised as an abbot you may lose your health. If the abbot is a small man, you will be betrayed by your sweetheart. To see several abbots together signifies approaching dishonour; if they are descending a flight of stairs you will be embroiled in a family quarrel.

ABDICATION To dream of a monarch abdicating his throne in any kingdom denotes anarchy and revolution there.

ABDOMEN It is an omen of contrary, when you are in pain in your dream; your health will be good, and your affairs will prosper because of your physical vigour. But if you dream of your unclothed abdomen, then it is an unfortunate omen – especially for lovers or married people, for you may expect unfaithfulness or even treachery on the part of some loved person. Do not rashly give your confidence after such a dream.

ABDUCTION To dream of being carried off by force means that you will carry out your plans against all opposition.

ABEL To dream of Abel, Adam's second son who was murdered by his jealous brother Cain, is a favourable omen, and indicates that you are coming up in the world. If you have a lawsuit, you will win. If in love, your partner will be kind and faithful. If you are about to go into business, your business will thrive, and you will become rich. In short, expect to rise to high esteem and affluence. If Abel speaks to you in your dream, be very careful to remember what he says, as otherwise you may reverse every benefit that fortune has in store for you.

ABHORRENCE To dream that you dislike anything or any person is an omen that depends on the circumstances. If your feeling of distaste disturbs you seriously, then it foretells difficulties in your path. But if you merely dislike any article, and can get rid of it, then you will overcome your worries.

ABJECTION To dream of feeling abject presages hard times, but only for a little while.

ABODE Strange houses show that your affairs are in an unsettled condition. If, in your dream, you go into a strange house, you will probably venture on some new undertaking before long. If you are refused admission, or find that you cannot get in, then be careful in your plans and avoid needless risk.

ABORIGINE A dream of any primitive peoples indicates that you will always be able to pay your debts.

ABORTION A warning as regards health or the happiness of your partner in marriage; be on your guard as to both.

ABOVE (Hanging and about to fall) Some danger awaits you, but may be avoided if the object does not fall.

ABROAD If a married person dreams that they are in a foreign country it indicates that a fortune will be left to them. To a lover, such a dream signifies constancy and happiness in married life.

ABSCESS A dream of illness is one of contrary meaning, and signifies that you will enjoy good health, or a speedy recovery if you are already ill.

ABSCONDING To dream that some person, whether stranger or acquaintance, has absconded with his employer's money, or otherwise done some serious wrong, is a warning to you of treachery among those around you. If you yourself are the person in question, the injury will be slight, and you will recover from your losses.

ABSENCE To dream of grieving over the absence of anyone is a sure sign that that person will soon return and your love or friendship will be stronger than ever.

To dream of rejoicing at anyone's absence denotes that you will shortly receive news you would rather not hear.

To dream of the death of a friend living abroad foretells good news. On the contrary, to dream that you have seen some absent friend alive and well foretells bad news.

ABSENTMINDEDNESS This signifies approaching good fortune.

ABSINTHE Drinking absinthe foretells sickness followed by good fortune and good health.

Selling absinthe signifies that you will suffer a loss; that you buy it, foretells a love affair.

ABSOLUTION To dream that you are granting absolution signifies that you will be robbed; that you have been granted absolution denotes that you will be scorned.

ABSTINENCE To dream you have signed the pledge indicates success in business, or happiness in some undertaking dear to your heart.

ABSURDITY Indicates happiness in love.

ABUNDANCE To dream that you have an abundance of anything is bad. Abundance of money means penury; of food, scarcity of clothing and a shabby appearance; of health, lingering sickness; of beauty, something that will spoil your personal appearance.

ABUSE To dream that someone is abusing you is a bad sign, but it applies to your business affairs only. But to dream that you are abusing some other person foretells success after hard work.

ABYSS To dream of any hollow space is a sign of difficulties ahead; it is an obstacle dream. If you escape from the abyss, you will overcome your troubles. But if you fall in, then be careful in your business affairs. Do not lend money, for it will not be returned to you.

ACACIA If in season this indicates disappointment, but to dream of this flower in winter is a sign of tender hopes which will be realised.

ACADEMY To dream that you are master or mistress of an academy indicates that you will be reduced in your circumstances; if single, that your intended marriage will be characterised by adversity.

ACCELERATION To accelerate speed in a vehicle indicates that you will achieve your goals. If you cannot remove your foot from the accelerator, beware of gambling and drinking.

ACCENT To dream of hearing speech in strange accents or a foreign tongue presages imminent news and a long journey.

ACCEPTANCE To dream that you have been accepted by your lover, or if a woman, that your lover has proposed to you and that you have accepted him, is generally considered a dream of contrary. It is a warning that your love affair will not prosper, or at least that it will be a long time coming right.

ACCIDENT To dream of having met with an accident foretells that you are about to go through a great trial. A railway accident signifies the loss of money; a road accident loss of health; an accident on board ship points to loss of friends.

To dream that you witness an accident without being involved signifies that you will profit by a cowardly action. If you give help to the victim you may expect to be betrayed by a friend who will cheat you of some money you expected to receive.

ACCORDION To dream you hear accordion music denotes pleasure and happiness in your home and family.

ACCOUNTS To dream that you are keeping accounts, if you are a business man, indicates loss of business by the failure and bankruptcy of those with whom you have had dealings. Unless you are very careful, you will incur other bad debts in the future.

ACCUSATION If you dream of being accused of a crime, beware of insincere flatterers.

ACE Diamonds mean quarrels; Hearts mean news; Spades indicate bad luck; Clubs indicate money.

ACHE This depends entirely upon the circumstances, but it is usually found to be a case of contrary meaning. If it is a trivial ache, it is probably due to some physical cause, and would be a sign of ill health. But if the pain is severe and obviously imaginary, it denotes some important event that will prove beneficial to you. To the business man, it foretells good trade, a fortunate season's business. To the lover, it indicates a favourable time to push a suit. To the farmer, it promises a good and profitable harvest.
To the sailor, it shows a successful voyage.

ACID To dream of handling acids foretells a dangerous promise. Fulfil your own promises and do not trust blindly in those of others.

ACORN Acorns are omens of wealth and happiness to come. If you eat acorns you will get rich very quickly. If you dream of picking acorns you will have a large family, probably including twins.

ACQUAINTANCE To dream of someone you know is a good sign, but it depends upon the degree of friendship and also upon what happens in your dream. If you quarrel, it is a bad sign, and often applies to the health of the dreamer.

ACQUIESENCE To comply with a wish, whether your own or somebody else's, denotes that you will shortly be engaged in several love affairs that will give you the greatest pleasure.

ACQUISITION To acquire something signifies profit. If the objects are necessities, it signifies to those who are poor a return of fortune; to the rich, success in their undertakings.

ACQUITTAL To dream of being accused before a court and acquitted foretells prosperity to yourself and failure to your enemies.

ACROBAT To watch other people performing clever gymnastic feats is a dream of contrary; be careful or an accident will befall you. Do not take long journeys for seven days after such a dream. If the acrobat in your dream has an accident or is unable to perform the attempted feat, then you will escape the full results of the peril that is hanging over you.

ACROSTIC Puzzles of almost every sort, when appearing in a dream, are a warning of coming trouble, probably caused by some hasty decision of your own. Postpone new ventures and take no unusual business risks.

ACTING To dream that you are acting denotes that you may look forward to a life of ease and comfort, after surmounting considerable difficulty.

ACTOR To dream of an actor means that a great deal of the admiration at present paid to you, which you think is genuine, is only make-believe. It can also signify that you can have confidence in your friend.

ACTRESS To dream of seeing an actress on the stage signifies that you will soon get into many difficulties, partly through your own indiscretion and partly from causes over which you have no control. Meeting her in private life in a dream indicates that you are about to discover how 'hand in hand with sorrow love is wont to go'. After dreaming of an actress, either on or off the stage, a single person should guard against jealous quarrels with their partner. A married person may look for temporary discord in domestic affairs.

ADAM and EVE To dream of Adam and Eve signifies that you will acknowledge as your own a child by adoption.

To dream you see Adam is a happy omen. If he looks pleasant, you will succeed in whatever you undertake. If you are in love, expect your partner to love you. If you are a farmer expect an abundant crop and that your livestock will increase, be top quality and fetch a good price. If you have left home, return if you can, for prosperity is there. If, however, he looks displeased and angry, use great caution in all your dealings; do not travel by sea, and do not borrow or lend money for at least a month or two. If he speaks to you, remember his words and observe them as faithfully as you can.

ADAMANT If you dream that you are adamant about something, you will fail to achieve one of your dearest ambitions.

ADAPTABILITY Your financial future is secure if you dream of having a flexible and adaptable attitude.

ADDER To fight with adders signifies the overthrow of enemies. Seeing them means you will become rich and marry into money. Adders signify arguments that will benefit you, especially if you dream they bite you. Beware of false friends when you dream of this reptile.

ADDITION If you are adding figures correctly in your dream, you will overcome personal difficulties. But if you have problems making your additions work correctly, then your success will be limited.

ADDRESS To have lost or be seeking for the address of anyone means that you are about to fall in with an old acquaintance in a place where you least expect to see them. If you dream of writing the address, be careful of your financial affairs, and do not enter into risky speculations.

ADENOIDS To dream of having your adenoids removed indicates social success.

ADHESION To dream of sticking or sticking to anything is a sign that you should employ prudence in your affairs.

ADIEU To dream that you are saying goodbye to anyone is an indication of misfortune due to ill health. Take no risks with regard to your health.

ADJUTANT To dream that you are in the company of an officer of the army is a sign of new friendship. The higher the rank of the officer, the more advantageous to yourself the friendship will prove.

ADMIRAL To dream of an admiral denotes loss of trade; to see one in a naval engagement signifies danger of drowning.

ADMIRER To dream that someone is admiring your looks is a sure indication that some wish particularly dear to you will be fulfilled. To dream that you admire someone indicates that someone will lie to you. To dream that you admire yourself signifies you will be the victim of deceit.

ADONIS To dream of Adonis signifies that you will be subject to the artfulness of your lover; or will employ craft to gain your own ends in love.

ADOPTION This signifies wealth and a ripe old age. If you dream of a child related to you by blood, you will shortly benefit from a legacy. If the child is a stranger, you may be sure of all that you undertake.

However for a young person to dream he/she has become the adopted child of some wealthy person may signify the death of father, mother or some near relative will soon take place.

ADORNMENT To receive a present of an article of jewellery is a sign that you will shortly suffer an affliction of a more or less serious nature, according to the value of the present.

To dream that you dress yourself up signifies that you have a rival.

ADRIFT To dream that you are adrift in a boat is a warning of difficulty ahead – it is an obstacle dream. If you reach land safely, you will overcome your troubles. But if you fall out of the boat, or if the boat should be upset by rough waves, then expect very serious difficulties. Even then you may swim to land, or be rescued, which would indicate ultimate success.

ADULTERY To dream that you are tempted to commit adultery and that you resist it is a happy omen, and it is a good time to begin business after such a dream. If you have a lawsuit, you will win. If you are in love, persevere, for your wishes will be gratified. To dream you have committed adultery shows you will be involved in arguments.

ADVANCEMENT This is a most favourable sign, and indicates success in some important undertaking. You may be your own master, yet if you dream that you are in some employment and are advanced, your success is certain.

This dream often occurs in connection with legal matters. But if you dream of the lawsuit itself, you will lose.

ADVENTURE To meet with exciting adventures in a dream predicts a surprising alteration in your fortune.

ADVENTURER You can expect a passionate relationship, but exercise caution in relation to your new lover.

ADVERSARY If you are continually being thwarted in some undertaking by persistent adversaries it denotes that there is much trouble and worry in store for you, from which you will eventually gain prosperity. To dream that you receive obstruction from an adversary shows that you will complete your business quickly.

ADVERSITY To dream of the adversity of your enemies signifies coming happiness; if you suffer adversity you will require courage in the near future.

ADVERTISEMENT Answering an advertisement foretells that you will shortly experience an alteration in your circumstances. If you were writing on blue paper, it will be for the better; if the paper was white, it will be for the worse. Looking over the advertisement in a newspaper or magazine denotes that you are about to attract considerable public attention by a judicious use of printer's ink. To dream that you advertise for a 'partner for life' is indicative of shortly becoming the victim of some practical joke or ludicrous hoax, in which your reputation for judicious conduct and wise behaviour

will be greatly tarnished. To read the same advertisement many times foretells good news coming from abroad.

ADVICE To receive advice, either good or bad, from an alleged friend denotes that enemies are working against you. The friend who is giving the advice, however, is not always a party to the wrong.

ADVOCATE To dream that you are a solicitor is a good omen and foretells success. If you are a barrister in your dream, then there will be a longer delay – but success is certain unless, in court, you dream that you lose your case.

AERIAL You will succeed in your plans despite all the odds.

AEROPLANE A sign that money is coming to you, but your methods may not be above suspicion. Study your plans carefully before you put them into effect.

AFFABILITY To dream of friendliness signifies madness.

AFFECTATION Seeing people giving themselves airs (for example, a healthy strong woman riding indolently on a horse, or the lover arriving casually to meet his loved one) signifies that the dreamer should avoid all quarrels because he or she is in danger of a serious fight.

AFFECTION To receive affection from someone signifies that you will be denounced by one you love.

AFFIANCE For a young, unmarried person to dream that he/she has suddenly become engaged to an attractive young person is not a favourable dream. Look out for a quarrel with your lover if you have one. If you do not have a lover, you will have to wait a long time before you marry.

AFFLICTION A great affliction to yourself or friends foretells an early wedding, if the dreamer is single. If married, then a change of residence will soon be required by an occurrence that will improve your social standing.

AFFLUENCE An increase in income will go a long way towards solving your immediate problems.

AFFRONT If you are affronted at the misconduct of some dear friend, look for a letter full of expressions of good feeling and kindness from a distant acquaintance

from whom you have not heard for a very long time, and whom you thought had entirely forgotten you.

AFRICA If you are on the way to Africa, you will soon have to take a journey for the benefit of your health; the doctors may be baffled by a sudden and serious illness which will prevent you from working.

AFTERNOON Dreams which take place in the afternoon are likely to portend better events than those happening in the morning or at night.

AGATE Agates or semi-precious stones signify sadness, sickness and setbacks.

AGE For a woman to dream she is courted by an old man is a sure sign that she will receive a sum of money, and be successful in her undertakings. For a girl to dream it shows that she will marry a rich young man and will have many children by him, who will all become rich.

For a man to dream he is courting an old woman, and that she returns his love, is a very good omen. It shows success in worldly affairs, that he will marry a beautiful young woman, have lovely children and be very happy. To dream that you have lived to an old age denotes that you will shortly hear of the death of a friend. To dream of the old denotes a peaceful and honest life.

**AGENT or
AGENCY** Signifies loss of inheritance.

AGGRANDISEMENT
Fairness and magnificence is bad, and shows death to the sick and poor success to lovers.

AGNOSTIC A dream of religious disbelief is a sign of a degrading experience with the opposite sex.

AGONY To be in agony, either from mental or physical pain is a very good dream. You will have general good health, business prosperity, and your domestic happiness will become greater than you have ever known it before.

To dream of witnessing a death agony foretells a legacy. If it is the death of an enemy it indicates that you will inherit from your father. The death of a stranger denotes unexpected benefits.

AGREEMENT For a business person to dream that they have made some advantageous agreement is a bad sign. Business will become dull, partly from failure of others and partly from general depression of trade.

Take care how you make your contracts after this dream; many have fallen from a position of prosperity and affluence from neglect of this warning.

AGRICULTURE Signifies unadulterated good fortune.

AIR If you dream the sky is clear, of a fine blue, calm and serene, then it is a good omen. You will be successful in your enterprises.

If you are seeking promotion you will obtain it; if you are in love, you will marry your lover; if you have a lawsuit, you will win; if you are a farmer, you will have good crops, your livestock will increase, you will get good market prices. Those who are married will have many successful children; journeys will fulfil your expectations; sea voyages will be pleasant and prosperous; debts will soon be cleared; prisoners will be freed.

To dream the air is full of thick, dark and heavy clouds is unfavourable; you will fall ill, perhaps seriously; disappointment will attend your business.

To dream the sky is streaked with white denotes that you will suffer many severe difficulties over which you will eventually triumph.

If the sky is fiery red, you will be successful in love, but not in business. It also warns of sickness and trouble coming to your family.

AIR BRAKE The sound of air brakes on a vehicle indicates problems and the failure of plans.

AIR GUN To have one given you means an enemy. To fire it is a warning to postpone decisions for a day or two.

AIREDALE A dream of this dog indicates a happy home life filled with simple pleasures.

AIRSHIP To be in a stationary airship denotes that you will have little success in life unless you work hard to get out of the rut into which you have fallen.

If the airship is moving very quickly, be wary of investing your money, as it foretells great loss.

AISLE To dream that you walk down the aisle of a church, or other place of worship, in company with a lover indicates that you will be deserted by your friends of the opposite sex. The person you see in your dream has never had the least thought of you, but may soon be in your company at a private party or ball.

ALABASTER Ill health or family disputes will follow.

ALARM An alarm clock ringing indicates profit and excitement. A fire alarm indicates personal fortune.

ALBATROSS Seen from the deck of a ship, an albatross indicates success in artistic pursuits.

ALBUM Looking over a photograph album predicts that a close relative will soon die and you will inherit a considerable sum of money.

ALCOHOL As a chemical, this is a favourable dream. As a drink, it is a good dream only if taken in moderation.

ALDER The alder tree is a portent of happiness.

ALDERMAN Dining with an alderman is a sign of falling into bad company, and you may be led into some bad behaviour unless you are careful. To dream you have been elected alderman means you will be reduced to poverty unless you are exceedingly careful.

ALE Hearty enjoyment of simple pleasures is indicated by a dream of drinking ale.

ALGEBRA To be working at algebra signifies successful speculation.

ALGERIAN Signifies you will enjoy the pleasures of love.

ALIBI Indicates marital discord.

ALIEN To dream that you are an alien denotes friendship and love.

ALIMONY Receiving alimony indicates a medical problem. Paying alimony is an indication of careless pleasures.

ALLEGORY A dream which appears to have a symbolic meaning indicates surprises, some of which will be disappointing.

ALLEY Walking along a dark alley indicates the loss of love. If you come to the end of a blind alley, expect your plans to fail.

ALLEY CAT To hear stray

cats howling indicates that you will associate with bad company.

ALLIANCE To dream of making an alliance with someone rich or influential portends problems in personal relationships.

ALLIGATOR In a zoo, alligators indicate travel on the horizon. Being attacked means that you will be laughed at by your enemies.

ALLOWANCE To receive an allowance portends happiness.

ALLOY Combining metals in a crucible indicates a happy marriage and healthy children.

ALLSPICE Romance will bring happiness.

ALLURE If you dream you are alluring to the opposite sex, expect invitations that will aid your social advancement.

ALMANAC Reading the almanac foretells that events that took place years ago will make you a richer and wiser person. Some purchase you formerly made in goods or shares will suddenly rise in value, or be sold at a price much above your expectations, and you will find out that you are well repaid for your investments.

ALMOND To see and eat almonds signifies difficulties and trouble. If the almonds are bitter, you will be subjected to a great temptation, that will lead to disgrace unless you can fight against it.

ALMS To be asked for alms which you refuse shows want and misery, but to dream you give them freely is a sign of great joy.

To give alms to a poor person is a good omen and indicates to a young woman that she is about to receive a most advantageous proposal of marriage, and to a man that he is about to make the acquaintance of an heiress who will fall in love with him and who, independent of her money, will be a wonderful partner.

For a person in employment to dream that he or she is bestowing alms is a warning to be careful in business, for the slightest mistake following this dream will lead to dismissal. If the dreamer has been in doubt over any enterprise he should take the advice of his best friend.

ALOE To dream of aloe

plants indicates bad news.

ALONE It is good to dream you are left alone. Your friends will never forsake you.

ALPHABET To learn letters means a benefit in store for the ignorant, but it will be accompanied by hard work and fear if you want a son.

To see all the letters of the alphabet in large characters is a sign that you will make great advancement as a student. You will be proficient in practical studies, and gain eminence as a theologian. If the letters of your name appear in succession before you, it indicates that you will be called to serve your native town or country in some very honourable position. Look out for a well-paid government situation.

ALPACA To dream of the material means a lucky find; of the animal, a valuable gift will be received.

ALTAR To uncover or discover an altar signifies joy and gladness. An altar signifies radiant hope; to erect an altar signifies gladness; to see one overthrown is a very favourable sign to those engaged in scientific, industrial or commercial enterprises.

To stand with your back to an altar is a sign of approaching sorrow and trouble. To be kneeling before an altar indicates that you are about to enter a successful marriage, have many healthy children and great worldly prosperity.

ALTERCATION   To argue with your lover means a happy marriage.

ALTITUDE   If you dream of looking down, beware of making wrong decisions which will cause you problems.

ALUMINIUM   Shiny aluminium indicates happiness in love; dull aluminium portends boredom and frustration.

AMATEUR   A handsome reward will come your way for a helpful action.

AMAZEMENT   An exciting experience is on its way.

AMBASSADOR   If you are talking to a foreign ambassador, expect a friend to betray you.

AMBER   To wear rings of amber is good only to women.

AMBITION   Indicates promotion and increased financial security.

AMBULANCE   An ambulance in a dream denotes that you will lose an inheritance. To see one filled with wounded people signifies a violent death.

AMBUSH   A pleasant surprise is around the corner.

AMERICA   If you have emigrated to America, you will remain in your present position and occupation, and your efforts to improve your present conditions will be successful. You will rise to a reputable and prosperous position through your persistent efforts. To hear good news from relatives in America signifies that you will soon hear news of business losses or domestic problems of those relatives who have emigrated.

AMETHYST   You will lose a relative or friend if you see an amethyst in your dream.

AMMONIA   Danger through illness or accidents; take no risks for a time.

AMOROUSNESS   If you dream you are of an amorous disposition it is a sign that you are likely to be the victim of scandal.

AMULET To dream you are wearing one means that you have an important decision to make shortly. Think well before choosing.

AMMUNITION Buying ammunition indicates that you will run into trouble for something you have forgotten to do.

AMPUTATION Indicates increased income.

AMUSEMENT If you are enjoying yourself, you have a bright future. If you are dissatisfied in the dream, trouble will be yours.

ANACONDA You will struggle in life.

ANAGRAM Personal difficulties will be resolved.

ANARCHIST A warning as to financial caution, especially if you dream of seeing more than one.

ANCESTORS A vision of an ancestor means illness in the family. If the dreamer has arranged a long journey he should abandon it, otherwise an accident is likely to occur to him. To see an ancestor arguing or fighting signifies an inheritance.

ANCHOR Seeing an anchor stuck in the sand signifies that someone of whose affections you are doubtful really cares for you and that circumstances will shortly make this fact plain.

A ship's anchor is a sign that you will receive a serious setback in business. If it is a large one, then you will come through the ordeal successfully.

ANCHOVY This fish usually denotes good fortune. To eat anchovies signifies pleasant but trifling love affairs. To sell them foretells ruin.

ANECDOTE A pleasant dream denoting social success.

ANGEL An angel or saint is an encouragement to live well and repent of sins; it also denotes good news, increase of reputation and authority. This is one of the best possible dreams. It is a sure sign of happiness, indicating long life, good health and the fulfilment of all reasonable wishes.

ANGER To quarrel with your fiancé denotes love and affection. To be angry with anyone means that person is one of your best friends. To dream of being angry with your partner signifies many violent scenes with him/her during the early part of your marriage, arising from the fact that someone has been telling lies about you, but common sense will prevail after a time and you will live peacefully.

ANGLING Angling signifies much affliction and trouble caused by something you want to obtain.

ANGUISH Signifies success to the dreamer.

ANIMALS To hear animals signifies gain. If you are attacked by fierce animals and beat them off you will make friends who will help you to rise in the world. If you are bitten by one of the animals, then you must be on guard against a false friend.

Animals in herds of different sorts signify abundance in your business and great prosperity. A few animals indicates news from an absent friend. To feed animals foretells fortune. If they speak to you it denotes illness and suffering.

ANISEED Aniseed denotes that there is someone preparing a present for you. To see the plant in flower signifies that you will benefit by a good action. Aniseed sweets signify that you must

exercise the greatest care in your business dealings.

ANKLE If your ankle is put out of joint it means you will soon suffer severe pains in the head, face or shoulders. To break your ankle means that your hair will begin to turn grey.

ANNIVERSARY Any anniversary or birthday celebrations are omens of happy family reunions.

ANOINTMENT To be anointed or painted is good to a virtuous woman, but to a promiscuous woman it indicates a speedy marriage.

ANNOUNCEMENT To make an announcement indicates business success.

ANNOYANCE To dream that you are annoyed about something signifies good fortune awaits your plans.

ANNULMENT To dream of having your marriage annulled indicates future happiness.

ANT To dream of watching ants at work indicates that you will for a time try to find pleasure in the idle and single life, but that you will at last discover that the truest happiness lies in hard work for the sake of a family.

Common ants are good, for they signify fertility.

To see a swarm of ants denotes that, providing you look for it, you will enjoy a large increase in your business.

To dream you see ants with wings is not good, for it indicates injury or a dangerous voyage.

ANTARCTIC Your favourite project will come to nothing.

ANTEATER An unfortunate dream. Take no risks.

ANTELOPE In a zoo, antelopes indicate disappointment. To see them in the wild portends an increase in income.

ANTHEM To hear an anthem played or sung denotes that you will visit a sick friend living some distance away from you. If the music is lively you will profit by the journey.

ANTIQUES Signs of happiness in the home.

ANTISEPTIC This indicates an accident in a vehicle.

ANVIL To hear the sound of the anvil is a good dream. It indicates hard work, good health, and brings gladness,

joy and prosperity.

ANXIETY If you suffer anxiety without being able to find out the cause, be wary if during the week following someone offers to do you a favour – it will be a trap.

APE All sorts of apes and monkeys signify malicious, weak, strange and secret enemies. To see an ape may denote that you are in danger from the society you frequent, of acquiring objectionable habits both of thought and expression. But to an engaged person this animal denotes a speedy marriage. A married person will soon be rejoicing over some domestic event.

APOLOGY A change of companionship; possibly a return to a former friendship.

APOPLEXY To be seized with a fit of apoplexy is a sign of inability of the blood to fulfil its functions. Lowness of spirit and general debility of the system will follow this dream, unless you strengthen your body with iron and tonics.

APPAREL If your apparel is suited to the season of the year it denotes prosperity and happiness.

Being dressed in fine

clothes means that you are in danger of indulging in extravagance which can have no end but poverty. If you dream of being in rags, your industry and common sense will in the long run be rewarded by wealth and reputation.

For a wife or husband to dream of wearing the other's clothes is an omen that the dreamer will outlive his or her partner. Buying clothes signifies honour and beauty. Going into company scantily dressed is a sign of vexation. If you see yourself gaudily dressed, misfortune will follow. But if you are dressed in rags, you will have nothing to complain of. If your clothing is scarlet, it is a warning of an impending calamity; if white, you will be successful in business and in love. Green predicts a long journey; black, bad luck in love; blue, happiness; yellow, jealousy and bickering over love affairs; crimson, that good news is coming to you from a distance.

APPARITION   To see a ghost is very unfortunate. If it is attractive and dressed in white, it shows deceit and temptation to sin; if you are in love it is a sign of unrequited love; someone is about to deceive you, and you are friendly with your worst enemy. Do not

undertake a journey at this period for it will be unfortunate.

APPENDICITIS   Keep to your own plans of action and your finances will improve.

APPETITE   To appease your appetite by eating something you especially like is a sign that you will shortly lose some of your robust and healthy looks; pallid cheeks and gradual weight loss will make your friends concerned at the appearance of decline.

APPLAUSE   To gain the applause of your friends means that you will become the object of libel or defamation of character in some of the newspapers. Lawsuits and quarrels may well follow shortly after this dream.

APPLE and APPLE TREES   To see apple trees and eat sweet apples signifies joy, pleasure and recreation; sour apples denote contention and sedition. To gather apples signifies vexation from some person or other. A boy giving apples to a pregnant woman means faithfulness in your sweetheart, and riches in business.

Seeing an apple tree coming into bloom is an encouraging dream for any who are in low spirits. It is a sign that fortune will shortly shine on them, and that the best of their days are yet to come.

APPOINTMENT To keep an appointment with a friend means that a secret you have tried to keep will be revealed.

APPRENTICE To dream of learning a trade indicates success in love and in business. If you dream of training an apprentice, you will have a chance to make money.

APRICOT To see or eat an apricot in season denotes good health and pleasure. But if you seem to eat them out of season, they signify vain hopes and business failures.

APRICOT TREE This fruit tree denotes pleasure and contentment. If it is loaded with fruits, exercise prudence, while if the fruit has been picked you will enjoy prosperity. To see it loaded with fruit out of season denotes unexpected success, though if the fruit is withered you must guard against boredom and laziness.

APRIL This signifies that you will obtain everything you desire and the greatest success will attend all those projects on which you have most set your heart.

APRIL FOOL To dream of being made an April Fool means that, after having arrived at considerable culture, you will marry one who is a philistine and so be exposed to unintelligent criticism and interference.

You may anticipate falling a victim to the false pretences of one in whom you are at present confiding, and may reasonably infer that your only safeguard is a little healthy suspicion.

APRON If you dream of tearing an apron, you will meet a young person of wealth who, with skilful handling and encouragement, will prove a good partner for life. To a married person the dream promises children who will be your pride in later years.

AQUAMARINE To dream of this jewel assures you of the affection of a very young friend or relative.

AQUARIUM A dream of an aquarium of any size indicates problems to come. If the fish are unusual, guard against accidents.

AQUEDUCT A good dream

if the aqueduct is running with water.

ARAB To dream of seeing an Arab is a sign that you will meet with a young person of orderly and sober demeanour who will speak of marriage but will not have the courage to carry that speech into effect.

ARBITRATION If you are acting as an arbitrator in an argument, you will have trouble in extricating yourself from difficulties.

ARBOUR To see an arbour means that you will hear secrets; to be in one, that your own secrets will be revealed.

ARCADE To dream of walking through an arcade indicates that you will find it difficult to overcome temptations.

ARCH To dream of walking with your sweetheart under a railway arch is a sign of opposition from his/her parents, or that you will be annoyed by the attentions of your lover's rival, who will come to your home or meet you in the street and entreat you to listen to vague promises.
  To dream of an arch signifies that you will be

flattered. You must take this dream as a warning against the flatterer.

ARCHBISHOP To dream of one, foretells danger in the night.

ARCHER To the single, this means a speedy engagement. If you are married, be true – danger is approaching.

ARCHITECT To dream that you have business with an architect is a sign that you will incur unexpected expenses, and will have trouble of a kind that you have never had before.

ARCHIVES To dream of archives signifies that an inheritance will be disputed in your family.

ARCTIC To dream of the North Pole indicates that you will achieve your ambitions.

ARENA A warning of danger – avoid crowds. If you are not alone in your dream, the danger is lessened.

ARGUING To dream you argue with intelligent people signifies profit and gain.

ARITHMETIC If you dream of struggling to solve arithmetical problems, expect to overcome your own difficulties after some hard work.

ARM If anyone dreams that their arms have grown bigger and stronger than normal, it signifies that their brothers or sons will help them gain happiness and profit, and they will become rich. To dream that you have strong arms signifies good fortune, restoration of health, or freedom from imprisonment. To dream your arms or elbows are covered in scabs or ulcers signifies annoyance, sadness and failure in business. If your arms are broken or thin, that is a bad sign, and if you are a powerful person, beware of a loss of authority or an illness attacking your son or brother. This same dream denotes problems, sickness and poverty to the children or brothers of ordinary people. If a woman has this dream, she is in danger of becoming a widow or at least of a separation from her husband. To dream that one of your arms has been cut off signifies illness or death of your father, son, brother or friend. To dream both arms have been cut off signifies imprisonment or sickness.

Some authors attribute the right arm to the father, son, brother and friend; and the left to the mother, daughter, sister, the friend and the loyal employees.

ARMCHAIR News soon.

ARMED MEN To see armed men is a good sign and denotes a fearless person; to dream you see an armed man run away is a sign of victory; to see armed men attack you signifies sadness.

ARMENIAN This signifies that you will be pestered by the curiosity of your wife.

ARMHOLE If you dream of putting your arms in the wrong armholes of your clothes, be careful in your relationships with the opposite sex or your reputation will be in danger.

ARMISTICE This presages promotion in business.

ARMOUR A warning to take precautions against enemies.

ARMY To see an army of soldiers denotes the loss of friends through circumstances over which you have no control.

If the army goes into battle, your goods will be wasted by those in whom you have placed the utmost confidence. To dream of a victorious army signifies that you will suffer sadness and grief. A vanquished army signifies the disenchantment of a long courtship.

ARREST To dream you are arrested signifies lack of wit and determination.

ARRIVAL Arriving at the end of a journey indicates the successful conclusion of a difficult task.

ARROW An arrow in flight is a good sign for any love affair that may follow. If, however, the arrow is lying on the ground or is broken, look for sorrow connected with your lover.

ARSENIC To dream of arsenic signifies poverty but good health. If you receive arsenic from a friend, your virtues will be rewarded. If you give arsenic, you will encounter opposition while trying to perform a good action.

ARSON An unfortunate dream. News of accidents at sea, possibly to yourself.

ART To admire or discuss art is a sign of advancement.

ARTERY To the healthy, this indicates a message. To the sick, it means a slow recovery.

ARTESIAN WELL If an artesian well figures in your dream, a moderate but steady income will be yours.

ARTHRITIS To dream of this problem indicates good health.

ARTICHOKE Vexations and troubles which, however, you will surmount.

ARTIST This dream means great misfortune; to a lover such a dream indicates that he or she will be jealous because of seeing someone in the company of their partner.

ASBESTOS To dream of using this as a protection against fire portends family discord.

ASCENT To ascend a mountain signifies that your wife will deceive you.

ASHES Misfortune and losses through carelessness.

ASIA If you dream of travelling to Asia, you will experience great changes in your life, but they will not necessarily bring you good fortune.

ASLEEP To dream that you are falling asleep is a bad omen for a busy person, unless it proves just a timely hint, because it signifies that he or she is likely to take great pains, but will work in such a drowsy way that the result will be small compared with the work involved.

ASP This portends enemies and if you are stung your enemies will do you harm. But if you kill the asps, you will triumph.

ASPARAGUS Signifies labour, reward and success. To cultivate asparagus denotes approaching fortune. To eat asparagus is a sign that you and your family will have reason for celebration. To sell asparagus signifies that you will receive money.

ASPHALT To dream of men laying a pavement or road predicts foreign travel.

ASPIC This signifies money, profitable partnership and an advantageous marriage.

ASPIRIN If you are taking aspirin, someone will spread unkind rumours about you. If you are giving the drug to someone else, do not repeat gossip or you will run into trouble.

ASS To dream an ass runs after you denotes that some slander will be raised against you by a foolish person, who will themselves become the victims of the scandal. To dream of seeing an ass denotes that you will spend much valuable time in trying to please everybody. But if the ass is looking away from you, you can take courage for you will end in being indifferent to the opinion of the others as long as you have the approval of your own common sense.

To dream you are riding on an ass can be the forerunner of a foolish quarrel. To ride an ass who carries you well is a sign of a good marriage. To dream that an ass has kicked you is a prediction of a very serious illness. To dream you are driving an ass denotes that you will experience some trouble, but will get the better of it.

ASSASSIN Misfortune will be yours.

ASSAULT To dream that you are being attacked signifies that those working for you have full knowledge of your most private secrets. If you are playfully attacked, it denotes that you will meet with well-earned success. To dream you are assaulted signifies suffering and misery.

ASSISTANCE This is a good dream, whether you give or

receive help, indicating success in a business deal.

ASTER This flower is an unusually good dream. You will attain proficiency in your occupation, and your judgement and intelligence will become stronger than ever; your love of justice, virtue and honesty will increase.

ASTHMA To dream you are subject to this complaint is a sign that you will be attacked by inflammation of the lungs, and may be so ill that the doctors will fear for your life. You will recover, however, to experience general good health.

ASTONISHMENT Signifies recovery from sickness.

ASTROLOGY To dream of any aspect of astrology indicates that your hard work will be rewarded with happiness and wealth.

ASYLUM To dream that you are in an asylum denotes that you will become famous through some great achievement.

ATHEIST If you dream of meeting or being an atheist, you will be disappointed in your plans.

ATHLETE This signifies adventurous undertakings or business negotiations.

ATLAS To dream that you study an atlas is a sign that you will have commercial transactions, if you are in trade, with some distant parts of the world where you have never traded before. If you are a retailer, foreign produce will be more in demand than before. A workman may have the offer of a situation in a distant part of this country.

ATMOSPHERE Blue skies and sunshine form one of the most fortunate of all dreams, since it foretells prosperity in money matters, happiness in domestic affairs, and the company of faithful friends. But clouds, rain or thunderstorms are all signs of trouble and misfortune, to be read according to their severity. It is less serious to witness a storm than to be at its mercy.

ATOM You will be deceived by someone you trusted.

ATROCITY To witness a dreadful event indicates a change of circumstance which may be for the better or for the worse.

ATTENDANT A speedy rise in position.

ATTIC A premonition of an engagement to the single. If married, avoid flirtation.

ATTORNEY Business worries are in front of you. Be careful of your plans and avoid all speculation in stocks and shares.

AUCTION A warning to be on your guard against being cheated by a plausible acquaintance. Trust only your dearest friends after such a dream.

AUDIENCE Social pleasures and distinctions to come.

AUGUST To dream of summer in wintertime foretells unexpected news.

AUNT To dream of close relations is a fortunate sign, and shows success in money matters.

AUTHOR To dream of a great author brings unexpected pleasures to the single; to the married, good fortune in the family.

AUTHORITY It is always good for a rich man to think or dream he is in authority.

AUTOMATON To see an automaton signifies that your child will be as mischievous as a monkey.

AUTUMN This season signifies a legacy and domestic happiness.

AVALANCHE Good fortune of an astonishing nature will soon befall you.

AVARICE To dream that you are avaricious or see other people's greed foretells that you will lose your money by foolish speculation.

AVENUE To dream of an avenue signifies an early understanding with the person you most desire.

AVERSION If someone is unfriendly towards you in a dream, it shows that you will be able to see through an attempted deception.

AVIARY An aviary full of birds indicates social advancement, but beware of spending too much time away from your business or you will lose financially.

AWAKEN It is a good omen if you awaken some person in the course of your dream, and it will go far to soften any unfavourable omen that may be present. This is especially the case if the sleeper is in bed, as the colour white then helps the good fortune and serves to confirm the fortunate issue of events.

AWARD   Receiving an award indicates good fortune.

AWL   Increased prosperity, but not through your own efforts.

AXE   A warning of danger which only your own forethought and bravery can avert.

BABOON   To dream of baboons indicates success in love or in business.

BABY   For a mother to dream that her baby is ill denotes its general good health, and prosperous times in her husband's vocation. To dream that her baby is dead is a sign of the early marriage of her eldest child, who will gain a wealthier position in life than its parents have done. To nurse a strange baby foretells sickness in your family. If the strange baby is ill, look for a death, but not necessarily in your immediate family.

BACCHUS   A sign of hard-working days to come.

BACHELOR   If the man is young it is a good sign, but if old, the dream indicates loneliness or the loss of a friend.

BACK   To see your back signifies bad luck and old age. To dream a man's back is broken, injured or scabby, signifies that his enemies will get the better of him and that he will be mocked by everyone.

BACK DOOR   To dream that you meet your lover near the back door of their employer's house means that you can feel certain that your lover will desert you for someone else living nearby, or will get into trouble which will force them to move.

BACKBITING   To dream that your character is the subject of scandal by backbiters is a sign that you will be able to gain the object of some of your wishes and have the satisfaction of knowing that others will not ridicule your efforts to do good, and lead an honourable and decent life. Expect to hear someone in authority speak very highly of your character after you have had this dream.

BACKBONE   To dream of the backbone signifies health and joy, and that the dreamer will take delight in his wife and children.

BACKGAMMON   To play this game is indicative of

advancement in theological study. You will become more studious in your habits and, by close application, become proficient in some of the sciences.

BACON To cut bacon signifies the death of someone, probably a close friend or relation. To eat bacon signifies gossiping, although you need fear nothing in business. But if you see fat bacon, be wary of an attempt to ruin you.

BACTERIA This is generally a favourable dream, but it should be considered in connection with other features of the dream.

BADGE You are under observation and will shortly be promoted.

BADGER Hard work is in front of you.

BADMINTON To play this game means that you will soon have a difficult decision to make that will affect your future.

BAG To dream of carrying a full bag means that you will never have much wealth, but that you will always have as much as you really need. To dream of carrying an empty bag signifies approaching

poverty. If the bag is so full that it is impossible to close it, you may expect to receive from somewhere so much money that looking after it will be a constant anxiety.

BAGPIPES Wind instruments such as bagpipes signify trouble, contention and losing a legal battle. To hear the music of bagpipes is a warning of trouble. For a businessman, it indicates failure.

BAIL If you are asking for bail, beware of accidents and unfortunate relationships.

BAILIFF To dream that the bailiff seizes your household goods for debt is a sign that you will have some unexpected favourable change in your circumstances. It will turn out that you are next of kin to some wealthy person who has died, either in this country or abroad, who has left you a very handsome legacy. You will do well to keep down your domestic expenses, as this dream repeated immediately sometimes has the opposite meaning.

BAIT Do not trust blindly in those who seek to please you.

BAIZE Exciting times to

come. Keep a cool head.

BAKER Good fortune is just around the corner.

If you dream of a baker or a baker's shop before applying for a situation or an increase in wages you may be sure that your application will be successful. In other circumstances, such a dream denotes everything that is good.

BAKERY For an independent person to dream they are in a bakery signifies that they or their spouse will lose their present employment, and will suffer from scarcity of food and clothing. For a young person to have this dream, their parent or parents, if living, will need social benefits.

BAKING To dream that you are engaged in baking something in an oven is a sure sign that enemies are about to harm you. Be careful of your so-called friends.

BAKING and BREWING To dream of baking and brewing means a bad housewife, who lies in bed when she should be at work.

BALCONY To dream that you are sitting on a balcony with your sweetheart denotes interruption in courtship from a quarter you little expected. Some lingering disease will afflict your lover and keep him/her in bed for a long time. You will also be afraid that some former sweetheart will gain his/her affections, but your petty jealousy will soon pass and you will enjoy undivided love.

BALDNESS To dream that you are bald or growing bald means that you are about to lose your heart, but it is at the same time a suggestion that that is no reason why you should lose your head. If a young woman dreams that her lover is bald, he will not live to marry her. To dream that one's own head is bald denotes worry.

BALE Good fortune, more or less, according to whether it is a bale of cotton or wool.

BALL To dream you see persons dance at a ball, or that you are at a ball yourself signifies joy, pleasure, recreation or inheritance. It is a good omen for lovers.

BALLAD To hear a ballad, beware of false judgements; to sing one, someone you care for thinks you unkind.

BALLAST Look to your

associates; one is not a true friend.

BALLET To see a performance of this kind at the theatre is indicative of your having attacks of gout or rheumatism, sometimes serious.

BALLOON To dream of an ascent of a balloon means that to gain what you want you will have to stoop pretty low and possibly undertake a perilous journey. But thanks to the lucky star under which you were born, it will not stop you from rising up again.

BALLOT A difference in position and surroundings is on the way; possibly for the better.

BALM True friendship is near you.

BALUSTRADE News of accidents on a river or at sea will soon arrive, possibly involving yourself.

BAMBOO Bamboo growing in a dream indicates relaxed and delightful company.

BANANA A good omen; if you dream you are eating a banana it is a sign you will be rich and happy. To dream you see bananas growing denotes success in love.

BANDAGE Fresh influences will surround you.

BANDSAW Using a saw in a dream means that you will be successful at work.

BANDINESS To dream that your legs have become crooked or misshapen is a sign that a young man will become tall, straight and good-looking. If an old person has this dream it means that in their old age they will become a good walker, full of vigour and energy, free from nervousness or other physical debility.

BANISHMENT To dream that you are driven from your place of abode, or exiled from your native country, is a good dream. You will live to a ripe old age, and your friends and acquaintances will agree that you are virtuous, a benefactor to those less fortunate, generous and kind.

BANJO Playing the banjo in a dream indicates quarrels with a lover.

BANK Paying a visit to the bank means, if you are in business, that you are likely to have many bad and doubtful debts, and that unless you adopt a system of prompt cash payment and no credit your ledger will present a long series of accounts balanced by death, 'running away', 'failure' and other similarly unremunerative items. A dream of a bank should be taken as a warning against investment for some time to come.

BANK BOOK To see a bank book in a dream is a bad sign, indicating that you will be a heavy loser by someone converting to his own use a cheque with which you have entrusted him. Should a bank book, however, be seen lying on the bank counter or in the hands of a bank teller, it signifies that, however long you live, you will never have any financial worries.

BANK NOTE To dream of having a bank note stolen foretells that you are about to lose money and be reduced to comparative poverty, but if you are philosophical about your loss you will be happier with little than you have ever been, or were likely to be, with a great deal.

BANKER' To dream you have business with a banker is a sign of losing part of your trade through great competition in the type of

goods in which you deal. If a person not in business has this dream it means that he will shortly lose part of his wages from slackness of trade or sickness.

BANKRUPTCY To dream that you have lost money and are now bankrupt should be taken as a warning. Some plan is not very creditable to you and should be abandoned at once, as trouble will follow. Be cautious in your transactions and seek the advice of friends older than yourself.

BANNER A good omen, this signifies a speedy rise to a good position or a wealthy marriage and prosperous life.

BANNS To dream that you are listening to your own banns of marriage is indicative of good and prosperous times for the dreamer, who will become a great favourite in his or her circle of acquaintances.

BANQUET To dream of banquets is a very good sign of prosperity, and promises promotion. To dream that you are at a banquet and do not eat denotes shortage of money.

BANTAM COCK An unwise plan which may succeed but will not satisfy you.

BAPTISM To be present at a baptism is an omen of riches or success in love, according to whether you are married or single.

BAR To dream that you are drinking at the bar of a public house is a good sign. You will avoid the society of those who are loud-mouthed, profligate and disorderly. Your children will grow up virtuous and wise.

To dream that you are called to practise at the bar as a lawyer signifies that you will take part in a trial from which you will come away victorious.

BARBARIAN If you have dealings with uncivilised people and have the upper hand, you will have success in business. If you are chased or captured, your future will have many problems.

BARBECUE To see animals roasted whole over an open fire portends the abuse of your hospitality. Cooking on a barbecue indicates disappointments to come.

BARBER If you dream of a barber or his shop, be careful to follow any advice you may receive from your friends during the following week. If you don't, you may experience loss and even poverty.

BAREFOOTEDNESS To go on a journey barefoot is a sign of prosperity. You will do well as a merchant, lawyer, artist or in any trade or profession you may take up. You will also enjoy your travels and meet with good and pleasant company. If you speculate, you will generally be fortunate in your ventures; you will make a fortune by careful trading, and retire in old age with a very handsome pension.

BARGAIN A warning to be steadfast and trust your own opinions.

BARGE You are about to travel some distance. Be careful.

BARK To gather the bark off a tree indicates an embarrassing experience with a member of the opposite sex.

BARKING To dream that you are barking denotes a fundamental improvement in your character. If you hear a dog barking, it is a sign that you will win a lawsuit; if you hear a dog nearby baying at the moon, you will be called upon to help someone. If you are being followed by a pack of barking dogs led by a servant, it signifies approaching danger due to some past folly.

BARLEY and BARLEY BREAD Eating barley bread indicates health and comfort.

BARLEY FIELD To dream that you go through a field of ripe barley at an unseasonable time is indicative of great trouble soon coming upon you; either you will lose relatives and friends, or you will be unfortunate in your choice of a partner in life, or sickness and poverty will strike before many months or years are over.

BARMAID For a young man to dream that he has made love to a barmaid is a sign that he will be called upon to leave his present home and occupation, and either emigrate to a foreign country or seek a situation in a distant part of his own country. To dream that you have married a barmaid means that you will fall into an easy situation and that it will not require either much skill or physical energy to do the duties assigned to your new job.

BARN To see a barn stored with corn signifies that you will marry a rich partner, overthrow your enemy at law, that you will inherit land or grow rich by trading or gifts; it also signifies banqueting or celebrations. If the barn is empty, be prepared for some calamity involving the loss of your money. A barn on fire means good fortune.

BARNACLES Barnacles indicate a peaceful retirement as a reward for your hard work.

BAROMETER This denotes change. If the barometer is broken, that change will be rapid and unexpected.

BARRACKS Your difficulties will soon be lessened.

BARREL A full barrel indicates good fortune. An empty one foretells distress.

BASEBALL To dream of playing or watching this game indicates that you will have many friends and be a popular companion.

BASIN For a man to dream of a basin signifies a nice working girl, and to dream you eat or drink from one shows you are in love with that working girl. For a man to see himself in a basin denotes that he will have children by a working girl.

BASKET For a man to dream of a basket is bad; it denotes poor business to a merchant, lack of employment to a mechanic and loss of place to a servant; but if a woman dreams she receives a number of baskets, it is good.

BASSOON To play this wind instrument is a sign that before very long you will be requested by a friend to take part in an amateur performance for the benefit of a charitable institution.

BASTING To dream that you are in the act of basting a fowl or joint of meat that is cooking is a sign that you will soon marry. In a mysterious and unplanned way, you will meet someone who will either propose to you or you to them, and you will lead a happy and prosperous life together.

BAT Bats or night birds of any kind are a bad omen and anyone who dreams of them must undertake no business that day. To dream that you see a bat flying about in the dusk of the evening signifies that you will meet a person of a deceitful disposition and character. They will propose that you become a business partner, but in fact they are only trying to swindle you out of your hard-earned income, and live at the expense of your forethought.

BATH To see a bath is a sign of suffering or grief. If a person dreams he goes into, or sees herself or himself in a bath, and that he finds it too hot, he will be troubled and afflicted by members of his family.

To dream of a bath is bad; expect after it to experience many hardships and sorrows; if you are in love, problems await you and your sweetheart.

BATHING Anyone who frequently sees others or themselves bathing naked are of a phlegmatic constitution and subject to delusions. To bathe in a clear fountain signifies joy, happiness, prosperity and success in love; if the water is dirty, it foretells shame, sorrow and a disappointment in love.

For anyone in trouble to dream of bathing either in the sea or in a river or lake means that the trouble is about to come to an end, and that a fortunate period will follow.

BATTALION For a young woman to dream that she sees a battalion of soldiers on parade is a sign that she will never gain the love of one who wears a service uniform.

BATTERY For a young man to dream he stands in front of a battery is a sign that he will be called upon to take the place of a fellow workman who is in the Territorials and on a training exercise in some distant part of the country.

BATTLE   To see a battle in the street forewarns you against secret enemies; if you are in love your sweetheart is false to you; it is also a sign of war and tumult. It implies that you will have a quarrel with your sweetheart, although much joy may await you afterwards. Dreaming of being present at, or engaged in, a battle predicts that you will shortly try to be the peacemaker between two friends, and that in consequence you will get yourself into a bad scrape.

BATTLESHIP   Seeing a battleship at sea indicates that your life will become easier. A fleet of ships indicates success in a business venture.

BAY   To be sailing in a calm bay indicates a peaceful and contented life.

BAY TREE   The bay tree denotes a rich and beautiful partner; and also failure of affairs because it is bitter. But it is good for physicians, poets and religious people to dream of this.

BAY WINDOW   Looking out of a bay window indicates many happy hours to come. If the window is broken, you will move house.

BAYONET   For a soldier to dream that his bayonet is broken is a bad sign. He will be brought into disgrace by misconduct; if he has obtained promotion he will be degraded to the ranks. If he sees his bayonet shining brightly he will gain the confidence of his superiors, and will soon gain advancement. For a soldier to dream that he uses his bayonet in a battle charge is indicative of his long enjoyment of peace.

BAZAAR   To help at a bazaar is a forecast that you will have many lovers; and if you marry early it will prove to be a wealthy match, though at the time it may not appear to be so.

BEACH   To dream of being on the beach indicates that you will have to explain your actions to a friend. If you are naked, you will soon undertake something unusual.

BEACON   Avoid misunderstandings. If you should unavoidably quarrel, take the first steps towards a reconciliation, or you will regret it.

BEADS   False friends or dissatisfaction.

BEAGLE   A beagle in the street is a sign of news from a friend.

BEAM   If you see a beam break or fall from a height, it is a bad omen, often predicting the death of someone near.

BEANS   Seeing the land sown with beans denotes affliction and trouble. To dream of eating beans signifies trouble, arguments and illness.

BEAR   To see a bear signifies a rich, inexpert, cruel and audacious enemy. If the animal pursues you, then look to your friends – one of them is trying to do you an injury. If, on the other hand, you stroke or pet the beast, you may be sure that your lover will be true to you and bring you much happiness.

BEARD   Anyone who dreams he has his beard trimmed will be in danger of losing a great part of his property, of being sick, or run the risk of losing his life by some humiliating death. If anyone dreams that his beard has

grown bigger than usual, he will grow richer. To dream you have a small beard signifies suits and controversies at law. To have a long beard signifies strength or gain; if he is in trade, he will thrive; if he is in love, he will marry his present lover who will bring him some money; if he is a farmer, it denotes good crops and an addition to his farm. To see your beard dry signifies joy. To see your beard pulled out by the roots signifies great danger. To dream you wash your beard signifies sadness.

If a married woman dreams of a beard, it is unlucky; it can foretell the loss of her husband, and that she will fall into great distress. If a girl dreams of a beard, it denotes that she will soon be married, and that her first child will be a boy. For a woman to dream that she has a beard is a very lucky omen, and denotes that she will speedily attain her greatest desires. For a widow to dream that she has a beard shows that she will remarry and have a loving husband again.

For orators, ambassadors, lawyers or philosophers to dream of a long, rough and thick beard shows success.

For a young child to dream they have a beard signifies

great danger, but to a young man it is a sign he will rise by his own efforts and achieve his greatest ambitions.

BEAST To dream any furious beast assaults you, such as a bull, bear, lion or dog, etc., denotes open enemies plotting against you.

To dream you have the head of a lion, a wolf, a panther or an elephant instead of your own is good. Anyone who tries something which is apparently beyond his power, if he has had this dream, will attain respect and dignity. To dream you have the head of a dog, horse or ass, etc., means pain and misery. To have a bird's head means you should not stay long in the country.

BEATING If a woman dreams that she beats her husband, that signifies fear, although her husband loves her. If she dreams she strikes her lover, that signifies she is insecure and her lover will get into trouble.

BEAUTY To dream that you are beautiful generally foretells an illness or disease of the skin, which will detract from your present good looks.

BEAVER Patient effort will be rewarded.

BED To see the bedposts on fire without being destroyed signifies good fortune to male children. To dream of sitting on a girl's bedside or talking with her is a sign of marriage. To dream of buying a bed denotes sickness. To dream you go to the bedside of your lover foretells a speedy marriage; if you dream you get into bed, you will have a child no less than 12 months after marriage, who will become rich and support you.

BED-BUGS You will receive bad news. If you kill the bedbugs in your dream, you will surmount your problems.

BED-MAKING To all those who never make beds, this means a sudden and provident joy. To change the sheets indicates removals, alteration of station or pregnancy.

BEDCLOTHES For a wealthy person to dream of bedclothes is very unlucky; it implies a change in circumstances for the worse. But for poor people to dream of bedclothes denotes a change for the better, especially if the bedclothes are clean.

BEDLAM To dream that you become an inmate of a madhouse is a sign that you will shortly be offered a post of responsibility and trust, where you will be required to take on many new responsibilities. You will be well regarded for your sound judgement and good conduct.

BEDROOM For a young woman to dream that she is in a very beautiful bedroom, well furnished with expensive furniture and drapery, is a sign that there will shortly be a very strange change in the circumstances of her life. Be prepared to hear that some wealthy old bachelor asks you to be his housekeeper; and if you refuse he will propose marriage.

BEDSPREAD To dream that your bedspread is torn can mean that one of your family will be born disabled. Or someone in your house is likely to be disabled by an accident. You will experience good luck if you see a hideous insect or reptile on the bedspread; you, your wife or children will inherit from someone you knew nothing about.

BEECH TREE A beech tree signifies promiscuous women, and these trees are good for those who are involved in shady business; to others they mean pain and hard work.

BEEF To dream of eating beef is a sure omen of the death of a friend or relative.

BEER If you are drinking beer you may take it as a prediction that, unless you are careful, you will lose a large sum of money. Above all, avoid horse-racing and lotteries. If you only see the beer without drinking it, an accident will follow.

BEE To see bees signifies profit to country people and trouble to the rich, but if they dream they make their honey in any part of the house that signifies dignity, eloquence and good success in business. If you are stung by a bee that signifies anxiety and trouble caused by envious people. You will lose your good reputation, and if you are in love, you will lose your sweetheart. To dream you see bees at work is a very lucky dream.

If the bees swarm over you, you will be happy in your love affairs. Should they be angry, be on your guard against receiving an evil account of yourself. If you take them in your hand, you will be notoriously lucky; if you kill them you will be overwhelmed by ruin. To dream you give bees away signifies a good marriage. To dream that bees fly about your ears shows you are being annoyed by many enemies but if you beat them off without being stung by them, it is a sign of victory and of your overcoming them. To take bees out of a swarm signifies profit and gain.

BEESWAX Dreaming of beeswax is a sure sign that you will receive a sum of money, or that you will become rich through the inheritance of an unexpected windfall.

BEETLE To dream that a black beetle creeps down your back is a sign that you will be the subject of a foul slander from those you thought were your friends. If they creep over your face it means that you are the subject of praise from people with whom you have not previously had much connection. To dream that you kill beetles means that you will shortly make active efforts to stop the slanderous rumours circulating about a friend or friends of yours.

BEETROOT Eating beetroot signifies freedom from trouble and expedition of business. Dreaming of beetroot indicates that you have an enemy who is trying to do you an injury, but this will turn out advantageously for you.

BEGGAR To dream of a beggar predicts a sudden change in your life which may be better or worse, according to how you act. Be very careful, therefore, and avoid confiding in strangers or acquaintances. To a person contemplating marriage, a dream of a beggar denotes there is a rival for his or her fiancé's affections, and they will have to act firmly to win. To dream that you give beggars alms indicates success in business, and that you will obtain, after much difficulty, the object of your affections. If you refuse them alms, it denotes misery, want and prison. To dream of poor people or beggars entering into a house and carrying away anything, whether it is given to them or not, denotes very great adversity.

BEGONIA To wear a begonia flower portends criticism from others for your extravagance.

BEHEADING To dream that you are beheaded according to the traditions of the Indians and Persians and that the head is separated from the body, signifies liberty to prisoners, health to the sick, comfort to those in distress and payment of debts to creditors. To anyone in authority it indicates good fortune, and that their problems and fears will be turned into joy and confidence in their servants and subjects. If anyone dreams that a person he knows beheads him, he will share with him in his pleasure and honour. If anyone dreams that a young child cuts off his head, he will not live long if he is sick, but if he is healthy he will gain honour. If a pregnant woman dreams this, she will have a boy and her husband will die suddenly. If anyone dreams his head is half cut off, these things will be fulfilled by halves. If anyone dreams that his throat is cut with a knife, he will be injured by someone. If he dreams he cuts the throat of one of his acquaintances, he will do him an injury; if he does not know the person, it will be done to a stranger. If anyone dreams that he is beheaded as a martyr for religion, that man will be elevated to the height of honour, and his soul will be happy in heaven. According to the Egyptian tradition, if anyone dreams he beheads an armed man, he will enter the service of some great person, where he will realise his ambitions.

BELCH   You will lose a good friend unless you act with more tact and consideration.

BELLE   To dream that you are at a ball and that you dance with the most beautiful girl is indicative of trouble coming to you from some of your female acquaintances. Expect to hear that a beautiful woman is claiming damages against you for breach of promise; or you will have your reputation tarnished by a report that you have been cruel to someone. You will be given leave of absence from work until any unpleasant affairs have been sorted out to the satisfaction of your employers. For a young woman to dream that she is 'the belle of the ball' means that she will meet with an arrogant, conceited fool who will try to engage her affections. If prudent, she will best serve her own interests by avoiding him in every possible way.

BELLS   To hear bells ring signifies an alarm, sickness, disturbance and commotions, especially if the dreamer is married. To play tunes on small bells signifies discord and disunion between employers and employees. Hearing the church bells ringing as if for a wedding indicates that your lover will shortly leave you for another, then another, all of which will be your gain, despite the fact that it will not appear so at first.

BELLOWS To dream that you fan a fire with bellows means that you can never gain the desire on which your mind is set. You will be thwarted on all sides.

BELLY If anyone dreams that their belly is bigger and fatter than usual, their family and property will increase proportionately according to the size of the stomach. If your belly has become lean and shrunken, you will avoid a bad accident. If anyone dreams that his belly is swollen but empty, he will become poor – even though he is well-regarded by many.

BELLY ACHE If anyone dreams his belly aches, he will suffer many family problems.

BELT To dream of putting on a belt indicates a happy future.

BENCH An unfortunate dream; attend carefully to work or you may lose your job.

BENEDICTION An unexpected and unwelcome wedding.

BENEFACTOR If you receive a boon from someone, be careful that people are not gossiping unkindly about you. If you give money to someone else, you will be successful at work.

BEQUEST To dream that you are bequeathing money or property to friends or relatives is a sure sign that you will soon receive money from an unexpected quarter.

BEREAVEMENT News of a friend's marriage soon to take place.

BERRY Social activities of a happy nature. If you dream you are picking many blackberries, it indicates financial gains.

BEST MAN To dream you are acting as best man denotes the failure of a plan of yours through a false friend.

BETTING To dream that you are betting warns you to be careful of your money for a time. Keep it on you. Do not lend any money, however small the amount may be, otherwise you will lose it all.

BEWILDERMENT You will receive a disquieting letter.

BEWITCHED To dream you are bewitched is a sign that you should take care in financial dealings or you will be hoodwinked.

BIAS To dream of cutting fabric on the bias indicates bad news from a friend.

BIBLE To see a Bible is a sign that you will be offered a position of trust.

BICKERING This is a sign of a quarrel with your loved one.

BICYCLE To dream of riding a bicycle means that for some years you will have constant change, always seeking for rest and comfort but only finding turmoil and problems.

BIER To see a bier carried from your house denotes the marriage of a member of your family within a short time. If a coffin is on the bier, it is a sign that the wedding clothes and rings for both bride and bridegroom have already been bought, ready for the big day.

BIGAMY For a man to dream that he is guilty of bigamy is a significant dream. He will meet with a partner soon if he is not married but, if he is, he will keep his wife

a long time (in fact, she will in all probability outlive him and re-marry after his death). For a woman to dream that she is guilty of this crime denotes great distress in the death of her present husband from a dreadful accident.

BILL To dream that you are paying bills denotes speedy financial gains; that they are unpaid, signifies evil speaking.

BILLIARDS Another dream of unusual occurrence, unless you play regularly, when the omen loses all significance. It indicates some difficulty; if you are in love, or engaged, it means that you will be opposed by your fiancé's family.

BINOCULARS Using binoculars at a sporting event indicates good fortune. If you are spying on someone, expect no good to come of your actions.

BIOGRAPHY Reading a biography indicates a serious illness in a member of your family.

BIRD To see many birds signifies lawsuits. To hear birds sing signifies love, joy, delight and news of a wedding. To hear a cock crow signifies prosperity. To see birds fighting signifies misfortune. To see birds fly over your head signifies prejudice by enemies. To see black birds signifies troubles. Birds entering a house foretells approaching losses, sometimes of friends but most often of money. To see several birds in a cage predicts a happy home life, although a long journey will tear you away from your friends for some time. To dream of a pair of birds or any other animal signifies the birth of a son. The croaking of ravens or screeching of owls signifies the death of friends.

BIRD'S NEST To dream you find a bird's nest is a good sign. To dream you find a nest without eggs or birds signifies great disappointment.

BIRTH This dream can signify the death of a sick person, because the dead are wrapped in linen clothes as children, and laid in the ground. For a woman to dream she is pregnant denotes sorrow and heaviness. If a woman dreams she has given birth to a child although she was not pregnant, it is a sign that she will happily accomplish her intentions. A girl who has this dream will quickly lose her virginity if she is not careful. For a man to dream that he sees two or three children born shows that he will have joy and meet with success in his business. When someone who has no children dreams they have many small children, it signifies they will have many anxieties and obstructions in their affairs. To dream of your birth is good for someone who is poor, but to a rich person it signifies that they will not be in charge in the house and that others will order them about against their will.

BIRTH CONTROL This is a good dream for those who are married, as they will have a wonderful family of which they will be very proud.

BIRTHDAY To dream that it is your own birthday is a fortunate sign for money matters or business affairs. To dream that it is the birthday of some friend or relative is a sign that they will benefit shortly, probably in connection with yourself.

BISCUIT To eat a biscuit denotes that you will suffer from indigestion and will have to follow a very plain diet. Your stomach will have to be treated very carefully, or other complaints will follow.

BISHOP Sudden death of a friend or relative.

BITE To dream you are bitten signifies you will suffer the pangs of jealousy.

BLACK This colour is unlucky to dream of. If you are in love, it denotes that your partner is very unhappy and is about to experience some problems. Black at a funeral denotes a struggle before success.

BLACK CLOTHES To see yourself in black clothes signifies joy.

BLACKBERRY To collect blackberries indicates that you will suffer setbacks in your plans. If you are eating them, you will suffer great losses.

BLACKBIRD To see blackbirds signifies tribulation, deceit and slander. To hear them sing signifies joy and delight.

BLACKMAIL Beware of promiscuous relationships or you will suffer a long period of bad luck.

BLACKSMITH To dream you work in iron and strike on the anvil signifies trouble and lawsuits.

BLAME If you are blamed for something, beware of hypocrisy among your friends. If you are blaming someone else, your peace of mind will suffer.

BLANKET To dream that you buy blankets in summer denotes that an affliction from a fever or severe pleurisy will trouble you. To dream that you buy blankets in winter indicates an attack of a very malignant fever.

BLASPHEMY If you dream you are cursing, it foretells bad fortune; if you are cursed, all your expectations will be fulfilled.

BLEACHING For a woman to dream of bleaching her hair indicates popularity with the opposite sex, but for a man to have this dream indicates humiliation.

BLEAT To dream that you hear the lambs bleat for their ewes in summer is a good sign. If the dreamer is young, it denotes that they will be a dutiful son or daughter, well regarded by all their friends because of their thoughtfulness.

BLEMISH For a woman to dream her face is blemished means that she will have many lovers. If the blemishes are on her legs, she should beware of promiscuity in her relationships.

BLESSING If you are blessing someone else in your dream, your path in life will be strewn with problems. If you are being blessed, your life will be happy and carefree.

BLINDNESS To dream that you are blind is a sign that you have placed your confidence in someone who is your inveterate enemy. Be warned to look out for mistakes and avoid them. It also denotes that your lover is unfaithful and prefers someone else; in business, it denotes that you will lose money, and that your employees lack loyalty. It can presage loss of children, brothers, father or mother, though it is a good dream to those who are poor or in prison. In the main, it is a bad dream for travellers, soldiers, traders, navigators, astronomers or astrologers. If anyone is searching for something they have lost, and dreams this dream, they will never find it.

BLINDMAN'S BUFF To play at this game signifies prosperity, joy, pleasure, health and harmony among friends and relations.

BLINKING Exercise your tact in your dealings with other people.

BLONDE Women who dream of being blonde are likely to suffer ill health. A man who dreams of blonde women should beware of difficulties at work.

BLOOD and BLEEDING To see blood is about as bad an omen as you can receive. If you are engaged, your sweetheart will lose affection for you, and your friends will prove false. To a businessman, failure in some big undertaking and robbery will follow.

To dream of bleeding denotes loss of goods and character, and that your lover will not marry you. To dream you see someone else bleeding indicates that someone who pretends to be your friend is about to take advantage of you. To dream you draw the blood of another denotes that you will recover a lawsuit, and be successful in love and business. To dream another draws your blood is a certain sign that you will be unsuccessful in love, business and everything you undertake.

To dream of vomiting a great deal of bright red blood is good for a poor person, for they will get a store of money. It is also very good for anyone who has no children or whose relatives are abroad. The first will have a child of his own and the second will be reunited with his family. To dream of carrying blood is not good for anyone who is trying to hide. To spit a little blood foretells sedition.

To dream of having a nose bleed signifies loss of goods and money to those who are phlegmatic and melancholy, but to the irascible and optimistic it signifies health and happiness.

BLOOD SUCKER Any animal which sucks blood, such as a leech or even a vampire, gives warning that you should choose your friends more carefully.

BLOODHOUND These dogs indicate faithfulness of a friend, unless they are hunting you – in which case they indicate that a friend will be deceitful.

BLOSSOMING of TREES To dream you see all sorts of trees blossoming is a sign of joy, comfort and recreation.

BLOT To dream you make a blot on a clean sheet of paper means a strange bed and some travelling to come.

BLOTTING PAPER Beware of talking too much; you may betray a secret entrusted to you by a friend.

BLOW To dream you strike a blow is a sign of a lawsuit. To dream you receive them means a reconciliation with your enemies.

BLUE Denotes happiness, prosperity and esteem from various people you want to please. To dream you are dressed in a variety of colours denotes a variety of fortunes are in store for you. If you are in love, a quarrel will take place between you and your sweetheart which, after much uneasiness, will be settled by friends.

BLUNDER This is one of the dreams that go by contrary and means that you will do unexpectedly well in your next undertaking.

BLUSHING Blushing in a dream indicates that you will be embarrassed by lies spread about you. If you see other people blushing, take care that you do not spread lies about other people.

BOA CONSTRICTOR This snake symbolises the devil, so

the dream is a bad one unless you kill the snake.

BOAR If anyone dreams they have hunted or captured a wild boar they will chase or take some enemy that has the same qualities as the wild boar. If anyone dreams they have the head of a recently killed wild boar brought to them, that predicts that they will soon obtain their desire from their most powerful enemy. To chase a wild boar indicates unsuccessful efforts; to be chased means separation.

BOAST Do not be impulsive, or you will cause trouble among your family or friends.

BOAT To dream that you are in a boat on a river, lake or pond of clear water is very good and signifies joy, prosperity and success, though if the water is rough and stormy, it means the opposite. If you are walking in a boat and enjoying yourself without fear, you will have comfort and success in your affairs. To be in a boat in danger of overturning is a sign of danger, unless the dreamer is a prisoner or captive; in that case it denotes liberty and freedom. To dream of being in a boat is a good omen, and if you are about to embark on

a new enterprise you can rest assured that it will be successful. If, however, the boat is drifting about in all directions, be careful that you do not get into trouble through some illegal transaction.

BOBBIN For a dressmaker to dream that her bobbins have no thread indicates business prosperity; if they have plenty of thread on them there will be a lack of both work and money.

BOG For a person to dream that they are in a bog or marshy piece of land, where they sink deep in the swamp, is a good dream. The dreamer will be eminent in trade, a profession or speculation. Success will attend their efforts; prosperity will crown whatever they put their hand to. Wealth, advancement and greatness will be the result of all their schemes.

BODY To see a beautiful body in a dream presages business advancement if the body is male, or social success if it is female.

BOIL Trouble with family matters or an unpleasant job to come.

BOILED MEAT Sufferings.

BOLT To dream that you are locked in a room with bolts and bars is a sign that your freedom of action in forthcoming legal problems is greater than you at first imagined. You will never suffer imprisonment or detention. The person who has this dream is often a great traveller.

BOMBARDMENT If you dream of being under enemy bombardment, your plans will come to fruition.

BOMBER Planes flying above you show that you will overcome your difficulties if you are decisive.

BONDSMAN To dream that you are bond for another person, either in money or criminal matters, is a sign that difficulties are ahead that will launch you into trouble and annoyance on behalf of people who are extravagant in their habits and expenditure.

BONES Signify misfortune which may or may not be overcome by courage.

BONFIRE To dream of helping to build a bonfire indicates that you are about to change your mind about many things, when you will burn much that you used to worship and worship much that you used to burn.

BONNET For a young woman to dream about wearing a new bonnet is a sign that she is about to land in difficulty through love of finery, desire for admiration and envy of the fancy clothes of some of her friends. But if a woman loses her bonnet, she must guard her reputation; if her bonnet is blown off, she will have something she dearly prizes stolen. A young man dreaming of a girl's bonnet, either in a shop window or on her head, may infer that he will marry before many months have passed.

BONUS If you are given a bonus in a dream, your professional life will continue to be successful.

BOOK To dream of reading a book, especially if in your dream you are surrounded by a considerable library, denotes that you are not likely to marry and will in all probability find consolation in literary pursuits. The chances against your marrying can be calculated by the number of books in the surrounding library. To dream of meeting a young lady in a bookshop signifies, in the case of a young man, that though he is fond of books he will marry a wife who will care little for them. Should you be reading the Bible, then you will be happy and respected by a large circle of friends. To dream that your bookcase is almost empty of books is a sign that you will become a scholar of great note, pass many examinations and ultimately be so proficient in your studies that you will become a certified teacher in a public school if you choose to follow that profession, or that you will either be a good accountant, a proficient astronomer, or else an expert in some physical pursuits. To dream that your bookcase is full of elegantly bound books is evidence that you will not have that taste for study which your opportunities offer to you. You will be behind most of your schoolmates in your education.

Books signify the 'life' of the dreamer. To eat books is good for schoolmasters or anyone who earns a living by books or strives to be eloquent. To others it signifies sudden death.

BOOKMARK You will keep an advantageous appointment.

BOOKSELLER If you dream this is your profession or that you meet a bookseller, you will have many friends.

BOOKSHOP If you dream of being in a bookshop, you should pursue your literary talents, but make sure that they do not interfere with other aspects of your life.

BOOKWORM Security and comfort will be yours.

BOOTS To have good boots or shoes signifies joy and happiness, honour and profit through your employees.

Old boots indicate a return to an old love.

BORAGE Eating borage signifies freedom from trouble and a business expedition.

BORROW To dream that you borrow anything is a bad dream. You will find the adage true:

He that goes a
borrowing,
Goes a sorrowing.

BOSOM To dream that your bosom is inflamed or painful is a sign of coming illness.

BOSS To be friendly with your boss in a dream is a good sign, but do not take advantage of his approval to be lazy at work.

BOTTLE Foretells bad fortune, bad news and, if black, the death of a friend. Empty bottles signify illness; wine bottles, prosperity; upset bottles, domestic troubles.

BOUND To dream that you are bound with rope or cord signifies that you will fall victim to a serious disease.

BOUQUET For a young woman to dream that her sweetheart presents her with a beautiful bouquet is a sign that her course in love will be interrupted by many unpleasant transactions on the part of her sweetheart. He will be given to flirting with other girls in her absence, and she will be annoyed by his thoughtlessness or want of consideration with regard to her feelings. For a young man to dream that he gives a splendid bouquet to a bride on her wedding day means that a death will take place among some of his dearest relatives or friends.

BOW To dream you shoot with a bow signifies comfort. To carry a bow signifies desire or torment.

BOWLS A fortunate dream, especially if you are taking part in the game, as this denotes future prosperity.

BOY Boys who are playing in a dream are a good sign to the dreamer.

BOY SCOUT One of your dearest dreams will come true.

BOX An empty box predicts unhappiness in love or trouble in marriage. If the box is full of useful articles, then the opposite can be expected.

BOXING MATCH An astonishing announcement will be made in your hearing which will lead to important events for you. Be wary of repeating or writing about it.

BRACELET For a lady to dream she is wearing a new bracelet is a sign that someone is slandering her. If she allows someone to fasten it for her, she will be ruled by the man she marries.

BRACKEN An adventure is awaiting you if you dream of lying in bracken, but its outcome will depend on the reason you are lying there.

BRAIN If anyone dreams their brain is large and efficient, they will be an able counsellor to those in authority, will govern themselves prudently and will achieve their ambitions with honour and profit. If, on the contrary, anyone dreams their brain is sick, damaged or painful, they will be unfortunate in their advice and enterprises, will pass for an inexpert and imprudent person and run into many problems.

BRAKE If you dream of applying the brake to a vehicle and it does not work, be careful of making commitments which you cannot fulfil.

BRAMBLES These represent difficulties, and indicate poverty or privation. If you push through, without serious harm from the thorns, then you will overcome your troubles.

BRANCH Trees are fortunate, being one of Nature's own blessings. If in your dream you see a tree with many fertile branches, it is a most fortunate omen. But be careful if you see any dead or broken branches.

BRANDY Denotes good news, no matter in what form it appears.

BRASS Observe your associates closely and do not let a false friend make you unhappy.

BRAVERY This warns the dreamer to keep a cool head and act with all courage, as an emergency is at hand that will test the nerve.

BRAWL If you are injured in a brawl, this indicates problems to come, but otherwise you will be fortunate.

BRAYING To dream that you hear the braying of a donkey is a sign that shortly you will hear of the death of some celebrated eccentric local character who has long been noted for oddities in conduct and behaviour.

BREAD To dream of eating white bread made of wheat signifies profit to the rich and damage to the poor. On the contrary, to dream of eating wholemeal bread denotes profit and gain to the poor, and losses to the rich. To dream of eating barley bread signifies health and contentment. To dream you carry hot bread signifies accusation. To cut barley bread signifies rejoicing. To dream of your usual bread, and eating it, is good. But if you eat a different sort of bread from usual, that means sickness if you are poor or accusations of false dealing if you are rich.

To dream that you throw

away bread is a prediction that you will suffer from slanderous reports spread abroad by a stranger. To dream you see a great quantity of bread denotes success in life. To dream you are eating good bread denotes that you will be married shortly.

BREAK A bad omen. If you break anything in your dream, be prepared for hardships and sadness for some time to come.

BREAKFAST To dream that you are eating your breakfast shows that you will do something for which you will be sorry.

BREAST To dream that your breast is beautiful is a good omen. For men, it is also a good dream if it is hairy as it is a sign of gain, but to a married woman it foretells widowhood.

BREATH If anyone dreams he has bad breath he will be despised by everyone.

BREEZE To dream you are in a strong breeze presages a successful speculation.

BRIARS To go through places covered with brambles means troubles ahead. If they prick you, unknown enemies

will slander you with your friends, and unfavourable rumours will cause problems with your lover; if you bleed, expect heavy losses in trade. If you dream you pass through them without injury, then you will eventually triumph over all your enemies and be happy.

BRIBE For a man to dream that he receives a bribe at an election contest is indicative of purity and honesty of character of the political parties to whom he is opposed.

BRICKLAYING You will increase your financial security by patient hard work.

BRIDE To see a bride warns you to beware of a rival either in business or love.

BRIDGE To fall off a bridge signifies obstruction. If the bridge is made of wood you may receive some honour; if it is iron, you will encounter many obstacles which will cause you trouble. To stand under a bridge for any length of time is very unlucky.

To dream you are crossing over a bridge is a good omen. It denotes prosperity through life and success in love. To dream you are passing under a bridge indicates that you will never be perfectly at ease. To dream a bridge breaks down with you on it denotes sudden death.

BRIEFCASE A business trip will be successful only if the briefcase is well worn; if it is new, your trip will fail through lack of preparation.

BRIGAND Dangers are in store, but you will surmount them.

BRONCHITIS To be troubled with this unpleasant disease is a sign that you will, with the proper cultivation of your voice, become a good singer, and if you devote much time and attention to the art you will become eminently popular and successful as a singer.

BRONZE A bronze statue indicates that you will not marry the person of your choice.

BROOCH To wear a strange brooch is a good or bad sign, according to the place where you see yourself in the dream. If you are wearing it at home, you will shortly discover something to your advantage in taking the advice of a friend who has partly succeeded in the construction of a new machine, and who wants you to join him in bringing it before the public as a patent. If you are wearing it before a number of strange people, you may expect to be waylaid on your way home and perhaps robbed.

BROOD For a mother to dream that she sees a brood of chickens gathered under the wing of the hen is a sign that, in spite of her care, earnest prayers and careful education of her children, some of them will go wrong.

BROOK Denotes vexation and sorrow. But if the water is exceptionally clear, wealth will follow the trouble. If the water is muddy, your sorrow will be a long one.

BROOM Beware of a false friend. The broom signifies that someone is seeking to take advantage of you.

BROTH A good sign which signifies profit and gain.

BROTHEL To dream of visiting a brothel is a dream of contrary and signifies a happy home life.

BROTHER For a girl to dream of a brother is a sign that she will receive a proposal of marriage before very long. For a brother to dream of a brother denotes a coming family quarrel.

BROTHER-IN-LAW   If you respect your brother-in-law in your dream, you may find that he has not been honest with you.

BROW   To dream you have a brow of brass, copper, marble or iron signifies irreconciliable hatred against your enemies.

For a young unmarried woman to dream that she is seated on the brow of a hill with her lover is a sign of an unpleasant marriage, if it takes place with the young man she dreams about. The match will be unsuitable because their tastes will be different, their desires will be opposite, their wishes will be contrary, and the conduct of each will be unacceptable to the other.

BROWN   To dream of anything brown is a sign that you are putting trust in false people.

BRUISES   A warning to all but the most robust that their health is suffering from overstrain.

BRUSH   Should you touch or use a brush in your dream your greatest wish will shortly be granted.

BRUTALITY   To witness a

brutal attack indicates a return to childhood haunts.

BUBBLES   A sign of gaiety. Avoid dissipation, or you may lose your sweetheart.

BUCKET   To dream of a bucket with the bottom knocked out denotes that you will shortly lose heavily by a great mercantile fraud unless you exercise proper precautions.

BUCKLE   For a woman to dream that she has lost the buckle of her belt is a sign that some important agreement she has made, or that has been made on her behalf, will be broken, and she will suffer from it.

BUGLE CALL   This announces success to your efforts.

BUG   A warning to act cautiously as there are unfortunate influences around you.

BUILDING   To dream you build or arrange for a house to be built signifies molestation, loss, sickness or death. Some venture dear to your heart will fall through. To dream of a very tall building denotes a long life and happiness. To dream of being among buildings denotes that you will change your present place of residence, and that you will make many friends in life.

BULL A bull signifies an important person; so if anyone dreams he receives either an injury or something good from a bull, he will receive it from someone in authority. An attack from such a creature is a warning that a supposed friend is slandering you. To be gored means injury from influential people; to kill a bull means suffering; two bulls fighting signifies brotherly love.

BULLDOG To dream that you meet with a bulldog is a sign that some friends whom you thought had deserted you will again renew your acquaintance and offer their assistance to you by good advice and financial help if necessary.

BULLET If you dream of bullets being fired in a dream, you are in danger, either physical or from unfaithful friends.

BULLFIGHT If you are enjoying a bullfight in your dream, an unpleasant occurrence will soon upset your family circle. If you are not enjoying yourself, prepare for foreign travel.

BULLOCK For a woman to dream that she is frightened by a bullock in the street is a sign that at some future time, when her children are in danger, or her husband is suffering from a serious and infectious disease, she will show great courage and rush to the place of danger to rescue or help those whom she loves most.

BULL'S-EYE For a young man to dream that he sees the centre of the target and hits it at the first shot is an unlucky dream, for he will never become a crack shot. To dream that you miss the bull's-eye is a good sign. By practice and perseverance you will become a very efficient and successful marksman.

BULLY To dream of being bullied or helping someone who is suffering means that you will be respected by friends and colleagues. If you are the bully in the dream, expect a long string of bad luck.

BUMPER To drink or see a large glass of wine indicates a merry meeting.

BUNION Presages the return of a traveller from a great distance.

BUNGALOW This signifies the friendship of those around you and possible social advancement.

BUNK You will have financial problems which will be difficult to overcome.

BURDEN Carrying a burden signifies you will depend upon others for help.

BURGLAR To dream that you fight with a burglar in your own house is a sign that someone who works for you is dishonest.

BURNING To see a burning light in someone's hands signifies that some mischief done will be discovered and the person punished and that there will be no possibility of excusing or concealing it. When the light is extinguished it means the opposite.

If you dream you see one or more houses burning with fire that is not violent or sparkling and that those houses are neither consumed nor destroyed, that signifies goods, riches and inheritances to the poor; to the rich it indicates honours, responsibilities and dignity. But if the fire is burning with a smoky, violent or sparkling fire and the houses fall and are destroyed, that denotes the opposite. When a man dreams that his bed is on fire and that he dies, that signifies injury or sickness to his wife. And if the wife dreams it, the same may happen to her husband. If you see the curtains or hall furniture destroyed by fire, that sometimes indicates injury or death to the owner of the house. If you dream that the kitchen is on fire, that could denote death to whoever does the cooking. When a man believes a shop is destroyed by fire, that signifies loss of goods and possessions. If the front windows of the house are burning, that might signify the death of a brother; if they are those of the back of the house, it could mean the death of a sister. If the gates are burning, that can signify death to the mistress of the house. To see the top of the house on fire denotes loss of goods, lawsuits or the death of friends.

To kindle a fire which burns immediately signifies that your children will be fortunate and honour their mother. If a woman dreams that she kindles or lights a fire it is a sign she is pregnant and will have a safe delivery of a fortunate child, whether it is a boy or a girl. If you kindle a fire with difficulty and it soon goes out, it denotes damage and dishonour to both you and your wife – and you are often the cause of it.

To see a castle destroyed by fire signifies injury, sickness or death to the owner, and to see a city on fire denotes famine, war or pestilence to that city.

To see a man publicly burned signifies loss in merchandise or sickness. If you see your clothes burned, it signifies vexation, injury, reproach, overthrowing at law and loss of friends.

Anyone who sees himself burning and in pain can expect envy, displeasure, anger and arguments. To burn your fingers signifies envy and sin. To dream you feel burning signifies great danger. To dream you feel burnt denotes a fever. Seeing a stack of corn burned and consumed signifies famine and death, but if it is not destroyed it denotes fertility and great riches to the dreamer. To hold a burning straw torch in public signifies joy, honour and the good management of affairs. To see a great fire in heaven indicates attacks by enemies, poverty and various misfortunes. A brisk, sparkling fire denotes anger and hasty news but a clear, moderate fire is good.

To dream of burning implies a sudden danger. For a man to dream he is burned signifies that he will be rich and respected, but if he imagines that he was burned by a fire that did not quite consume him he will inevitably perish in the end. To burn yourself can sometimes mean good fortune.

To dream you see burning lights descending from heaven is a very bad sign indeed and portends some dreadful accident to the dreamer.

BURIAL To be buried signifies that you will have as much wealth as you have earth laid on top of you. To dream that you are buried alive is an evil omen and signifies prison or captivity. If anyone dreams he is buried alive he is in danger of being unhappy and unfortunate during his life.

To dream that you inter or bury your best friend or nearest relative is a sign that you will hear of good fortune attending some of your friends or relatives who have emigrated, who have prospered in business, and with whom the climate agrees very well indeed. If you see someone you know at a funeral it is a sign that a friend or relative dear to you will die. In most cases it proves to be a rich relative.

BUS Travelling in a bus in a dream indicates difficult times ahead.

BUSH If the bushes are green and luxuriant, expect protection and favour where you least anticipated it. If the bushes are bare of foliage, luck will not be on your side and scandals may follow.

BUSINESS To dream you manage a very important business signifies obstruction. For a working man to dream of business affairs denotes a legacy. To dream of bad business concerns signifies that your ideas will in future turn to religion.

BUTCHER To dream of seeing a butcher is in general a very unlucky omen and usually foretells some injury to the dreamer. If you are in love, expect disappointments. If you are in trade, someone will defraud you. If you are a farmer, your livestock will fall ill. If you see a butcher cutting up meat, some of your friends may die, while you could experience misery and poverty.

BUTTER Surprises; to make butter signifies a legacy.

BUTTERCUP Walking through buttercups indicates that you will have a happy marriage and healthy children.

BUTTERFLY To dream of a butterfly is a sign you have an inconstant lover or sweetheart. Domestic troubles may follow.

BUTTERMILK To drink buttermilk indicates disappointment in love. To the married, it means trouble, sorrow and losses.

BUTTERSCOTCH Someone close to you will be marrying soon.

BUTTOCKS Disaster will follow if someone kicks your buttocks. If you are doing the kicking, expect social advancement but a consequent loss of respect among your colleagues.

BUTTON If buttons enter into a girl's dream she will marry a man much older than herself. For a bachelor, such a dream denotes that he will not find the right partner until late in life. To dream of light buttons is always good; if they are fabric-covered, it means sadness. If a man dreams that he has lost all the buttons on his clothes it is a sign that he will not live long.

BUYING To dream that you are making extensive purchases foretells a run of extravagant pleasures which will not be good for you. To dream you are making a purchase is profitable; to witness trading indicates that you should exercise economy. Should you purchase an everyday article, beware of approaching loss.

CACTUS If you prick yourself on a cactus, it indicates minor annoyances will upset you.

CAB To dream of riding in a cab promises good fortune in many respects. Generally it predicts travel in a foreign country which will lead to the amassing of great wealth. If married, your children will rise to good positions in life.

CABBAGE To see cabbages signifies riches and happiness; to eat cabbages, unexpected sorrow, loss and illness.

For a girl to dream she sees cabbages growing is a sign that she will soon receive a proposal from a man earning his living in the country.

CABIN To dream that you are in the cabin of a ship foretells domestic troubles.

CABINET To dream of a cabinet is a sure sign that you have an enemy in possession of a secret, the divulging of which will do you a deal of harm. To dream that you are hiding something in a cabinet

implies that you have a design against some young person not very creditable to yourself, and which will greatly injure your character.

CABINET MAKER To dream that you are in love with a cabinet maker indicates that you will marry someone of expensive habits, who will keep you poor and unhappy.

CACKLE The married woman who hears ducks cackling in her dream will be blessed with a large family of boys and girls.

CAD To dream that you hear your sweetheart called a cad indicates that he will suffer from much unjust talk and be made the subject of slander. All will come right, however, and you will marry and have a fine family.

CADDY You will receive a present which should have arrived sooner.

CAFÉ If you are buying food at a café, expect a windfall from an unexpected source.

If you drop the tray, it is a sign of ill health for you or someone in your family.

CAGE To dream of seeing a bird in a cage is a sure sign that although there may be some problems at first, you will make a happy marriage and live in total harmony.

To dream of an empty bird's cage denotes that some unforeseen circumstance will cause you to leave home; it signifies disappointment.

To dream that a girl lets a bird out of a cage is a sign she will not keep her virginity, but will part with it as soon as she can.

CAIN An unusual dream, distinctly warning the dreamer to retrace their footsteps and tread a different path.

CAKE A great deal of joy awaits the person who dreams they are making cakes. But if the curious combination of cake, cheese and butter appears, they must be careful in love affairs.

CALENDAR To dream that you are searching the calendar for a date you cannot find signifies that you will soon be making arrangements for getting married. If, however, the dream ends before you find

the date, you will very likely have cause to cancel your engagement.

CALF For a young woman to dream that she sees a calf in front of her when out walking with her lover is a sign that her young man after marriage will become a good husband, a faithful and devoted provider for his children and a strict but affectionate father. He will be respected by others for his wisdom and kindness and gain the confidence of his employers by his punctuality and conscientiousness.

CALICO Over the next twelve months, you will experience extremes both of happiness and sadness.

CALLING To dream of calling on a friend and finding him/her out means that someone with whom you are at present very intimate will be lost to you forever through marriage.

CALM The end of trouble and the beginning of happiness. The meeting of old friends.

CALUMNY You will be respected.

CAMEL If a person dreams of a camel, it is a sign that

someone who wants to marry them will be lazy and slothful in later life. If, however, these traits can be cured, they will amass great wealth, become rich and live through extraordinary changes and circumstances.

CAMEO BROOCH For a young woman to dream that she wears a cameo brooch is indicative of success in the art of musical education. She will excel at playing the piano. If she dreams that her cameo brooch is broken, a rupture will take place between her and those she loves at home.

CAMERA To look into one, someone will deceive you.

CAMOMILE You will attain a fine old age.

CAMP To dream that you are in a camp of soldiers means, to a young woman, an offer of marriage from a civilian. To a young man it means that he will fall in love with a woman who, either as a soldier's wife or daughter, has seen service in the camp. It also means he will have no taste for service in the army.

CAMPAIGN To dream you enter upon the duties of a campaign means that you will be called upon to do duty at home for a sick partner, if you are married. To an unmarried man it means he will join the army and do garrison duty for a short time.

CAN Good news. To drink out of a can, great joy.

CANAL To walk beside a muddy canal is a sign that some trouble will shortly afflict you, either at home or in your business relations. If the waters are clear you will have prosperity in your commercial transactions, and peace at home. If you fall into a canal you will shortly be involved in business engagements of an entirely fresh nature from those you have been accustomed to, and all your time and attention will be required to make your new calling successful.

CANARY Through someone who is taking an interest in you, you will rise to a life of luxury and ease. To hear a canary sing indicates a happy marriage to the single. To the married, joy and comfort.

CANCER This is a good dream. You will feel your bodily health so robust that you will become proficient in athletic or aquatic sports.

CANDLE To see a clear, shining, lighted candle on a

table or cabinet is a good sign to the sick, as it denotes recovery and health. If you are unmarried, it signifies that you will soon marry, you will be successful and will gain credit. The same interpretation can be made of a lantern or flaming torch. To see any of these extinguished or darkened signifies sadness, sickness and poverty.

Many candles burning brightly foreshadow much merrymaking and an important occurrence. If they burn dimly, expect misfortune. If a girl sees a candle being lighted, she will soon receive a proposal of marriage. A bachelor will come into money. To dream that new candles are brought in denotes that all your disputes will be amicably resolved.

CANDY   To dream of candy is a sign of domestic tranquillity.

CANE   Cane is considered a most inauspicious dream, and some authors forbid the dreamer to undertake any business on that day.

CANNIBALISM   If anyone dreams he has eaten the flesh of a man or woman, he will enrich himself by injuries and reproach. If anyone dreams he has eaten the flesh

of a man who has been hanged he will be enriched by foul practice and some secret crime.

CANNISTER   Should you enclose anything in the cannister, you will soon have a secret to keep. Should you open one, you will discover a friend's secret.

CANNON   To hear or see a cannon fired foreshadows a long but not fatal illness. You will meet with opposition and trouble.

CANOE   To paddle down a river in a canoe is a sign that you will make application to a friend to help you financially in your business, but they will refuse. In fact, nearly all your life you will be left to fight your way without the help of any other person, except perhaps your partner. Self-reliance is the principle and practice you must cultivate.

CANOPY   To sit under a canopy means that you will soon have to move from your present home to another house, for the circumstances of your life will change for the worse.

CAP   To dream that you put on a cap indicates that you must be careful in your love affairs; to take one down shows that the thing you wish to hide will be discovered; if you receive a cap you will soon get married.

CAPE Be cautious and you will be able to overcome the problems caused by a bad decision.

CAPERS To dream of capers is not good, unless you dream at the same time of banquets and great feasts.

CAPON To dream that you hear the capon crow signifies sadness and trouble.

CAPSULE Taking a capsule of medicine indicates that your next business deal will be successful.

CAPTAIN Advancement, prosperity and hopes fulfilled after great difficulties have been surmounted.

CAPTIVE A sign of an unhappy marriage.

CAR You will be able to make a good living and overcome run-of-the-mill obstacles.

CARCASE of an ANIMAL Happiness and long life.

CARDIGAN If you dream of

wearing a cardigan you will have to explain your unusual conduct to others.

CARDS To dream that you are playing at cards is a sure sign that you will soon fall in love and marry. If you are hoping for a new job you will get it and if you are in business it will be successful. If you hold a great many picture cards, your marriage will make you rich and happy; if your cards are mostly Diamonds, the person you marry will be of a sour and disagreeable temper; if they are mostly Hearts, your marriage will be loving, you will be very happy and have many children; if they are mostly Clubs, you will get money by your marriage; if they are Spades, your marriage will turn out very unhappy and your children will be undutiful and subject to many hardships.

CAREER To dream of a career signifies that the dreamer will have many lovers but will not marry.

CARESS For a mother to dream that she caresses her child is a sign that the child will soon suffer from a common but serious childhood illness. She will have days of anxiety, and nights of eager watching but the child will, with great care, recover.

CARGO To dream of cargo loading onto a ship indicates travel.

CARNATION To dream of wearing a pink carnation indicates success in love; wearing a red carnation means adventure.

CARNIVAL To dream of being at a carnival foretells many party invitations, but beware of drinking too much.

CAROL To sing carols indicates a happy marriage.

CARPENTER Should a carpenter figure in your dream a calamity is threatening you, although it may not be felt for some years to come. However, the difficulties will soon be arranged to the satisfaction of everyone.

CARPET For a lady to dream that she has bought new carpets means that shortly, she or her husband will be called upon to pay additional income tax; to dream that your carpets are worn out means success in your employment. To dream you sell carpets is a sign that you will be expected by your relatives to amass a large fortune, which they intend to inherit!

CARRIAGE A carriage without horses foretells a calamity, and a long journey should be avoided during that week. If horses are attached to the carriage, honour awaits you. Should you be sitting in a carriage which is not moving you will suffer from scandal. To dream that you are riding in a carriage indicates that you are never likely to become wealthy.

CARRIER Through work and patience you will attain independence.

CARRION CROW *See* crow.

CARROT To dream of carrots, signifies profit by inheritance.

CARRYING To dream that you are carrying someone is better than to dream you are carried; to be carried by a woman, a child or poor person means profit and success; by a rich person the opposite. To dream of carrying a girl means cheerfulness.

CART To dream of riding in a cart is a sign that your character is being assaulted, and this will lead to serious trouble unless you can find the guilty party. Your business will not go smoothly and you will be hard put to it to make ends meet.

To dream of being fixed in a cart to draw it like an ox, an ass or a horse denotes servitude and pain to everybody.

To dream that you are carried in a cart or coach that is drawn by men signifies that you will have might and authority over many or have well-behaved children.

CARVING To see a quantity of wood carvings is indicative, if you are a young woman, of your having a husband who has a taste for the arts and sciences. He will be fond of the ornamental part of everything, and pride himself in making his house as beautiful as possible. If you are carving, then expect prosperity. If you are single, expect success in love.

CASCADE Mediocre happiness and success. Nothing brilliant, but you will not be in need.

CASH To dream of handling cash indicates future financial success.

CASHIER To dream that you are a cashier means that

you will have cares and annoyances in life on account of others, of which you had no idea before. You will be denounced as dishonest by malicious and evil people and you should make sure you are correct and accurate in all your dealings.

CASSEROLE To dream of cooking or eating a casserole signifies a bright social future.

CASTLE A castle in a dream foreshadows a good match, but an unhappy married life.

CASTOR OIL For a young woman to dream of taking castor oil is a sign of increasing good looks.

CAT The cat signifies a cunning thief, so that if anyone dreams he has met or killed a cat, he will commit a thief to prison and the thief will die. If the dreamer thinks they eat cat's flesh they will have the goods of the thief that robbed them. If they dream they have the skin, then they will enjoy all the thief's goods. If anyone dreams they are fighting with a cat that badly scratches them, that signifies sickness or affliction.

A cat washing itself signifies that you will command respect and love where your affections are placed. If the cat is restless, be wary of treacherous friends; it denotes to the lover that his/her sweetheart is treacherous.

CATACOMBS To dream of walking through skeleton-filled catacombs is an indication of future health.

CATAMARAN To dream of this type of boat indicates good fortune in business unless you capsize.

CATARACT To dream that you see a cataract is a sign that you will, if you see the waters clear and bright, have good success in your domestic affairs. You and your children will have sound health and good looks. You may also expect to receive birthday gifts for your children from a quarter where you do not expect them. If the water of the cataract is muddy and dirty-looking, expect trouble and sickness to overtake some of the members of your household.

CATARRH For those in love, this signifies a happy relationship.

CATECHISM To study the catechism is a sign that you have a retentive memory. You

will be a good scholar in mental arithmetic and adding up accounts.

CATERPILLAR To dream you see a caterpillar signifies bad luck and misfortune caused by unknown enemies.

CATHEDRAL To attend a service in a cathedral predicts an early marriage to a person of title. You will be protected from everything bad if you see a cathedral. If you enter the cathedral and pray, expect happiness, joy and success in everything.

CATTLE Fat cattle denote prosperity, and unexpected success, then misfortune. To dream of buying cattle is a sign that some project which you have in hand will not prove successful. If you are about to be married when such a dream comes you will be wise to postpone the ceremony until you have made sure you have really chosen the right partner. If you are married, beware of gossiping tongues which try to make domestic trouble for you.

CAULIFLOWER To dream that you are eating cauliflower is a very good dream. You will have joy and peace in all aspects of life. You will abandon any bad habits and replace them with domestic happiness and contentment.

CAUSEWAY Your troubles will increase and then cease abruptly, especially if you should dream you cross over one and if your work is of an artistic nature.

CAVALIER Indicates restlessness and much trouble. You are likely to go into rowdy company.

CAVALRY To dream that you see a regiment of horse soldiers on parade is a sign that, if you are unmarried, you will meet with a partner for life who will be able to keep you well by his own industry and thrift, and that you will have children who will at some future period of their lives want to lead a soldier's life. For a young man to have this dream means that he will meet with a young woman of a staid, peaceful and affable disposition.

CAVE To be in a cave indicates many and considerable changes in your happiness.

CEILING To dream of sitting in a room where the ceiling collapses is a sign of the sudden loss of a friend or relative.

CELEBRATION Your future will be brighter than you expect if you dream of enjoying a celebration.

CELERY To dream that you are eating celery is a sign that the dreamer is a person of very robust constitution, full of vigour up to an old age.

CELL You will lose a friend because of your inaction or indecision.

CELLAR To dream of being in a cellar denotes that you will travel and make many new friends. If the cellar is full of wine, however, be careful of these friends, for one at least will prove unfaithful. If there is coal in the cellar you may expect to hear good news.

CELLO To hear a cello being played indicates that a new turn of events will bring happiness into your life. If the cello is badly played or is out of tune, the events will bring discord.

CEMENT A present is soon to be given you, which will lead to more important events.

CEMETERY You will overcome all problems.

CENTAUR You will receive

some shocking news concerning one of your family or close friends.

CENTIPEDE   To see centipedes signifies ill luck and misfortune by unknown enemies.

CERBERUS   To dream you see the dog Cerberus, the porter of hell, signifies sin and arrest.

CERTIFICATE   You do not attempt to see things from other people's point of view. Try to be more sympathetic in small ways and big events will ensue.

CESSPOOL   This dream signifies that you should avoid promiscuity in your sexual relationships.

CHAFF   To dream of chaff signifies that your plans will not succeed.

CHAIN   To dream of a chain with long links of which you see both the beginning and the end foretells that you will carry on a long correspondence with someone beginning formally, becoming very friendly, but eventually ending on a cold and formal note.

If you dream of a broken chain you may reasonably look forward to a change of business which will be good for you. If unbroken, the reverse; your wife is preventing all success in your affairs and is a hindrance to you instead of a help. If you are married your relationship will not run smoothly until you have experienced some disappointments.

Chains of pearls, precious stones, and all jewellery of the hands and necks of women are good dreams for women; to girls they signify marriage; to those that have husbands and children, purchases and riches.

CHAIR   To sit beside an empty chair signifies that you are about to meet and talk with one who for several years has been on your mind a great deal.

CHAIRMAN   You will advance at work and will be popular among your colleagues.

CHALET   You will make other people happy, and thereby find your own happiness.

CHALK   A dream of vast quantities of chalk foreshadows disappointment in business or matrimony. To a farmer it is a sign that his cattle will die of disease.

CHAMBER POT To dream of seeing a fish in a chamber pot is bad for those in authority or the sick.

CHAMBERMAID For a young, unmarried man to dream of courting a chambermaid means that he will either marry a cook, housemaid or nurse. He will cause a rupture in the family he visits, for no one can tell which one of the girls he professes to be engaged to.

CHAMELEON Beware of false friends.

CHAMPAGNE To dream that you are drinking champagne means that you will, in spite of the warnings and entreaties of your parents, keep company with someone who, though they promise well, will turn out to be worthless; they will be deficient in education, loose in moral character, and profligate in habits.

CHAMPION To dream that you are the winner in any kind of competition is a sign that despite study and practice on your part, you will not gain the efficiency and success you desire. Try some physical employment rather than a mental one.

CHANDELIER A brightly lit chandelier indicates success in business.

CHANGE To dream of changing anything – changing sides, or changing clothes, or changing books at a library, or changing money (but not changing houses, for which see Removal) – means that you are about to enter on a period of unrest. It will turn out for the best if in your dream you gained by the change you made.

CHAPEL If you see the outside of a chapel, then you will become rich. If you are inside and see the priest, be careful of your actions. It indicates that a trap is set for you, and if you fall into it you will regret your mistake all your life.

CHAPPED HANDS To dream that your hands have become chapped is a bad sign. There will be a great deal of problems in your family from one of your children. They will be troubled with a desire to take other people's goods, for no other reason than that they have an unaccountable desire to possess them. They will suffer from that curious problem known as kleptomania, which will continually recur to disturb your peace of mind.

CHARADE   To act in a charade at a private party is a sign that your friends will fight shy of your society, and not extend their invitations to you as they have done before. This will cause you trouble, but you will soon find out the cause and put matters right.

CHARCOAL   If you dream that you are sitting beside a fire of charcoal you will soon hear news of an exciting character from friends abroad.

CHARIOT   For a woman to dream that she rides in a chariot means poverty from sickness and lack of employment. For a young man to have this dream means that he will soon have to move, because he will lose his job due to fierce competition.

CHARITY   For a rich person to dream that he is charitable signifies loss of fortune.

CHART   For a person to dream that they are studying a chart signifies a change of direction in their life. Choose the course with care.

CHASE   If you dream of being involved in a chase, you will be hardworking but eventually successful.

CHASTISEMENT   For a parent to dream that they scold their children for disobedience means that the children will be good tempered and obedient.

CHATTER   A runaway marriage will cause much gossip.

CHEATING   To be cheated at any game of chance, or in any purchase, is a sign that you will become more circumspect in your trading, and will therefore make very few, if any, bad debts.

CHEEK   To dream of your cheeks is a good omen. To a person employed in business it denotes that they will be successful in surmounting all their difficulties, and will rise to the top of a large business. To dream that you have plump, rosy cheeks is a good sign, especially to a woman. But to dream that you are lean, pale and full of wrinkles signifies grief and heaviness.

CHEERING   If the sound of cheering enters your dream, you will soon have cause to shed many tears.

CHEESE To eat cheese signifies profit and gain. A girl who dreams of cheese should be careful not to give too much credence to any tale she may hear about her lover. The dream foreshadows a small loss for a man.

CHEESECAKE If a young woman dreams of eating cheesecake, she will soon meet a witty, humorous, intelligent, fair young man who will invite her to take a walk in the moonlight. Act discreetly, judge his character, think of his promises, and see how you can sum up his worth. If he is good at heart, good will come of your moonlit walks.

CHEMIST For a person of a sharp temper to dream of a chemist's shop is a sure sign that, unless that person takes care to improve the fault, married life will be a failure, and much sorrow will be brought about by a sudden death. To a person of milder temperament the dream gives warning of sickness and the failure of some long-cherished scheme.

CHEQUE To dream that you have received a payment of money by cheque is not so pleasant as it may at first appear. Be wary of an imposter, who will be so plausible that you will be tempted to advance him money which will never be returned.

CHERRY Dreaming of cherries indicates disappointment and rejection in love and vexation in marriage. To see the fruit growing is a disappointment in love or marriage. To dream that you are eating cherries presages a great disappointment or a series of petty worries.

CHESS The game of chess represents a field prepared for battle. The two players are the two generals of the armies and the tables and the chessmen are the soldiers that make up the two armies. If anyone dreams they are playing chess with an acquaintance, it is a sign that they will fall out with somebody that they know, and if they imagine in the dream that they win, they will be victorious over their enemies, or vice versa. If the dreamer imagines they have taken many men in play, that foretells they will take many of their enemies prisoner. If a ruler or general of an army dreams they have lost their chess board or that it is broken or stolen, they will lose their army, either by the enemies' assault or else by plague or famine. To dream that you see others play chess signifies loss by craft.

CHEST If you dream of a large empty chest, prepare for disappointment in love.

CHESTNUT and CHESTNUT TREE To dream that you are eating chestnuts is a sign that wisdom will be one of the most prominent features in the character of your partner. For an unmarried woman to have this dream means that she will meet with a very bashful young man who is deeply in love with her, but has not the courage to talk to her on the subject.

CHEWING Overlook another's faults if you wish to know true happiness.

CHICKEN To dream of chickens is unlucky. If they are roosting, then the bad luck will affect your domestic affairs, and will not be very serious; if they are strutting about, the trouble will be more severe, and will extend even to your own or your partner's business. If you are a farmer, you will have a bad crop, and lose many of your poultry. If you are in trade, some con-man will defraud you. However, a dream of catching hens signifies joy and happiness.

CHICKEN POX If your child is suffering from this illness in your dream, he or she will have a successful future. If you are ill, minor setbacks will follow.

CHILBLAINS A misunderstanding will be cleared up.

CHILDBIRTH If a woman dreams she gives birth to a child without being pregnant it is a sign that she will happily accomplish her intentions. To dream that a woman is in labour and the child is stillborn after a difficult and painful labour shows that she will work hard for something that will never be accomplished. If the child is alive, she will achieve her ambitions but through hard work. To dream you see a child born denotes a speedy marriage and that you will be very happy with your family.

CHILDREN Male children bring good success; daughters signify that you will be put to a good deal of expense, if they are your own. To see other men's children is good when they are fair and attractive, for this signifies that a good and happy time is at hand. If anyone dreams that he sees himself wrapped in children's clothes it signifies a long sickness unless his wife is pregnant, for then they should have a son born like himself. If his wife has such a dream she will have a daughter. But if anyone in prison has such a dream, the accusations against them will be such that they will not be freed.

If someone with no children dreams that they have many small children and that they seem to run about the house, that signifies that it will be very difficult for them to have any, and that they will have many cares and obstructions in their affairs. When anyone dreams they see an infant wrapped in swaddling clothes and suckling at his mother, that signifies a chronic and dangerous illness unless his wife is pregnant; if so it signifies that the child will be delicate. If a woman dreams this it is a sign that she is or will shortly be pregnant and have a daughter, unless she is sick or her husband dies.

To see a beautiful, fair, naked child denotes joy. If you see many children playing innocently together you will become wealthy. If the dream is the opposite and the child is ugly or deformed, especially about the genitals, then you will know shame and reproach. To dream of anything happening to small children which is not relevant to their age, such as boys having beards and grey hair or little girls married with children, signifies a crisis for the dreamer. To dream you see a child die imports that you will experience some heavy misfortune.

CHIMNEY To see a tall chimney indicates fortunate events to come.

CHINA To dream of china is a sign that, providing you persevere in your occupation, you will make a big success and die rich.

CHINAMAN To see a Chinaman in a dream is a warning that someone whom you have trusted will prove false and cause you trouble.

CHIP A business success or wager won.

CHIROPODIST To dream about a chiropodist means that you will soon be on the move, either changing home or job.

CHISEL A public appearance of some kind.

CHOCOLATE To dream of buying chocolate is a prediction that you will bring sorrow on yourself by a foolish action unless you keep a firm hold on yourself during the following nine days. If you are eating chocolate, however, you will receive a gift from someone you despise.

CHOIR The singing of a choir means that you will soon be speaking to an old sweetheart. If the music is solemn, however, you must be wary of any advances he may make, for he does not mean half he says.

CHOKING To dream that you are choking is significant. You will be praised by some of your friends for your proficiency in the studies of science and intellectual culture. In physical health you may be troubled with indigestion from time to time, but careful diet will help you through the most painful part of this disease and give you vigour in your old age.

CHOLERA To dream that you are suffering from this disease is indicative of some accident happening to you before long. If you are about to start on a journey it will be prudent for you, after having this dream, to remain at home for a while, especially if the weather is foggy, windy or stormy with a heavy downpour and thunder and lightning.

CHORISTER To dream that you are a chorister in a church choir is indicative of success in the art of public speaking if you cultivate your abilities. You may be able to enter, through the influence of friends, into a college and become a student for the ministry. For a young woman to dream that her lover is a chorister means that she will meet with one who has a desire for singing, but not for sacred songs; sentimental and comic songs will occupy his attention more than oratories and sacred music.

CHRIST To talk with Jesus Christ signifies consolation. To see Christ's body signifies honour.

CHRISTENING For a young woman to dream that she is at a christening ceremony is indicative of the sudden illness of some of her nephews or nieces. Perhaps before very long some of those who are peculiar favourites in her family will be seized with croup or bronchitis. For a young man to have this dream is indicative of trouble on account of his religious beliefs.

CHRISTMAS A dream connected with this season denotes a reconciliation between two old-time friends who have quarrelled, with much jubilation as a result. Or, if you have not had a disagreement of this kind, you may expect to hear from a friend or relative of whom you have lost all trace for some time.

CHRISTMAS TREE To dream that you see a beautifully decorated Christmas tree is a sign that the festivities of the Christmas season will be remembered for a long time, because you will meet with someone under the holly who has never spoken to you before, but who will seek your company, first as a friend, afterwards as a lover, and lastly as a marriage partner. Your marriage will be long and happy.

CHURCH To dream you are in church and praying devoutly to God signifies joy and comfort. To build a

church signifies that one of your relations will receive a present. To see yourself sitting or lying in a church signifies change of clothes. To dream that you do nothing but talk and sing idly at church signifies envy or sin, and the persons dreaming this, if wicked, should alter their way of life. To dream of seeing the sacrament administered in church is a good dream.

CHURCHYARD To dream of walking in a churchyard is an omen of a pleasant surprise, with a probability of wealth to come.

CHURNING To dream that you are churning milk is good. You will gain the respect of social, jolly company because of your powers of reciting some of the best pieces of favourite authors. Your company will be much sought after and enjoyed by both young and old. But to attain greater proficiency you must practise regularly.

CIDER Good fortune follows a dream of cider, and if you drink it the luck will be even better. For a student it signifies honours in an examination.

CIGAR To dream that you are enjoying the luxury of a

first-class cigar is a significant dream. You will have much to be thankful for; and even if you do have problems, the fumes and flavour of your finest brands will help to lighten the load of trouble that would otherwise weigh you down.

CIGARETTE   To dream you are lighting one signifies new plans; a half-smoked cigarette in your hand is a post-ponement; to smoke it to the end means a successful conclusion to your hopes.

CINDERS   To sweep up cinders is a sign that you will have trouble with some of your relatives. Some of them may even decide to tramp the country; in all probability they will become vagabonds and be a disgrace to their family.

CIRCLE   To dream of drawing circles is a sign that you will fulfil your ambitions.

CIRCUS   Examine yourself well after dreaming of a circus, for it proves that you are developing some bad habit, probably selfishness, which, if not checked, will make you unhappy.

CITY   A large city denotes ambition. If you enter the city, your ambitions will be realised.

CLAIRVOYANT   If you dream of talking to a clairvoyant, your love life is likely to be problematic.

CLAM   You will have difficulties in your life ahead, but through patient effort you will overcome them.

CLARET   To dream that you are drinking this wine is a sign that there is a pretty handsome fortune in store for you, if only you have the means to redeem it from those who have heavy mortgages upon it. Some of your relatives have been too extravagant and have not lived within their means, and the consequence is you may lose your inheritance through their extravagance.

CLARINET   To dream that you hear music from this kind of reed instrument is a sign that you will have a taste for piano music, and could become adept at playing this instrument if you practise carefully. But if you allow your energies to remain un-used, they will be of no use to you at all. Your ideas of harmony and time will be very correct.

CLARION   To play or hear playing on wind instruments, such as a clarion, signifies trouble, contention and losing a court case.

CLASSROOM To dream of a classroom indicates that you are likely to marry or become emotionally involved with an old school friend.

CLAVICHORD To dream you play, or see someone else play, a clavichord signifies the death of relations or funeral obsequies.

CLEAN SHAVEN If your face is clean shaven, it signifies sudden shame and problems. To see the back of the head shaven signifies poverty and bad luck in old age, although it is good for anyone appealing to the legal profession, or anyone who is afraid about something. It also signifies to a prisoner that he will escape.

CLERGYMAN For a young unmarried woman to dream that a clergyman wants to meet with her is a sign that she will be disappointed; the man she most desires as a husband is engaged to someone else, and she will marry someone she loves less. She will, in the end, marry a craftsman, a mechanic or an unskilled worker. She will never rise to a position of affluence.

CLIFF A dangerous dream; avoid taking risks.

CLIMBING If someone dreams of climbing a great tree, they will be promoted to some honour or dignity, and will have authority over others. To ascend a ladder signifies honour. To ascend a very high mountain, the same thing. To ascend up to heaven signifies grandeur. To dream of attaining the summit of a hill signifies that the dreamer will get his desires, but if you fall before you gain the top you will not attain your ends.

CLOCK To dream of a clock, especially when it is the chief clock in the house, having stopped means that you are in danger of a serious illness, but if the clock is wound up and set going again in your dream it is a sign that the illness may be averted by the strictest attention to the rules of health.

To dream of a clock that has stopped working indicates that you will be mixed up in sickness and a business loss. To dream of a clock breaking is dangerous, especially to the sick, although it is better if the hour is before noon than afterwards.

To dream you hear the clock strike denotes that you

will be speedily married, and that you will be moderately successful in life.

CLOGS If you are putting them on, prepare for a wedding shortly.

CLOTHES If someone sees their clothes destroyed by fire it signifies vexation, injury, reproach, legal problems and loss of friends. If anyone dreams they have a suit on, which they like, it signifies joy, profit and good success in business. If a woman dreams she is dressed in a hood, that indicates damage and dishonour. If someone dreams they are dressed very expensively, it signifies honour. To dream your clothes are embroidered signifies joy and honour. If a man or woman dreams they are poorly dressed, it signifies trouble and sadness. If anyone dreams their clothes are filthy, or that they have tattered clothes, that signifies sin, blame and shame in the world.

For a girl to dream of putting on new clothes means that she will soon marry.

For a wife or husband to dream of wearing the other's clothes is an omen that the dreamer will outlive his or her partner. A dream of buying clothes signifies honour and beauty.

To dream of white garments is good only to priests; to others it signifies trouble. To dream of a black garment signifies good luck and good health. To dream you are wearing clothes of many colours or scarlet for priests or actors is good; to others it signifies troubles and dangers resulting from the revealing of secrets, and to the sick, that they will become seriously ill. To dream you see a woman in a fine dress is good only to actors or to those who are unmarried. To the married this dream sometimes foretells the illness or loss of their partner. To dream that you have a dress in the fashion of a foreign country signifies good luck to someone who is about to travel or live there; to others it signifies sickness or problems. To dream you have a delicate and sumptuous dress is good for everyone, as it indicates increased prosperity. To dream of a coat, short cloak or skirt of woollen cloth signifies anger, but it is better to dream you lose them than that you find or have them. But the loss of any other garment is evil, for a garment lost signifies loss from evils that are associated with them. It is always better to dream of having good, attractive and clean clothes than old and dirty ones.

CLOUD To see a cloud coming for a short while over the sun denotes that the friends of your partner will place barriers in the way of your relationship. For a time these will seem insurmountable. However, the tide of fortune will eventually begin to flow in your favour, and you will be welcomed by those who formerly would have nothing to say to you.

If the clouds are thick and heavy, you will shortly be mixed up in a quarrel which will leave you with fewer friends, and the dispute will not end satisfactorily for you. If, however, the clouds disperse, you may look for happiness after the trouble is settled.

To dream of white clouds signifies prosperity; clouds mounting high denote voyages, the return of the absent and revealing of secrets.

CLOVE Your offspring will be a source of great pleasure to you.

CLOVER Health, wealth and happiness await the person who dreams of walking in a field of clover. Look forward to the future with hope, for it will be bright and happy. To the young and the lover it foretells a happy marriage.

CLOWN Others think you stupid.

CLUB You will meet with people whom you have not seen for a long time. Do not let them influence you.

COACH To see a coach drawn by black horses means that you will be present at a funeral. If, however, you are riding in a coach, you may look forward to a spell of luxury and idleness. Be on your guard against some disgraceful act, if you dream of alighting from a coach. If you are in love, your sweetheart will be idle and bad-tempered. If you are in trade you will become bankrupt, and if you are a farmer your goods will be seized. It also denotes that the dreamer will shortly be put in prison.

COAL To dream of putting coals on the fire means that in, at most, a few days you will meet with a stranger who will have much to do with your future life. A young man dreaming of taking coals off the fire can assume that he will change his mind about his current sweetheart, and from thinking her perfect will come to find no end of faults in her. To see coals burning brightly foretells success in love. To dream of coals which are not burning is a very unlucky omen. It denotes many problems. To dream you see the coals extinguished and reduced to cinders denotes death, either to yourself or some near relation or friend.

COAL-MINE   If you dream of walking in or looking down the shaft of a coal-mine, be careful that your partner in life is not a widower or widow. Unhappiness will follow such an alliance if you ignore the warning. For a young woman to dream that she is wandering in a colliery means that she cannot obtain all her desires. In love, her imagined perfect partner is far above what the reality will be; he will be a faithful lover, but not wealthy, and she will be compelled to moderate her ambition. She will also be disappointed in other things, but not as badly off as many. She will have a comfortable home, though it will not be as elegant as she wishes, but it will be contented and peaceful.
To dream of being in the bottom of a coal-mine signifies marrying a widow, but whoever marries her will never fully understand her intentions. To be in or near a coal-mine warns you of danger.

COAT   To dream that you have torn your coat is a sign that your mature years will not be happy. Your children will desert you and offer no financial support when you need it. To dream you tear the sleeve of your coat is a sign that you will commence a new business and work hard to be successful, but it will not live up to your expectations and desires. To dream that you are wearing a beautiful and fashionable coat is a sign that financial problems will shortly overtake you.
   To dream of a coat of mail warns you to be careful in all your dealings.

COAT-OF-ARMS   To dream of a shield with a coat-of-arms on it is an excellent sign. A powerful friend will protect you.

COAXING   A dream signifying a dangerous request probably to be made to you. Do not accede to it.

COBBLER   You will cope with your problems and experience good fortune to follow.

COBWEB   To brush one away means a triumph for you over an enemy.

COCK You will be loved by the opposite sex if you see a cock. To dream you see or hear a cock crow signifies joy and prosperity and is the forerunner of good news. To see two cocks fighting denotes quarrels and fighting in your home. To dream you see a cock in the house is a good sign for anyone about to marry. It also signifies that you will earn enough money to live comfortably. It is a bad omen for the sick since it indicates feverishness. It also foretells that secrets will be revealed.

COCKLES Expect bad news from abroad.

COCOA To dream that you are drinking cocoa is very good. You will live a contented life. The things that once troubled your mind will not affect it now.

COCONUT Eating coconut indicates that you will exercise determination when faced with problems.

COFFEE To see or roast coffee indicates unhappiness and persecution.

COFFEE HOUSE To eat your meal in a coffee house is a sign that you will have pretty general good health; you will also be popular among your work colleagues and, even when some trifling difficulties arise in the conduct of those you work with, you will not be blamed, because you will be of a very peaceful turn of mind and disposition.

COFFIN To dream of seeing a coffin is a very bad omen, suggesting a downward turn in all your affairs. If you are about to go to a wedding, it denotes sickness for the bride or bridegroom during the first year of married life.

COGWHEEL Introductions will cause a fresh outlook on affairs. Take new hope and achieve your plans fearlessly from now on.

COIN To dream of coins is a very significant dream. If you dream of a large number of copper coins it is indicative of plenty. To dream you see a large quantity of silver coins means an average crop, trade or business, and fair weather. There will not be many independencies made for some time; want of confidence in the money market and on the Stock Exchange will prevent much business being done. But to dream that you see a great quantity of gold coins is indicative of commercial depression; for some time the scarcity of work and wages will be so great that want will be felt pretty keenly in some families.

COKE To dream that you see a bright fire of coke is a sign that either your father or mother are about to fall ill, or there will be slackness of work and you will be short of money and need to borrow to obtain the necessities of life.

COLD To dream that you are suffering from a cold or chill denotes a falling-off in affection, either of a friend or a sweetheart. Though you may have many problems, in the end you will be happy.

COLLAR For a young woman to dream that she is putting on her collar before a mirror is a sign that there is a young man in her neighbourhood who wants to marry her. He may meet her when she doesn't expect him; she has never met him before, but he has wanted to meet her for some time and has been calculating the best way to approach her.

COLLAR BONE To dream that your collar bone is broken in an accident means that some unpleasant affair will happen in the circle of your friends or acquaintances and some of your friends will break a limb.

COLLECTING To dream of collecting something indicates that you will soon meet a celebrity.

COLLEGE For a young man to dream that he is a student in a college is a sign that he needs to further his education before he will rise to a position of eminence and trust.

COLONEL For a young woman to dream that she is in the company of the first officer of a regiment is a sign that her husband will never be of the first rank in any profession. She need not look so high for a partner for life. Her husband will be a good man, but not a leader in authority.

COLOURS If you dream about flags or decorations in many bright colours, it signifies continued prosperity and success in all your undertakings.

COLLECTION Should you dream you are contributing to a collection, you have to travel a long way soon but will meet with good luck abroad.

COLLISION A sign of mental strife. You will need all

your self-control to overcome the effect of bad tidings.

COLUMBINE   The flower is a sign of a visit to luxurious surroundings.

COLUMN   This presages future success and honours.

COMBAT   It is not a good sign to be engaged in a fight in a dream. If you are successful, all will come well, but only after difficulty and worry.

COMBING   To dream of combing the hair is a sign of prosperity following grief. If you are combing another person's hair you will be obliged to accept a low situation, but unless the comb breaks you will rise to higher things. Your work will be heavy and profitless if you find difficulty in combing your hair, but if easy and the hair is beautiful it means eventual gain and a new friendship.

COMEDIAN   For a young girl to dream that a comedian has fallen in love with her is a sign that she will have a desire to go on the stage as a professional actress. It would be best to stifle the desire, as there will not be that success attending her efforts that she should wish.

COMEDY or FARCE   To dream you see a comedy, farce or some other recreation signifies that you are not well thought of by others and will meet with trouble and loss of reputation.

COMET   To see several comets, or other stars with streaming tails, signifies future evils such as war, epidemics and famine. A comet in a dream is a forerunner of evil, and often forebodes shattered hopes and wrecked affections. This dream warns you to avoid all changes; do not travel or walk on an unmade road.

COMFORT   To dream you comfort anyone means injury and mishap to the rich and happy, but to the poor and suffering, aid and comfort.

COMMANDING   To command anyone signifies trouble. To see someone in command signifies anger and authority.

COMMITTEE   To dream of being on a committee is a sign that you will be involved in a social or public cause.

COMMUNION   Happy love, enjoyment. Your friends will always stand by you.

COMMUNIST You will be misunderstood by your friends.

COMPANION A fortunate omen indicating immediate success.

COMPASSES To dream that you are working with a pair of compasses is a sign that some of those who are studying with you will be far ahead of you in the branches of study in which you are spending your time. More close application is required before you will be able to pass examinations with flying colours.

COMPETITOR To dream that you are a competitor in either racing, jumping, swimming or rowing races is a sign that you will soon lose your physical strength by an accident.

COMPLAINT You will make new and important friends if you dream of lodging a complaint against someone. If someone is complaining about you, you will quarrel with your family.

COMPLEXION A dark-complexioned man is a sign of success.

COMPLIMENT To dream that you are receiving compliments from a stranger is a sign that you will arouse the jealousy of your sweetheart through appearing to appreciate the attentions of a third party.

CONCERT To dream of taking part in a concert as a member of the chorus denotes, if the concert is going off successfully, that you will play an important part in society, and work harmoniously with your friends and colleagues. Should the concert of your dream, however, be remarkable for bad tune and bad time, this predicts that you take more pleasure in spiting your enemies than in pleasing your friends, and that you will soon discover this to be a mistaken policy.

CONCERTINA To hear one of these instruments played in a dream means that you will become fond of dancing, and you will become adept by practice.

CONDUCTOR A dream involving a train or bus conductor signifies foreign travel. A conductor of an orchestra signifies financial reward.

CONFECTIONERY To dream you make sweets, pies, cakes, or tarts signifies joy and profit. To taste sweet things signifies that you will meet with advantages and success.

CONFERENCE You will be able to turn circumstances to your own advantage.

CONFESSION Guard the confidences given to you by others. You will soon be tempted to reveal a secret.

CONFETTI Minor social disappointments on the way.

CONFIRMATION To dream that you attend the confirmation service and are a candidate of that ceremony is a good sign. You will become a scholar in theology and able to defend the doctrines of the church of which you are a member.

CONFRONTATION To dream that you confront someone who has deceived you, is a sign that you will not have courage to speak in your own defence when opposed by someone who does not believe, or practise some of the principles, which you adopt.

CONFUSION Dreaming of things about you being in confusion is a sign that the many plans on which you are at present engaged require weeding out, for some of them are worthless and wasting your time and energy.

CONGRATULATIONS These signify cause for condolence, but better times to come.

CONGREGATION To dream that you see a large congregation of people assembled in a chapel or other place of worship is a sign that you will be left alone when you are ill. Very few of your friends will call on you as they did before, probably because someone has been spreading lies about you.

CONJURER To dream you see a conjurer perform is a sign that you will be deceived by the words of a deep, designing person, who uses great cunning and coaxing to get what he or she wants.

CONSCIENCE A dream of contrary; if you are worried by your conscience, all will go well. The more self-satisfied you feel, the less your chance of prosperity.

CONSENT If you consent to a request, you will lose something valuable.

CONSERVATORY If you are in a conservatory in your dream, expect to marry soon.

CONSUMPTION To dream that you are subject to this lingering disease is a sign that you will have a strong voice, healthy look, sound body and fair complexion. If you work at a desk job you had better have a change, one that will be for the better preservation of your health.

CONTENTMENT Another 'contrary' dream. Be careful of fires and enemies alike for a time. There is danger for you in both.

CONTRADICTION Your wish will be granted.

CONUNDRUM To dream that you compose a conundrum is a sign that you will never become adept at solving intricacies or explaining mysteries. You will feel your want of suitable language when trying to tell a story.

CONVENT An engagement speedily followed by a happy though not wealthy wedding.

CONVICTION To be convicted of fraud, theft or murder is a sign that all your life you will be a law-abiding citizen, highly respected, well regarded and much loved. Your integrity, virtue and love of justice will raise your character very much in the minds of those of your friends who know you better than any strangers possibly can do.

CONVULSIONS To dream you see someone in convulsions means an invitation to a concert.

COOK To dream you see a cook in the house is good to those who want to marry and also to the poor. But it also signifies the revealing of secrets, for the cook's apparel is white and is seen by many.

COOKING Either roasting or frying, stewing or boiling represents the approach of evil times.

COPPERS These are luckiest when you dream of giving them to someone. Otherwise they signify loss.

COPYING This foretells legal affairs, probably to your advantage.

CORAL To dream you are wearing it predicts the return of an old friend or a meeting with a former sweetheart.

CORD To knot a cord means the strengthening of a friendship; to unravel it means the breaking of an engagement.

CORK If you dream that you are extracting a cork, it is a sign of some good news of a friend. If you are pushing a cork into a bottle, it shows a visit to you unexpectedly.

CORKSCREW To dream of using a corkscrew is indicative of a long illness, but not necessarily of the dreamer. Probably a near relation will fall ill and cause anxiety. To dream that in using this article you break it is a sign that you will suddenly lose a dear friend through some infectious disease.

CORN and CORNFIELDS To see a stack of corn destroyed by fire signifies famine and death, but if it is not destroyed it denotes fertility and great riches to the dreamer. To dream that you gather ripe corn signifies profit and riches. To dream that you see stacks of corn signifies profit and abundance to the dreamer. On the contrary, to see a small quantity signifies famine and need.

To dream you see cornfields denotes success in business, joy to the lover or a prosperous voyage to a sailor. A field of corn denotes plenty, with poverty to follow, unless you are careful to put by for a rainy day when you are prosperous. To dream that you are among unthreshed corn, is a very favourable omen; it announces that you will marry and become rich and happy. To dream of seeing a barn full of corn indicates marrying a good wife or overcoming enemies.

CORNER To dream that you stand in a corner with your sweetheart is a sign that your marriage is not to take place yet; perhaps years may intervene before you set a date. Make a decision, for unless you set a wedding date you may go off with someone else and regret it later.

CORNET To hear a cornet being played foretells strife and family quarrels. If you like the music, you will be involved in the unpleasantness.

CORNS To dream of corns on your feet means that you will grow rich proportionately to the number of corns.

CORONATION Long-distance travel is around the corner.

CORPSE If you see the corpse of a near relative, do not enter into a hasty marriage, for unhappiness will follow. A little thought will probably show you that your prospective partner differs from you in so many things that such a relationship would be foolish. To see your own corpse signifies that you will soon find much happiness in ministering to the wants of others. If the corpse is that of a complete stranger, someone will take an interest in your welfare and bring much happiness into your life.

COSMETICS A woman dreaming of using make-up in private will have good luck, but she should be careful of arguments with lovers if using cosmetics in public. Men dreaming of using cosmetics must watch their professional reputation.

COTTAGE For a young unmarried person to dream that they are sitting with their spouse in a newly-furnished cottage is indicative of an argument and unpleasant problems in their relationship because of their different tastes and because they are unaware of each other's failings. You have to learn that give and take is vital in any relationship.

COTTON To dream that you see great quantities of cotton is a sign that the manufacture

and demand will be scarce. Those who work in manufacturing will have short time and poor wages.

COUGH To dream that you are troubled with a violent cough is a sign that you will have great strength of lungs and chest. You may well be attacked with a bout of gout or rheumatism, however.

COUNTENANCE To dream you see a very handsome face signifies joy, contentment and health. To see a beautiful face, unlike your own, signifies honour.

COUNTERPANE The sign of an accident if it is torn or pulled from the bed.

COUNTING the HOURS To dream that you are counting the hours, if it is in the morning, indicates happiness and that your partner is true to you, but if it is in the afternoon, that you will suffer problems and that your lover is unfaithful.

COUNTRY To dream of the country promises success to some project you have in mind, if only you apply yourself seriously to it.

COUNTRY TOWN To dream of having moved to a country town is a sign that by your present pursuits and general course of life you are liable to fall intellectually asleep, and that prudence suggests your taking steps to counteract that danger.

COURT of LAW To dream you are giving evidence in a court of law foretells that you are about to incur a heavy bill for legal expenses. Should the counsel examining you have a piece of paper in their hand, you may infer that you are to get into trouble through writing a letter of importance and neglecting the wise rule of going over it afterwards and striking out all the adjectives.

COURTSHIP For a young person to dream that they have started courting is a sign that they will have many followers, but will not like any of them. Through being too particular as to appearance, they will not marry until late in life.

COUSIN To dream that your cousin writes to you is indicative of news from an old lover, who wants to renew a loving relationship.

COW To dream you see or have one cow means good luck; many cows signify wealth and plenty.

COWARD To dream of being a coward is a dream of contrary; you will be steadfast when faced with difficulties.

COWSLIP If in your dream you see cowslips in full bloom, there will be a sudden and unexpected change in your circumstances. A young wife may become pregnant; a young person may find a new lover, although they will not marry.

CRAB Beware of the law.

CRADLE For a mother to dream that her child's cradle is broken means the illness, possibly a serious one, of her youngest child. Or she will have nights of watching and days of anxiety over the sick bed of one of her favourite children, but by care and attention the child may recover. To dream that the cradle rocks itself, the mother may expect twins to be her next charges.

CRANE To dream you see a flock of cranes on the wing foretells the approach of enemies and thieves. In winter it signifies bad weather.

CRAWL To dream you are crawling on the floor is bad, but to dream you are crawling on the roof of a house is good.

CREAM To dream you see cream spilt on you signifies the infusion of some grace by the Holy Ghost.

CREPE To dream that you wear this emblem of mourning is a sign that you will soon receive a piece of wedding cake from an old schoolmate or some other dear friend of your youth.

CREW To dream that you see the crew of a vessel hard at work, reefing their sails and doing other duties on board, is a sign that storms at sea will be frequent, in some of which your friend or friends will be exposed to shipwreck or loss of goods.

CRIBBAGE Taking part in a game indicates important decisions. If you are watching a game, your advice will be sought. Think carefully before you give it.

CRICKET If you see a cricket or hear it chirp, beware of a stranger who will attempt to flatter you. To dream that you take part in a game of cricket is a sign that you will suffer from an injury to your legs.

CRIES If in your dream you hear cries of distress, expect glad news; some of your relatives who have been married for some time and are childless will soon be expecting a baby. If the cry is one of joy you must look out for someone bringing or sending you news of the death of a close friend. If the cry is one of despair, as in the case of shipwreck or fire at sea, either you or your partner will in due course gain a great deal by speculation.

CRIME Your undertakings will be crowned with success.

CRIMSON Denotes pleasant news from an unexpected quarter.

CRINOLINE For a woman to dream that she is wearing a large, old-fashioned crinoline means that she will be forced to save money at home, both on clothes and household expenses, because money will be short.

CRIPPLE A warning to be kind to those around you.

CROCHET WORK For a young woman to dream that she is crocheting is a sign that her hobbies are carried on at the expense of her more important jobs.

CROCODILE   Dreaming of seeing a crocodile indicates that your good nature is at present imposed upon by one who enjoys the triumph of gaining sympathy by telling lies to people.

CROCUS   To dream that you see a number of these early flowers of spring is a sign that peace and domestic happiness will be yours.

CROSS   To dream you see a cross carried along signifies sadness. To see a cross of gold is an indication that you will marry well and be happy; or, if you are already married, your marriage will continue to be a happy one. If the cross is of wood, however, and you are single, your marriage will not be a wealthy one, but it will be happy all the same. If married, you will have your share of petty worries, but nothing serious will spoil your domestic bliss.

CROSS PURPOSE   To dream you play at cross purposes signifies prosperity, joy, pleasure, health and harmony among friends and relations.

CROSSBONES   Indicates health throughout your life and absence of want.

CROSSROADS   To dream of standing at a crossroads means that you have an important decision to make which will affect the rest of your life.

CROW   To dream you see a crow in a clear sky signifies completion of successful business. To dream of a crow and other birds of prey flying in cloudy weather denotes anger, loss and misery. To dream you hear a crow croaking unpleasantly is bad luck.

CROWD   Your happiness is assured and will increase.

CROWING   To dream you are crowing, or that you hear others crowing, denotes bad luck, especially to lovers. But to dream that you hear pigeons cooing is good, especially to those who are newly married, as it denotes happiness.

CROWN   To dream you are wearing a gold crown signifies that you are appreciated by those in authority and will receive many presents. To carry a gold crown in your hand signifies honour and dignity. A crown of precious stones predicts that you will shortly receive an invitation to a wedding which will give you great pleasure. A crown of gold or silver denotes enemies, of whom you must be wary; of brass or iron signifies illness and distress.

CRUCIFIED To dream you are crucified in a town signifies that you will obtain property or a job in that town.

CRUELTY To dream of seeing this means that someone near to you is in need of help.

CRUMBS To dream of birds pecking at crumbs foretells both gifts and good tidings.

CRUST To dream that you are forced to beg for a crust of bread is a good dream. Though your parents may not have been well off, you will rise to be a wealthy and respected member of society.

CRUTCHES To dream you are walking on crutches is a very unfavourable omen. To dream you see someone else walking on crutches denotes that the unfavourable things will happen to some friend. If you are married, then your partner is unfaithful.

CRYING If you weep in your sleep you will have reason to smile when you are awake.

CRYSTAL To dream that you see a crystal substance is a sign that those whom you have respected will lose their good character and prospects by succumbing to some temptation that is presented to them.

CUBS Take a friendly hint and you will avert danger.

CUCKOO If a young person dreams of hearing the cuckoo, they can tell how many years will elapse before they marry. The number of years will be the same as the number of times the bird is heard calling in the dream.

CUCUMBER To dream of eating cucumber denotes hope and recovery to the sick, and that you will soon fall in love, or that you are in love and you will marry.

CUP An empty cup is a sign of troubled times ahead. A full one tells of good opportunities coming your way, which you must grasp without hesitation if you want to make a success of life.

CUPBOARD If you dream you see a cupboard burning, that signifies sickness or death to the owner. To dream that your cupboard doors open by themselves means that there will be plenty of the essentials in your home, but you can expect the breadwinner to fall ill before long.

CURATE For a young woman to dream that she marries a curate is a sign that a lawyer will seek her company and want to marry her. It may, however, prove a very long engagement, if in fact they do marry.

CURLS A complete change in your affairs; new environment and better times are in view.

CURRANT Black currants are forerunners of good fortune, and if you are eating them your married life will be happy and you will have a large family. Red currants are not such good omens, for false friends and sickness follow in their wake. White currants indicate success.

CURSE Hearing curses or rough language indicates a ceremonial visit.

CURTAIN To dream of a curtain means that someone is hiding something from you which, if you knew of it,

would make for good fortune. If you touch the curtain, the thing will be revealed to you at an early date.

CUSHION To dream that the cushion of your chair is torn is a sign that you will have sciatica, or severe pains in the back. It will be best for you to consult a skilful doctor.

CUSTARD To dream that you eat custard is a sign that you will have severe dental problems in a few months or years, and will require the skills of a good dentist.

CUTTLE-FISH Important decisions to be made in a great hurry.

CYCLING To dream that you are cycling indicates a visit you will make at some distance. If you see people cycling, friends will visit from afar.

CYPRESS TREE To dream you see a cypress tree denotes death, affliction, obstruction in business, or that bad news is about to come to someone who is dear to you.

DADDY-LONG-LEGS This dream signifies an amusing experience.

DAFFODIL All early spring flowers are fortunate omens. Daffodils particularly concern your love affairs, not your business concerns. A happy future is certain for the one who dreams of these beautiful spring flowers. But for the best results, they should be seen out-of-doors.

DAGGER To dream of seeing a dagger, either held by yourself or anyone else, portends that you are about to have a serious argument with a close acquaintance which will end in your becoming enemies for life.

DAHLIA To dream of these flowers is a sign of thrift and that you or your partner will make money rapidly.

DAIRY If you are helping in the work of a dairy you will marry someone in the same station of life, but you will have plenty all your life. If you are already married your social position will improve.

If you are skimming milk and taste the cream, you will have a windfall of money from an unexpected quarter.

DAIRYMAID For a young man to dream of seeing a dairymaid busy at work denotes that he will fall in love with an industrious girl whose business will be a great help to him, and aid him in his prosperity in financial affairs.

DAISIES To dream about gathering daisies is exceedingly fortunate. It foretells that you will obtain your wishes whatever they may be. But beware of trusting strangers; you will be deceived unless you are very careful.

DAMSON If you dream of eating this kind of plum when it is out of season expect great trouble, annoyance and vexation. Some of the affairs of your life will be very complicated and difficult.

DANCING To dream you see other people dance at a

ball signifies joy, pleasure, recreation and inheritance. To dream you are dancing at a ball foretells that you will shortly receive some joyful news from a long-absent friend that you are about to inherit some unexpected fortune; it foretells success and happiness. But to dance without music foretells want of money.

DANDELIONS   If you dream that you see these flowers in profusion it is a sign that news will shortly come to you of the marriage of one of your closest male friends. To dream of gathering dandelions is ominous; you have many new enemies forming, who will injure you behind your back. If one in love dreams of dandelions, it denotes that his or her sweetheart is or soon will be unfaithful to them.

DANGER   To dream of being in danger shows success in life; to shun it, misfortune.

DARKNESS   To dream of groping about a strange place in darkness denotes that you will receive an urgent message calling you to an unfamiliar location where sorrow awaits you. To dream you are in a very dark place, or that you are in the dark, is a very unfavourable omen.

To dream you get out of darkness denotes good to the dreamer. Expect good news from a distant country.

DARNING   To dream you are darning denotes the introduction of a new and kindly friend. To see it is a warning against gossip.

DATES   You are likely to be admired by a member of the opposite sex.

DAUGHTER   For a newly married woman to dream that her first child will be a daughter denotes that her husband will be presented by her with a fine, healthy chubby-faced boy.

DAWN   To see the dawn, days of storm and stress lie before you.

DEAD MARCH   To hear this played is a good sign for your dearest friend. He or she will have reason to rejoice at an early date.

DEAFNESS   To dream that you are afflicted with deafness denotes that, through the kind actions of a stranger, you will miss hearing something which would cause you unhappiness.

DEATH If you dream you are dead, you will work for someone in authority, will grow rich and live a long time, although not without much envy. To those who are married it foretells young children and that they will be dutiful and give you great comfort.

If it seems that you are put into a grave and buried, that indicates you will die poor, although some people believe that to dream you are dead and buried means that you will inherit property, the size of which will be in relation to the amount of earth under which you are buried.

To dream you see another person dead denotes friends will abuse you; if you are in love your sweetheart will prove false; if you are in a trade, you will be conned; if you are a farmer, you will lose money and may be robbed. If you dream of seeing a friend who is dead it is a sign of hearing of some friend or person whom you have not seen for a long time. If you dream you see someone who is dead and you believe him to be alive, that signifies that he is bringing God's message and should be listened to. If you dream that a dead man takes away your clothes or robs you of money or food, it may be a sign of death to one or more of your nearest relations and friends. To dream you see a man who is already dead die a second time signifies the death of one of your relations of the same name and surname. If you dream you were involved with a dead woman you will be loved and maintained by some great person. To dream that you give anything to someone who is dead signifies loss. To dream that you stand beside the death-bed of one of your friends or relations is indicative of marriage.

To dream of talking with dead people is a good, auspicious dream, and signifies a boldness of courage and a very clear conscience.

To dream of seeing the spirits of the dead, whether relations or friends, means long life to the living, combined with good health and easy circumstances.

DEATH TICK To dream that you hear the approach of death means that you will commit the error of marrying in haste, and will repent at your leisure.

DEATH-WATCH BEETLE A speedy marriage is ahead.

DEATHSHEAD *see* Skull.

DEBT   To pay a debt in a dream denotes a loss of money through carelessness. If you dream that a debtor is paying you, be on your guard against lending to a friend. His or her story of woe will be false.

DECAPITATION   To see someone decapitated, you will overcome enemies. It also indicates the return of a long-lost friend.

DECORATING   To decorate a room means poverty either of yourself or your friends. Some unfortunate circumstance will shortly happen to reduce your style of living.

To dream you decorate yourself in beautiful clothes means want of neat clothing. You will have difficulty in obtaining fashionable clothes.

DEER   To dream you have killed a deer, and that you have the head or skin, signifies that you will inherit the estate of some old man, or that you will overcome deceitful, cowardly and irresolute enemies. To dream you see a deer running signifies great wealth gained by application and subtlety at sport. If you see a deer in a forest and attempt to pursue it, you are wasting your time over some project which will

never be brought to a successful conclusion. If the animal is dead, you will be the innocent cause of pain to your dearest friend.

DEFEND   To dream of shielding or defending someone denotes at least one loyal friend.

DEFORMED   To dream that you are deformed, you have to fear shame, humiliation and sadness.

DELICACY   For anyone to dream their health is delicate, if they are ill it means recovery is at hand. For a healthy person to have this dream it means a greater robustness and strength will be enjoyed.

DELIGHT   To dream that you are really delighted with some event in your life means sorrow and trouble will shortly cross your path from some unexpected source.

DELIRIUM   To dream of being delirious signifies danger through a secret; to see someone else in that condition means a friend trying to help you secretly.

DELUGE   Business loss.

DENTIST   To dream you

visit a dentist is indicative of digestive problems becoming a source of illness to you. You had better take care of your health.

DERBY A lucky dream; financial gain will come your way.

DERELICT To dream of a derelict building or property signifies that you are having problems with your business but will eventually succeed.

DESCENDING To dream you descend a ladder signifies damage, sickness and ill health.

DESERT To travel in the desert indicates difficulties and dangers.

DESK To dream of sitting at a desk means that you are about to receive news that will be important or not according to how near to or far away from the window you are. A closed desk signifies that a frequent correspondent is about to have a serious illness which is likely to prove fatal. If a stranger is sitting at the desk, you will have dealings with a lawyer before you are many years older.

DESPAIR To dream that you are thrown into a state of despair by some sad event means that you will soon have cause for joy and rejoicing. Your children will show great success in their education, or some of your friends will become more devoted to you by some act of great kindness towards you. Expect some very favourable turn of fortune from this dream.

DESSERT To dream that you eat a dessert of unripe or unseasonable fruit is a very bad dream. You will have trouble and sorrow on all counts. You will soon learn that troubles come in troops, or quickly follow in succession.

To dream that you eat a dessert of ripe and seasonable fruits is a good dream; no event will happen that will trouble or annoy you, but a succession of happy and prosperous things will take place in your life.

DESTRUCTION To dream of destroying something of worth denotes that an acquaintance will shock you by performing a mean act, and will try to drag you into the trouble that will follow. Keep a guard on your tongue and avoid scandal.

To dream you destroy any place signifies deceit.

DETECTIVE To dream of having dealings with a detective is a sure sign that you will never find yourself in a court of law or have reason to apply to the law for protection.

DETESTING To dream that you detest a person means that you will shortly lose a valuable friend through some wicked slander which will be started by an enemy.

DEVIL If anyone dreams that they see the devil, it is a very bad sign; for such a vision cannot bring along with it any good tidings; to the sick it can foretell death and to the healthy it signifies melancholy, anger and violent sickness. If you dream you have seen the devil and that he was tormented or frightened, that signifies that the dreamer is in danger of being rebuked or punished by a magistrate. If you dream you strike the devil, it is a sign that you will beat your real enemies. If anyone dreams they are possessed by some evil spirit, they will receive benefits from the government and be long-lived. If anyone dreams that the devil speaks to them, that signifies temptation, deceit, treachery, despair and often the ruin and death of the dreamer. To dream you are carried away by the devil is a worse dream; yet often this is a delightful dream to the dreamer, because when they wake up, they feel delighted that they have been freed from so great an evil. To dream you see the devil as he is drawn by painters and poets – black and hideous, with horns, claws and a great tail – signifies torment and despair.

DEVOTION As with most dreams concerning religion, this is a good sign.

DEW To dream of the dew glittering in the morning sun is a very lucky omen. It means to the lover encouragement, to the husband and wife happiness in the home, to the businessman wealth, to the literary man reputation, to the musician applause – in short, to everyone their heart's desire and the reasonable reward of all their hard work.

DIADEM To dream that you wear a crown is a sign of degradation. You will not have a happy life but will be dogged with failure and difficulties.

DIAMOND If diamonds are seen in a dream they have a different meaning, depending on whether they belong to you or to someone else. If they are owned by someone else, they mean for you wealth and success in all your endeavours. Should they, however, be your own, then you may infer that you are in danger of getting into severe problems caused by debts or that you will be mixed up in some gossip that will lead you into serious trouble – you may even lose your job. To eat diamonds indicates much profit, wealth, success and happiness.

DIARRHOEA   Illness, loss and sorrow.

DICE   To dream you play at dice and win signifies deceit and craft and that you are in danger of losing your money to some wicked person, but good fortune in marriage or business should follow a game of dice if you lose the game.

DICTIONARY   This denotes quarrels and the loss of a friend.

DIFFICULTY   If you imagine in your dream that you are in great difficulty, or in personal danger of any kind, it is a favourable sign, as such dreams always go by contrary.

DIGGING   Much depends upon what you dig. If it is a grave, you may look for good fortune for yourself in some small affair, and the reverse for a friend. To dig up treasure of any kind signifies that you will soon have need for all your spare money. To dig a ditch or trench means illness.

DINNER   Being present at a dinner party indicates that you are about to be an innocent sufferer from the actions of someone in whom you have placed confidence. If you see any guest referring to a piece of paper, the probability is that you will be taken in through accepting a valueless cheque which will bounce. If someone present is making a speech beware of flattery, which will lead you astray unless you keep a guard on your actions. To dream that you are dining alone at a table laid for several people and that your meal is a frugal one denotes that after trouble there will be reason to celebrate.

DIPLOMA   To dream that you have obtained a diploma for the practice of medicine, it is a sign that you will become skilled in surgery, if you study it. Anatomy will be the most valuable study for you to follow.

DIRT To dream of filth and dirt denotes dishonour and sickness. To dream of falling in the dirt shows disgrace and malice. To walk through dirt indicates misfortune. If your clothes are dirty, it shows sickness and trouble.

DISASTER These are always dreams of contrary.

DISAPPOINTMENT To dream you are disappointed assures the dreamer of success in the very matter dreamed about.

DISCUSSION If the discussion is between yourself and a number of people you will make a success of life by your own individual efforts rather than from anyone's help. To have a friendly discussion with an acquaintance means rapid promotion in your business, or an improvement in the affairs of your husband or sweetheart.

DISEASE To dream you are stricken with a serious disease foretells that you will develop a liking for drink, which will lead to your ruin unless a friend keeps a watchful eye on you.

DISGRACE To dream that you fall into disgrace by some thoughtless act is a sign that in most of your affairs you will display prudence of a kind that will bring you into the favour and reputation of your friends and acquaintances.

DISGUISE If your friends appear to you disguised for a fancy dress party it means that you will have a visit from some old school friends, whose altered personal appearance will prevent you from recognising them.

DISGUST If you are disgusted by something horrible in your dream, expect to meet influential people.

DISH To dream you have broken a pewter dish means that you will have a greater loss in a short time; some of your relatives will fall ill.

DISHONESTY An important document will be mislaid. If you are dishonest in your dream, it will be a document affecting your affairs.

DISINFECTANT Take care to avoid infectious diseases.

DISLIKE This dream depends upon the circumstances. If you dream that someone does not like you, and that you are worried, it is a bad omen. If, however, you do not appear to be upset at all, then your difficulties will be overcome.

DISLOCATION If you dream of dislocating a limb, be careful of changing your job or making other career changes you may regret.

DISMISSAL To dream of being dismissed from a business position presages a rise in position.

DISOBEDIENCE To dream of your own disobedience denotes a difficult choice before you, possibly regarding marriage.

DISPUTE To dream that a dispute happens between you and some person with whom you have business is a sign of bad luck. After such a dream you should be careful of yourself, and be as gentle and reasonable as possible so that you do not give anyone any advantage over you.

If you are in love, someone has attempted to injure you with your partner and has in some degree succeeded; you should, therefore, after such a dream, be particularly thoughtful and attentive.

DISTANCE A dream that you are separated from your

friends or family is a bad sign. But if you dream of some person who is separated from you, then you will hear good news.

DISTRESS Great distress in a dream is a sure omen that some person will make you indebted to him or her all your life. Probably they will help you make advances in life.

DISTRUST To dream that you have reason to distrust a person generally means bad luck for a friend, or illness for a relative of whom you are very fond. If someone distrusts you, your friends have been talking about you, and you will have cause to regret ever having known one or more of them.

DITCH To see great ditches or precipices and that you fall into them signifies that you will suffer a great deal of injury and hazard, both to you and your property by fire. To go over a ditch on a small plank signifies deceit by lawyers. To dream of a ditch containing muddy water is a sign that you will narrowly escape from a bad accident. If you fall into a ditch, whether dry or otherwise, you may look for serious trouble through an accident caused by your own carelessness. To dream of leaping over ditches indicates troublesome children, of which you will have a good share.

DIVING If you dive into water, some speculation in which you are involved will turn out unfavourably, or you are placing trust and confidence in someone who will let you down. The young may infer from this dream that their lover is deceiving them.

DIVORCE Fidelity and love.

DOCKS To visit the docks of a seaport town is indicative of being confined at home to your room from gout, rheumatism or some other painful and severe illness.

DOCTOR To become a physician signifies cheerfulness, fortune and health – a rise in life. To open the door to a doctor portends good news, which you will receive by word of mouth. If, however, you see the doctor tending a sick friend or relative, you will meet a friend whom you have not seen for many years and will renew the old friendship.

DOG A dog denotes fidelity, courage and affection, if it belongs to you and is friendly. If you have had a quarrel with a friend or sweetheart, you will make up to your advantage; if you are in love, your sweetheart will marry you and make you very happy. Dogs denote health, riches and honour. But those that belong to strangers signify infamous enemies. If they are barking and snarling at you, then your enemies are secretly endeavouring to destroy your reputation and happiness; if you are in love, be careful of your present sweetheart – if you marry him/her you will be unhappy and poor. If you dream dogs bite you, then you will experience some loss; if you are in love, your sweetheart will deceive you, and make you very unhappy.

To dream that a dog barks and tears your clothes signifies an enemy is slandering you or trying to deprive you of your livelihood. To be disturbed by dogs barking signifies success over adversaries. To dream of seeing a dog begging means that you will experience the misery of waiting and watching for favours from those who are farther advanced in life than you.

DOLPHIN To dream you see dolphins playing in the water denotes the loss of your sweetheart and the death of some near relation or friend. It is an unfavourable dream and signifies that your present pursuits will not be to your advantage. You would do well to move on.

DOMINOES Taking chances will not benefit you.

DONKEY Your love-life will be successful, unless the donkey kicks or throws you.

DOOR To dream of a door opening unexpectedly is an intimation that you ought to be saving as much as possible, because if you accumulate a certain amount of capital a chance will occur which will enable you to make a lot of money. To see many doors indicates a visit from a person whom you distrust. If you are knocking at a door of a strange house and gain admittance you will make a new friend shortly, but if the door is not opened you will be disappointed in an engagement.

DOORBELL Exciting adventures with a member of the opposite sex.

DOUGH Kneading dough signifies good health and nourishment.

DOUGHNUTS You will travel around the world.

DOVE These birds are omens of good fortune to come. If married, your partner in life and your children will make you happy, and never cause you a moment's anxiety by reckless behaviour. For the businessman, the birds bring promise of increase in trade. If the birds are feeding out of your hand it denotes a removal to the country, where you will be greatly respected.

DOWRY To dream that you have received a dowry with your spouse is a sign that they will keep you poor all your life by extravagant ways.

DRAGON To see a dragon is a sign that you will see a person in authority and power. It also signifies riches and treasures.

DRAGONFLY A sea voyage is in prospect.

DRAMA To dream you see tragedies played signifies travel, fighting, injury and a thousand other evils. But to see a drama with a happy ending means that you will also experience a happy ending to your affairs.

DRAUGHTS
Playing draughts means your affections are being trifled with – beware.

DRAWBRIDGE You will undertake an unexpected journey.

DRAWER To find your drawer open is a sign of the security of your property, if you have any; if not, of the security of your character from scandal.

DRAWING To draw pictures signifies joy without profit; expect good business increase.

DREAM To dream you relate your dreams to anyone shows that something unexpected will take place.

DRENCHED An unfortunate dream, presaging danger of fever for you or someone near to you.

DRESS To dream of a new dress predicts that you will live to want; of an old one, that you will be comfortable all your life, but never really rich. White dresses mean good and kind friends; black ones indicate the death of a friend or relative; a torn dress shows misfortune.

DRINK To drink clear water signifies good times to come. To drink hot water signifies sickness and problems. To drink stinking water signifies violent illness. To dream of drinking unreasonable quantities signifies that you will suffer from some violent disease. To dream that you are drinking from a stream or fountain is another sign of sickness.

To dream that you are suffering from thirst and someone gives you a glass of wine means that you will make a discovery through a friend which will bring you happiness. If, instead of wine, you receive water from a man, you will be married within the year if you are not engaged; and, if married, your spouse will introduce you to a friend of whom you will become very fond. To dream you drink wine in moderation is good. To dream you drink sweet wine and see beautiful women and sleep under shady trees means success in love to anyone who wants to marry. To dream that you drink cocktails is only good if you are accustomed to drinking them. To dream you drink oil signifies sickness from poison. To drink from vessels of gold, silver or earthenware is good because it signifies tranquillity. All vessels of horn are good because they are unbreakable, but vessels of glass are evil.

DRIVING To dream of driving is a sign that a habit

you have acquired will lead you into serious trouble. To a man or woman in business it denotes a falling-off of customers or clients, and to a lover disappointments brought about by their own foolishness.

DROP If you are measuring out drops of liquid, you will shortly have a small sum of money left to you, or it will come to you from an unexpected source.

DROPSY To dream that you have dropsy is indicative of decline of health from diabetes. You will have good health for a long period, and then this complaint will set in.

DROUGHT For a farmer to dream of seeing their crops or grass drying up for want of rain denotes that an accident will happen to the farm during a storm, or that some of the livestock on the farm will die or meet with an accident.

DROWNING To dream you are drowning or see another person drowning is good, and denotes that you will be preserved through many strange difficulties. If the scene takes place at sea, then the trouble will not arrive for some time; if on a river, the

first signs may be looked for immediately. Eventually, however, you will overcome your problems. If you are a lover, it denotes that your sweetheart is good-tempered and wants to marry you; if you are a traveller, it foretells a pleasant and prosperous voyage.

DROWSINESS To dream of having a feeling of drowsiness is a sign of bad luck, and may be interpreted as meaning that you are working too hard and that you will accomplish more by finding time for some rest and relaxation. If you push yourself too hard, you will not gain your ambitions.

DRUM To hear the beat of a drum or drums foretells fame and popularity for you or those around you.

DRUMMER For a young man to dream he is a drummer in an instrumental band is a sign that he will become a musician of another kind.

DRUNKENNESS To dream you are drunk is one of those dreams by which the dreamer is forewarned of things they know nothing about. For example, it might indicate that someone you have not met will become a very good friend, and promote your welfare; through their means you will acquire money and reputation, especially if you dream of having drunk a sweet and pleasant drink. However, if you dream you are drunk without drinking any alcohol, it is a bad omen, and you run the risk of being disgraced by some criminal action. If you dream you are drunk with pure water, you will boast of your wealth without reason and praise another person's strength. If you dream you are drunk and vomit, you will run the risk of losing money because you will be forced to account for any illegally acquired money, or because you lose everything through betting.

DUCK   To dream of seeing ducks walking or flying is an omen of good news coming by post. If the birds are swimming, good health and a contented mind will be yours for some time. You will overcome all evil spoken about you and all problems.

DUEL   Trouble from friends and relatives is indicated by this dream. You have treacherous enemies and should beware or they will succeed in their plans to harm you.

DUET   To dream of singing a duet with someone of the opposite sex shows that you can win your lover if you want. To hear a duet sung denotes business troubles, or troubles from friends or relatives.

To dream of dancing a duet indicates that you will have a light-hearted approach to life which will not be altogether bad. But you should be careful not to act in too frivolous a manner, otherwise other people will suspect your intelligence or sincerity.

DUMB   For a married person to dream their spouse is dumb is a bad sign. Gossiping will be a source of serious problems for some time to come.

DUNGEON   To see a dungeon means difficulties and doubts in connection with love or home life. If you dream of being a prisoner in a dungeon, you will be hampered all through life by a weakness of will which will give other people the advantage over you.

DUNGHILL   For a poor man to dream he sleeps on a dunghill signifies that he will accumulate considerable wealth. To the rich it signifies public estate, office and honour.

DUSK To dream that you walk with your lover in the dusk of the evening means that the relationship will soon be made public among friends and acquaintances.

DUST To dream of being in a dusty house signifies that you will soon marry, but that you will not be a good housekeeper and your surroundings will be untidy. To dream of dusting a room predicts a short engagement. Being blinded by dust indicates business difficulties and losses in the family circle.

DWARF If you see a dwarf in your dream, it is a sign of difficulties in your domestic circle.

DYE To dream that you dye your hair is indicative of a vain and conceited character, fond of appearing in company to the best advantage, determined to be fashionable at all costs. Affected and conceited in deportment, you will become the laughing-stock of the prudent friends and companions you meet.
To dye clothes indicates slight pleasure. To see clothes being dyed, your confidence will be abused.

DYING If you dream you are dying, you will receive empty promises.

DYNAMITE If you dream of dynamite, your plans will be destroyed.

EAGLE To dream you see an eagle perched on the steeple of a church, or on any high eminence, is a very good omen – especially to those who are in business and to soldiers. If you dream that an eagle lands on your head or carries you into the air, it signifies death to the dreamer. If a woman dreams that she gives birth to an eagle, that foretells that the child she is pregant with will be a great person, and that he will have many under his command. If anyone dreams he sees a dead eagle, that signifies death to a powerful man, but profit to the poor. If eagles are seen flying overhead in a dream you may infer that you are entering on a period of unusual prosperity, in which you will not only obtain much personal advantage but be the cause of many benefits falling to others. The higher the bird soars the greater your triumph will be. To the lover, it fore-tells success in love and a happy marriage.

To see an eagle in its nest is a sign that laziness, not necessarily your own, will cause you trouble.

EAR To dream a man has many ears signifies that he will gain the love of his employees and they will work well for him. To dream that a man picks his ears signifies that same thing. To dream his ears are full of corn signifies he will inherit money from his parents. To dream you have asses ears signifies servitude. To dream you have the ears of a lion or of any other wild beast signifies treachery or deceit by your enemies and those who envy you. If you dream that your ears have become larger than usual, you will prosper with the person to whom you communicate your secrets. If anyone dreams their ear is hurt or cut or you have lost them through an accident, they will be offended by a friend to whom they have entrusted their secrets. If it seems that the ear is completely cut off, their friendship will be destroyed. If anyone dreams their ears are stopped, it is a sign they will alter their resolutions and will deceive those who confide in them.

Dreaming of having a pain in one of your ears is a sure

sign that you are about to be made the subject of a false charge, your innocence of which it will be exceedingly difficult to prove. To dream that your ears are washed shows you will hear good news. To dream of a singing in the ears portends false news. To have your ears beaten foretells bad news. To dream that you are suffering from a disease of the ears indicates that you will hear of a death that will bring you a legacy.

If you dream your ears are quite attractive and well shaped, it shows you will become well known. But if you dream your ears are ugly and deformed, it shows the opposite.

To dream you have ants crawling into your ears is good only to philosophers and schoolmasters, for the ants represent children who are forced to listen to such pedants. To others it foretells death.

EARACHE For a person to dream that he or she is suffering from earache is indicative of some part of the body being affected with scurvy, or a swelling will paralyse the leg or arm.

EARRING If a young man dreams of buying earrings, he will shortly quarrel with his sweetheart. For a girl to dream of receiving a present of earrings is a sign that she will fall in love with a man who does not return her affection.

EARTH If you dream of seeing the earth, you will come into money.

EARTHQUAKE To dream of an earthquake warns that your affairs are about to take a very great change. If you see many houses tumble into ruins, then it will be a great deal for the better. To dream of great ditches or precipices or the land split by the violence of the earthquake and you falling in them signifies that you are in danger from fire. To dream that the whole earth quakes signifies a Government announcement that will shock everyone. If you dream that the house shakes, then the announcement will affect your property; it indicates the loss of goods and legal problems. If the walls and top of the house fall in because of the earthquake, that denotes the destruction and death of the chief persons in the house. To hear a shaking signifies deceit which will happen to the dreamer.

To dream of a house falling on you shows the dreamer to

be oppressed by some superior hand, but if the weight seems removed you will regain your former station.

EARTHWORM To dream of earthworms signifies enemies that try to ruin and destroy you.

EARWIG To dream of having an earwig in one of your ears means much the same as that of having a pain there. Both suggest that you are to be the victim of slander and ill will. To dream of seeing a swarm of these insects is a sign that you will be pestered by gossips concerning your love affair or domestic life. But you need take no steps to find out the mischievous party, for they will bring about their own punishment.

EASEL To dream of purchasing an artist's easel is a good dream. For the single it signifies marriage; to those who have no children it indicates that they will have children; and to those who are married with children, it means purchases and riches.

EAST You are about to be sent on a long journey with an important result; perhaps a religious mission.

EASTER To dream of this season is a prediction that someone with whom you are only slightly acquainted will cause you happiness by introducing you to a stranger.

EATING To dream you are eating is unlucky; it denotes disunion among your family, losses in your trade, disappointments in love, and is a sure sign of quarrelling. In business it means that you are about to lose money through carelessness in not taking a receipt, the amount being in proportion to the quantity of food you have in front of you. In love affairs it signifies separation, coldness and quarrels. To dream you see others eating means the opposite; and foretells success in all your present enterprises; if you marry the present object of your affections, you will grow rich, be happy and have dutiful children. To see silver eaten signifies great advantage. To dream of eating human flesh signifies labour and distress; to eat lard or salt signifies gossiping; to eat cheese signifies gain and profit; to eat apples signifies anger.

EATING HOUSE To dream that you are having a meal in an eating house is a sign of inducement being given to you to become a commercial traveller for an insurance company, or for the sale of books or other merchandise.

EAVESDROPPER To dream that you are playing eavesdropper to some private conversation is a sign of approaching trouble. You will be assailed by unscrupulous enemies, and be hard put to it to defend your home and reputation.

EBONY A voyage to a foreign country.

ECHO To dream of listening to an echo means that your marriage partner will think they are particularly clever, and expect you to share their opinion.

ECLIPSE of the MOON To dream you see an eclipse of the moon, denotes that you will lose some female friends – your mother, if she is alive.

EDEN Look out for flatterers who do not mean well towards you.

EDITOR To see an editor working means that you should take stock of your career and finances.

EEL When seen in a dream these indicate difficulties,

which you can overcome if you persevere.

EGG To dream of lots of eggs foretells anger, and is a sign that you will shortly be involved in violent arguments between relatives and friends. Keep a guard on your tongue, for you will be in danger or trouble through over-plain speaking. To dream that you are carrying eggs and break some or all of them indicates unfaithfulness and sorrows. To dream of eating eggs is a sign that you will be spared a great evil which is threatening you. You may soon have a child. To dream you are buying or selling eggs is a more favourable omen.

ELASTIC This dream denotes an improvement in your fortunes.

ELBOW To dream of a pain in, or any trouble with, your elbow may be taken as a sign that you will have need of all your strength in an emergency which will soon arise.

ELDERBERRY For a lover to dream of this fruit is a warning that he or she must be on her guard in dealings with the opposite sex, otherwise much trouble will ensue. For a married person the fruit is an omen of sickness in the house.

ELECTION To dream that you are assisting at one means a speedy success for your own hopes.

ELECTRICITY Something will happen to surprise you greatly. Guard against small losses.

ELEPHANT If someone sees an elephant, it may be taken as a sign of stability in love and domestic happiness. If someone dreams that he gives an elephant anything to eat or drink, it is a sign that he shall work for some powerful person, to his advantage. A herd of these animals indicates a big surprise.

ELF This is a very fortunate dream, for it shows that the little people are friendly.

ELM To dream of a tall elm tree is an omen that your partner in life will rise to distinction through his intelligence. It denotes a long life of luxury.

ELOPEMENT To dream of eloping with your sweetheart is a sign that your honeymoon will be marred by some unforeseen happening. To elope with a stranger is an omen of a happy marriage.

EMBANKMENT Your hopes will not be fulfilled, but someone you have known formerly will shortly return into your life.

EMBARKING To dream you embark in a small vessel signifies sickness.

EMBARRASSMENT Do let others change your mind against your better judgement.

EMBRACE To dream of embracing anyone does not have a good meaning. Beware of the friend or lover who embraces you in your dream; he or she is deceiving you. But should you see your sweetheart embrace another, be content that you are well loved.

EMBROIDERY To dream of embroidery signifies an affection that is returned.

EMERALD To an engaged person, a dream of an emerald is a warning against a rival. To one who is married it tells of petty annoyance from an enemy.

EMIGRATION A friend in a foreign country will write to you shortly enclosing a present.

EMPEROR To dream of an emperor signifies disquietude. To see kings and emperors together denotes much success in life.

EMPLOYMENT To dream that you are seeking employment and cannot obtain any is a sign that you will not change your place of occupation many times during your life. If you obtain lucrative employment it is a bad sign, and you will probably be seen looking for a situation.

EMPTINESS To dream you are pouring from an empty jar signifies unexpected gains, but an empty barrel means poverty.

ENCHANTMENT To dream you are enchanted signifies secrets and sorrows.

ENCYCLOPAEDIA Using an encyclopedia means that your career will be successful.

END OF THE WORLD You will hear of something very surprising leading to good times for yourself.

ENEMY To dream you are obstructed by an adversary signifies success in business. To talk with your enemy signifies you must look out for him. To dream of meeting an enemy is an omen of success for you and trouble for him.

ENGAGEMENT To dream you enter into an engagement is a good or bad sign, according to the kind of engagement you make. To dream of a matrimonial engagement is a sign that you will not be married for many months or years. If you have a lover, look out for a quarrel. A trade engagement is a sign of difficulties besetting your career as a businessman. An engagement to meet a friend means an unfortunate encounter with a creditor of yours, in which you will quarrel; coldness, if not absolute hatred, will follow, and you will become alienated from the intimacy of your friend.

ENGAGEMENT RING To see or wear one means a new attraction or to be engaged, a speedy wedding.

ENGINE To stand beside a steam engine at work is a sign that you will lose your physical strength through illness, or lose something else dear to you. To dream you are riding on a railway engine is indicative of your having an offer of railway shares at a very cheap rate, or of a disagreement with someone engaged on the railway.

ENGRAVING To dream that you are engraving your name on metal denotes that you will have an offer of good, regular work at a new company. Someone connected with you will marry a wealthy man but will be left at home while he is engaged abroad.

ENJOYMENT When a married person dreams that they are enjoying themselves, it is a sign that they will soon have to undertake a disagreeable journey, but will eventually profit by it. To a single person it predicts a quarrel over a love affair, but not with the sweetheart. On the contrary, the lover will be faithful and defend you from the malicious attacks of others. To a man or woman in business the dream predicts worry.

ENLISTING For a girl to dream that her lover or someone for whom she has a great regard has enlisted is a sign that she will marry but will lose her husband early in life. If a man dreams that he has enlisted, he should look out for a new job – he will soon be in need of one.

ENTERTAINMENT If a young person dreams of enjoying themselves at a place of entertainment, they will do well to take a ticket for a concert or some such entertainment and use it, for there they will meet the person who will eventually become their partner. For a married person the dream foretells a happy family and a contented mind, especially if at the time of the dream, things are not as comfortable as they might be.

ENTOMBMENT Be warned not to put yourself forward too much. Your actions will speak for themselves.

ENTRAILS If you dream you have excreted your entrails, some of your family will be engaged abroad in a quarrel which will cause you damage and suffering. If you think that you have eaten your entrails, you will gain by the death of someone who works for you; if you dream you have eaten the intestines of someone else, you will enrich yourself by the estate of another. If you dream you are dead and see your innards, it is good if you are poor, for you will have a child and gain financially. But to a rich man, it means shame and dishonour. To dream that you are cut open

but cannot see your entrails
signifies that you will leave
your house and lose your
children; it also indicates
death by sickness. This
dream can, however, be a
comfort to anyone suffering
from problems because you
will lose those things which
are causing pain and grief.
For example: the heart or
lungs signifies a man; the
liver signifies a son; the gall
bladder indicates melancholy,
money, women and wives;
the spleen signifies pleasure
and laughter; the belly and
guts signify children.

ENVELOPE   To dream of
seeing a packet of envelopes
signifies that you may expect
to receive many Valentines on
the next 14th of February. If
you see many directed
envelopes you will have
problems collecting money
owed to you.

ENVY   If you are envied in a
dream you will be admired.

EPAULETS   To a man a
dream in which epaulets
figure denotes early
promotion. To a girl it is a
sign that she will fall in love
with a soldier or sailor who
will rise in the service of his
country.

EPICURE   Sickness.

EPITAPH   A wedding; or a
new addition to the family
should you be already
married.

EQUATOR   Think hard
before making decisions that
will alter the course of your
life, but be careful not to let
opportunities slip by.

ERMINE   This signifies a
letter from, or some
association with, those of
high rank. But to the sick it
means a slow recovery.

ERRAND   To dream that you
are out on an errand and
have forgotten your mission
is a sure sign that someone in
authority will cause you grief
through a thoughtless act or
speech. If the errand is a
difficult one and you
accomplish it to your own
satisfaction you may look for
a present of money from a
quarter in which you least
expect it.

ERUPTION   To dream that
an eruption breaks out in
some part of your body is a
sign of illness from exposure
to cold; bronchitis or
inflammation of the lungs
will attack the dreamer, but
the illness will not be very
severe.

ESCALATOR   If you dream
of an escalator moving up,

you will find new friends and fulfil your ambitions. If it is moving down, you will have to work hard to avoid problems.

ESCAPE Inability to escape indicates trouble will overtake you; a successful escape means you will overcome your present difficulties.

ESKIMO If you have been trying to borrow money, you will be unsuccessful. You may find a coolness in your love-life.

ESTATES If you dream that you own considerable fenced lands, you will have a beautiful or handsome spouse, to compare with the goodness of the land in the dream. But if the land seemed spacious and not enclosed, that denotes pleasure, joy and riches, comparable with the extent of the land. If it seems that the enclosed lands have lovely gardens, fountains, fields, pleasant groves and orchards adjoining them, that signifies that you will marry an attractive and sensitive person and will have very handsome children. If the land is sown with wheat, that signifies money and profit with hard work. If it is sown with any kind of pulse, that denotes affliction and

trouble. If it is sown with millet, that signifies vast riches to be gained with ease and much delight.

ETCHING You have good taste.

EUNUCH Unhappiness, loss and difficulties.

EVE To dream that you are Eve, or, in fact, naked, is an unfortunate omen for a woman. Problems are in store for you.

EVENING A prosperous time to come later in life. Your earlier worries will be happily ended.

EVERGREEN Evergreens in profusion, either plants or branches cut for decoration, portend good fortune throughout the year. This is a most favourable dream indicating happiness, honour and success. To pick them, you will have the true friendship of some person.

EVIDENCE To dream of giving evidence against a criminal in court, denotes a friend whose reputation you will be able to save.

EVIL SPIRITS A very serious omen, unless you succeed in driving them away. Be careful in your business.

EWE A large family and prosperous times to come.

EWER To dream that you break a water jug is a sign of unpleasant interruption to a correspondence with your lover. Some mischievous local busybodies will contrive to obtain possession of the love-letters that pass between you. The secrets of your conversation may become a source of gossip among the neighbours where you live.

EXAMINATION The student who dreams that he or she is sitting an examination, and is in difficulty over the problems set, will come through the course of study with flying colours. To dream of passing an examination with ease is a bad omen.

EXCHANGE For a person in business to dream of success in exchanging goods is a sign that someone will try their best to swindle him out of his property by trading with him in inferior goods. Much care and forethought is needed after the revelation of this dream.

EXCISEMAN If a woman dreams of an exciseman she must expect a brother or close male relative to gain a financially rewarding Civil Service post.

EXCITEMENT To dream that you are feeling unpleasantly disturbed denotes a successful ending to your plans.

EXCREMENT For a man to dream that he puts excrement in his bedroom signifies great sickness or divorce of his wife, but probably a change of lodging. It is very bad to dream that you relieve yourself in a church, market or greenhouse as it signifies that you will suffer humiliation and pain by the revelation of unfortunate secrets.

EXCURSION Be on your guard against a married associate who may not be a true friend.

EXCUSE For a young woman to dream that she puts off with a paltry excuse a young man who asks her to take a walk is a sign that she will shortly meet with a fair-haired, light-complexioned young man who will desire her company and take no denial.

EXECUTION To dream of execution signifies that you will be asked a favour. To imagine yourself present at the execution of a criminal is a good omen. You will get on in life and will soon be in a position to administer charity, which will make you well regarded by many.

EXECUTOR To dream that you are the executor of some person recently deceased is a sign that you will be called upon to pay money on another person's account. Either you will be bondsman in a money club or surety for a person who has committed a breach of the peace and you will have to forfeit the bond, or you will give your word of honour for the payment of goods they wish to possess, and they will fail.

EXERCISE To dream that you are taking vigorous exercise is a sign of hard work to follow.

EXHAUSTED To dream you are exhausted from some violent exercise or passion is indicative that a change in your disposition will shortly take place. You will become more accustomed to hard work and also used to a great deal of worry.

EXHIBITION To dream you visit an exhibition is a sign that you will form a liking for some indoor amusement. Cards, dominoes, draughts or chess will be the game that will keep you in your home each evening after work.

EXILE To dream you become an exile in a foreign country is a sign that you will be more in love with your native land than ever. At the first public or private convivial or social party you will be called upon to give the loyal toast, which you will perform to the satisfaction of everyone and make a speech that will surpass any you have ever delivered before.

You may be offered a job working for someone who is about to become a foreign ambassador.

EXPEDITION To go on a dreary expedition or a voyage of discovery is a sign of removal to some other locality through fear of a house being badly drained, or because of unpleasant or unhealthy smells continually coming from various parts of the lower rooms.

EXPLOSION Danger to a relative.

EXPRESS If you are travelling on an express, beware of your superiors in business.

EXPRESSION To dream of a cloudy look denotes want of money; or being blind in both eyes denotes the loss of both children or parents. But for anyone who is poor or in prison, it is a good dream; for soldiers or merchants, the opposite.

EXTRAVAGANCE   To dream that you are spending extravagantly is a sign of success in your domestic arrangements. You will have many home comforts which will make you enjoy your home more than ever. For a woman to have this dream means that you will be a good financier, and your husband or those dependent upon your management will be pleased to stay beneath your roof.

EYE   The eyes are the windows of the soul, and the Ancients represent by them faith, the will and the light of understanding. If you dream you have lost your sight, you will violate your word, or else you or your children are in danger of death, or you will never see your friends again. If you dream that you have grown bleary-eyed, you will commit a dreadful crime and afterwards repent of it. You are also in danger of losing your property. To dream you have a good and quick sight is an extraordinarily good dream; it means that you will succeed in your enterprises. But a troubled and weak sight signifies want of money, failure in business and

sickness to anyone with children. To dream that your eyesight is failing means that you are in danger of wasting your best years and your choicest thoughts on someone who is quite unworthy of you. To dream of an injury to the eyes or a disease affecting them is a sign that you have enemies seeking to take away your good character and many problems will fall on you, ending in the death of a dear friend. To dream you lose your eyes denotes change of circumstance for the worse, loss of friends and disappointments in love. If a pregnant woman dreams of it, it denotes that the child she is carrying will be very unhappy and will be imprisoned before it grows to maturity. To dream of having three or four eyes is good for those who are married and would like to have a family. To dream of having someone else's eyes denotes the loss of one's own. To be haunted by a pair of staring eyes is an omen of good fortune.

EYEBROWS   To dream your eyebrows and eyelids are more attractive and larger than they usually are is a sign you will be honoured and well regarded by everyone, that you will prosper in love, and grow rich. If you dream that you lose the hair of your eyebrows, or your eyelashes, the opposite will happen.

EYEGLASS   Good news from a friend, or sometimes a fortunate business deal.

EYELASH   Secrets someone shares with you could lead to problems.

EYELID   To dream of any trouble to your eyelids is a sign that someone you know is in distress but hesitates to ask for your help, although you would freely give it if you knew it was wanted.

FABLE If you dream that you are reading a fable it is a sign that you will become attached to an unfit young companion, with whom you will only keep company for a short time. Some of your friends will advise you to drop the acquaintance.

FABRICS You will follow an artistic career.

FACE To dream you see a black face signifies long life. To see a beautiful face, unlike your own, signifies honour. To dream you wash your face signifies repentance of your sin. To see a strange face is an indication that you will soon be changing where you live, either permanently or otherwise. To see your own face reflected in a mirror is a promise of a long life to yourself and your sweetheart or spouse. A number of faces familiar to you is a sign that you will soon receive an invitation to a party or a wedding. To see a beautiful face reflected in water indicates a long and happy life.

FACTORY To dream that you are in a factory denotes some change in your health. You will be surprised by the news of a son, daughter or other near relative suffering some accident from machinery, or some unforeseen calamity from fire and water.

FAGGOTS To dream of faggots signifies that you will receive bad news.

FAILURE To dream that you fail in anything indicates success by your own efforts.

FAINTING To dream that you are fainting is a very sad omen. It foreshadows family arguments and disgrace for someone in whom you have trusted. If you faint in a crowded street, beware of some infectious disease, and if in a place of entertainment look to your sweetheart's or partner's health. They will have a serious breakdown unless you take great care of them. To dream that you are tending someone else who has fainted is a sign that you will lose money through robbery.

FAIR To dream you are at the fair denotes that some pretended friend is about to do you an injury. You may grow dissatisfied with your sweetheart's attentions and find someone more thoughtful. To dream of being at a fair in company with your sweetheart indicates a separation caused by jealousy.

FAIRY Whatever happens in a dream about fairies, the opposite will take place. If the fairies are helping you, look out for the evil tongue of an enemy who will try to do you harm.

FAIRYLAND To dream of being in fairyland signifies that you will be inventive and creative.

FAITH Feel free to make decisions which you have been postponing. They will work to your advantage.

FAITHFUL You will have a happy and productive period in your life.

FAITHLESS To dream that your sweetheart is unfaithful is a good dream. You will find that your lover is true to you, even though a richer person tries to tempt them away.

FAKE Do not act without proper thought; things may not be as they first appear.

FALCON To see birds of prey or falconry signifies increase, riches and honour. To dream you carry a falcon on your fist and walk with it signifies honour.

FALLING If you dream you have fallen from a tree, and been scratched by thorns or otherwise injured, it signifies that you will lose your job. To fall in the dirt signifies treachery, or disturbance by some person or other. To fall into the water signifies death or personal danger. To fall into a clear fountain signifies honour and gain. To fall into a pit or ditch signifies sudden surprise or danger, the loss of a cause or lawsuit. To fall into a troubled fountain signifies accusation. To fall on the ground signifies dishonour and scandal. To fall from a bridge signifies obstruction. To dream you fall from a high place denotes many troubles will follow. If you are in love, it indicates that you will never marry your present partner. To the tradesman it denotes decline of business, to the sailor storms and shipwreck. A fall from a stool or chair is indicative of loss of dignity through some thoughtless action. To dream of falling and falling without landing means that you will shortly become very depressed, imagining that the whole world is going wrong, but will after a time rediscover your equilibrium. You may suffer a breakdown in health.

FALSEHOOD To dream that you have told a serious lie is an indication of an upright nature. If you hear someone else tell a lie, you will be the recipient of good news concerning someone dear to you.

FAME To dream of sudden fame is a sign that you will have to strive your utmost to make ends meet for some time to come, and you would do well to start saving while your affairs are prosperous. To dream that a friend or lover has achieved fame is an indication that you will be disappointed by an action of that person.

FAMILY To dream of a large family is a good sign of prosperous times in store, and also to dream of relatives (as long as they are friendly).

FAMINE A dream of famine is the reverse of fame. You will have no cause to complain of the successes which will come to you in life. Prosperity, health and happiness will be yours.

FAMOUS To dream that you have become famous is a bad sign. It shows loss and a change for the worse.

FAN To dream of a fan indicates a flirtation which will lead to trouble unless you keep a grip on your good sense and nip the affair in the bud.

FAREWELL To dream of saying farewell to a friend about to leave you for good is a sign that you will never have cause to doubt the fidelity of your acquaintances. If you should be the one who is leaving, you will make new friends.

FARM To dream that you are staying as a guest at a farm denotes unhappiness, quarrels and bickering in your family. To dream of working on a farm is a sign of steady improvement in your affairs, but nothing wonderful.

FARMER For a young woman to dream that a farmer wants to take her out is good; she will meet with a young clerk, who, though he is not particularly well paid, knows how to use the means at his command. He will be a faithful and devoted sweet heart to her. To dream you become a farmer signifies hard work.

FARMING To manure and cultivate the earth signifies melancholy to those who are usually cheerful, and to labourers it signifies gain and a plentiful crop. To dream you are in woods or in meadows and looking after animals signifies profit. To dream you do business in the fields signifies joy, profit and health.

FASHIONS To dream that you are studying the fashions, either in a magazine or in the shop windows, is a sign of some small change, for good or ill.

FAST If you dream that you observe a fast day you will inherit wealth although it will come late in life.

FAT To dream you are stout is a sure indication of riches. To see fat children, many happy years are in store for you.

FATE To dream that fate is against you is indicative of prosperity in whatever you may put your hand to.

FATHER To dream of your father is a sure sign of his love for you.

FATHER-IN-LAW To see your father-in-law, either dead or alive, is bad luck – especially if you dream that he uses violence or is threatening since it signifies vain hopes and deceits.

FATIGUE To feel tired in a dream is a sign that you should try to put up with present difficulties and inconveniences because there is fame and profit in store for you, and not in a very distant future either.

FAULT To dream that you commit some fault and receive censure for it from your friends is a sign that you will become more loved by those who know you best. You will be esteemed and respected for your wisdom and integrity. Some of those who would criticise you will be compelled to admit your good character and honesty.

FAVOUR This is a dream of contrary, for if you dream that someone has done you a favour it shows a loss of money in some business transaction.

FAWN If the creature is running, be on your guard against a danger threatening you. Disappointment in love and inconstancy may follow. If it is standing still, things will go well with you.

FEAR   If you are afraid of a mysterious event, it is a sign that you will feel great joy. You will receive news from a lawyer some way away that a wealthy relative has left you a legacy of a large amount of money. Your children who have left your home have obtained good positions in their different employments, and are making money in speculations of various kinds.

FEASTING   To dream you are at a feast denotes that you will meet with many disappointments, particularly concerning the thing which you are most anxious about. In love it forbodes much uneasiness, and to those who are married it foretells problems with children – with many heavy losses.

FEATHER   To dream of seeing feathers floating in the air is a sign that you will have cause to be anxious over some matter concerning yourself or someone immediately connected with you. If you are wearing the feathers, dishonour will come your way through a member of your family. To see white feathers is a good dream and indicates that your credit and honour will never be called into question.

FEATURES   To dream of a strange face with features which you can remember on waking indicates important introductions. Blue eyes indicate a new friendship; dark eyes a lover; bearded face, a traveller will return; smiling face, a wish will be granted.

FEEBLE   To dream that you are feeble and weak in your health means that you will soon become noted in your neighbourhood for your physical strength and powerful body. Great exertion will develop your powers; and by exercise you will become an expert in a field of gymnastics or physical skill.

FEEDING   To dream you feed or bring a lamb to the slaughter signifies torment. To dream you feed cattle is a good sign. To dream that you are feeding cattle, horses, poultry or pigs means that you will have success in your work, whatever it may be, and that, providing you are thrifty, your old age will be financially secure, with your children also well provided for.

FEET   If you dream you have three or four feet you are in danger of being crippled in the legs or feet by an illness or accident; nevertheless this dream is advantageous to merchants, and those who work on the sea. To dream you have fire at your feet is a bad sign. To dream you are nimble-footed, and that you dance well signifies joy and friendship. To dream your feet or legs have been cut off signifies pain and damage. To dream you see the feet of your little children signifies joy and profit, good health and pleasure. To dream that you have an ulcer on your foot signifies assurance in business. To dream you are near a river or fountain and that you wash your feet signifies humility and success. To dream you kiss the feet of someone signifies repentance, contrition and humility. To dream you see a serpent or some other creature that will bite your feet signifies envy; and if the creature bites you that signifies sadness and discontent. To dream that anyone scratches the soles of your feet signifies loss or flattery. To dream that anyone bathes your feet with herbs, or perfumes them with beautiful scents, signifies honour and joy from employees. To dream your leg or foot is dislocated signifies that an employee will receive loss and damage, or die, or that they will be prevented from making a journey.

FENCE To dream of building a fence is an omen of good fortune provided you have no difficulty with the work. If part of the fence falls down, misfortune will mar the good fortune at one part of your life, but it will not banish it for ever. Climbing a fence indicates a sudden rise in life; creeping under a fence is a warning to avoid shady transactions.

FENCING To dream you are fencing is a sign that you will be fond of dancing, and do your utmost to get into the company of party-givers.

FERMENTATION A period of turmoil and reassessment will follow.

FERN To dream that you see a large number of ferns growing luxuriantly is a very good dream. You will have great cause for joy; if you are married you will have children, some of whom will grow up to fill good positions in life. Your second son will show a quickness of intelligence that will put him at the head of his profession. If in your dream you see ferns which are stunted in their growth it is a sign that you will meet with nothing but misfortune; your children will not rise above mediocrity, and gloomy prospects will blight your life.

FERRET If in your dream you see one of these little animals it is a sign that you will have a desire to search out difficult things, explain problems, unravel mysteries and understand puzzles.

FERRYBOAT To dream you ride a ferryboat is a sign that if you are single you will marry someone who is afraid of going in a boat. But if you are married and have children, one of them will have a great desire to go to sea, and when you give your consent and they are employed on a merchant ship, they will desert and go on a long voyage on another vessel; eventually they will beg to be taken home again.

FERTILITY Your income will increase suddenly.

FESTIVAL To dream that you are at an annual celebration of a society is a sign that you will soon have to remain at home because of the illness of one of your children. You will suffer considerably from the loss of a respected friend; or you will yourself suffer from headaches.

FETTERS To dream that you have fetters placed on your legs as a criminal is a sign that your liberty will be curtailed by some complaint such as gout or rheumatism. Someone will claim that you owe them money, but when you produce your settled account the difficulties will be sorted out.

FEVER To dream that you are suffering from fever is a sign that you will have no serious illness for some time to come. Should you be nursing a person suffering from a fever, however, you will lose a close relation.

FIANCÉ A disagreement or argument soon overcome.

FIDDLER To dream you hear a fiddler play is a sign that one of your children, if you have any, will be out dancing without your knowledge. It also means that you had better get a musical instrument into your home, or some games for evening amusement, to keep those whom you love from bad company.

FIELD To dream of wandering in a field is a token that your life will have no great events to relieve the monotony. If the field is ploughed, however, your own exertion will bring you success, while if it is planted with corn you will have either children or a legacy late in life. If it is sown with any kind of clover it denotes affection and trouble; if sown with millet it signifies vast wealth which can be achieved easily.

FIEND If you see a fiend or evil spirit it is a sign that one of your family will have a strong desire to become either a clergyman or dissenting minister. Cultivate their powers of public speaking and give them as good an education as possible so that they can go on to theological college.

FIFE If you hear music from a fife you can make preparations for going on a long journey; for either son or brother has enlisted, or a sister has married a soldier, and you will want to see them before they join their regiment.

FIG To dream you see figs in season signifies joy and pleasure; out of season, the opposite. Figs are the forerunners of prosperity and happiness; to the lover they denote the accomplishment of their wishes; to the tradesman, increase of trade; they are all indicative of a legacy. You will never be short of the good things of this world, even though you have ups and downs in the early part of your life. Dried figs indicate rejoicing; green figs signify hope.

FIGHTING To dream you are fighting forebodes much opposition to your wishes, with loss of character and property; to the sailor it denotes storms and shipwreck, with disappointment in love. To dream you win a fight shows you will get the better in a lawsuit.

FIGURES To dream of any number above one and below 78 means good fortune to the dreamer, but 49 is the most lucky. All numbers above 78 are uncertain except 343, and that is a very lucky number.

FILBERT To dream of filberts forebodes much trouble and anger from friends.

FILE To see a metal file is a sign that one of your sons will express a desire to become a mechanic; if you help him to achieve this, he will become an excellent workman. To dream of dealing in files indicates a busy life.

FILM To dream of a film signifies a possible journey abroad in the near

future and much discussion –
guard against your tongue.

FILTH If you are not careful,
your circumstances will
deteriorate quickly.

FIND To dream of finding
property, either accidentally
or after a search, is both
lucky and unlucky. It means
you are sure to get on in
business, but by no means
sure of winning the one you
love.

If you dream of finding a
purse, see that your savings
are in a safe place, otherwise
you will lose them. To pick
up an article of jewellery,
such as a brooch or a ring,
means success in love but
disappointment in business.

FINGER To burn your finger
signifies envy and fun. If you
dream your hands or fingers
have grown slimmer than
usual, you will find that your
employees cheat you and do
not like you. To dream the
fingers have been cut off
signifies loss of friends or
employees. To dream that
you have six or seven fingers
on each hand signifies
friendship, new
acquaintances, good fortune
and inheritance or benefits.
To dream that your fingertips
or nails have been cut off
signifies loss, disgrace and
arguments with your relations

and friends. To cut your
fingers, or see them cut by
someone else, signifies
damage. To dream of cutting
a finger is a warning that,
unless you interfere less with
other people's affairs, you
will be led into a quarrel
which will have serious
consequences.

FINGER NAILS To dream
of long nails signifies pain;
and to dream of having your
nails pulled off indicates
great misfortunes.

FINGERPRINT Follow an
unusual lead and you will
find a true friend.

FINISH To dream of
finishing something signifies
the start of a new era in your
life.

FIR TREE The dark
colouring peculiar to fir trees
suggests the misfortune of
black, softened by the more
fortunate toil of the green.
Work hard and all will go
well; slacken, and you may
expect losses.

FIRE People who dream of
fire often have a fiery temper.
To dream you have been
burnt indicates a violent
fever. To see a moderate fire
in your grate without smoke
or sparks signifies that you
are in perfect health. If a

sensible person dreams that a fire is put out, it can mean his death. When someone dreams their bed is on fire and that they are killed, it signifies that their spouse will suffer an illness or acident. To dream you have handled a fire without hurting yourself signifies that you will not be harmed by your enemies and you will achieve your ambitions. To see fire burning signifies a deluge, or change of place. To dream you see burning lights descending from the sky is a very bad sign indeed, as it portends some dreadful accident to the dreamer such as breaking your legs, or, alternatively, getting into prison or other strange happenings. To dream you quench a fire denotes overcoming anger and recovery from sickness. To dream you see a cabinet on fire denotes the death of its owner. To dream of seeing a stack of corn burnt down is a sign of death and famine. Flashes of fire show sudden death. To dream of lighting a fire in a grate is an indication that you will hear important news in an unexpected manner. If you see your own house burning, you will have reason for happiness at an early date. To dream that you witness a big conflagration, such as the burning of a

factory, is an omen of a big improvement in your affairs if you are married, and an advantageous engagement if you are single. To dream you see a clean, pure and clear fire is threatening to people in powerful positions because it indicates the approach of enemies, poverty and famine. It is an even worse dream to carry fire.

FIRE ENGINE To dream that you see a fire engine is a warning for you to insure your property against fire and take every sensible fire precaution.

FIRE ESCAPE You will need to be careful to avoid owing money.

FIREARMS To dream of using firearms indicates a quarrel of a long-standing nature. To see another person using them means slander.

FIREMAN Adventurous circumstances await you.

FIRESIDE To dream of sitting by the fireside with someone you love means, to the young, a speedy happy marriage, and to the old and middle-aged it foretells that what remains of life will be contented and happy, although neither splendid nor brilliant. If you imagine yourself sitting by the fireside talking to a close companion you will have no cause to complain of lack of comforts when married, and your partner will always love you. For an elderly person it signifies a peaceful death at an advanced age.

FIREWOOD   Your life will be happy, traditional and contented.

FIREWORKS   To dream of taking part in an exhibition of fireworks denotes that before long you will be in great danger of losing your temper with an acquaintance, and that you will be tempted to assault them to ease your anger and frustrations. To dream that you witness a display of fireworks is a sign that you will be deceived by appearances. Someone will offer to sell something to you which will turn out to be worthless. Be careful if you are buying cheap articles at auction sales.

FIRMAMENT   To dream that you see the heavens red is a sign of fair weather; if the heavens are murky or dusky, do not take a journey at present, as there will be very severe storms; if there are mackerel clouds, the weather will be reasonable, but there will be no sunshine, and the nights will be cold. If you see the sun rise blood-red, there will be storms; or if you see the moon shining silvery bright, there will be some days of continued fine weather.

FISH   To see many large fish is a sign of good health and good fortune; small fish mean good health and a fairly easy life. An unmarried person who dreams of eating fish will marry well; a married person will have a large family. Dead fish signify quarrels and disappointments. A pregnant woman who dreams she gives birth to fish instead of a child will have a stillborn child, or one who is premature. To catch sea fish is a bad sign.

FISH POND   Fish ponds denote that you will do well.

FISHING   To dream that you are fishing signifies that someone will try to draw you into a plot against a friend. To see other people fishing means a discovery that will cause you pain. If you catch any fish, you will be successful in love and business. If you catch none, you will never marry your present sweetheart, nor succeed in your undertakings. To dream of eating the fish foretells better fortune, signifying that you will be successful in the studies which you are currently following, and that you will get a good reputation for the soundness of your knowledge and the brightness of your intellect.

FISHING NET To dream you see fishing nets signifies rain or change of weather.

FIT To dream of having fits is good or bad, according to the kind of fits they are. To dream of having a stroke means your physical strength will be increased. To dream of having fainting fits is bad; guard against the consequences of being disappointed in your expectations. To dream of having paralytic fits is a bad dream, and the dreamer should be careful to follow a balanced and a healthy lifestyle.

FLAG To dream of a flag is a sure sign that one of your friends is in distress, and that you will hear from that person only just in time to prevent a disaster.

FLAGON To dream that you see a flagon of beer, wine or any other alcoholic drink is a sign that you will be deceived by some unscrupulous person who will tell you to take useless medicines. You will try them, but they will not benefit you in the least. To dream that you drink from a flagon of wine or beer means that you have recently become careless in your tastes and habits. Indigestion and liver problems will trouble you from time to time.

FLAME If in your dream you see flames ascending into the air you will find that some of your acquaintances are making light of your character by spreading slanderous reports. Be careful with any gas fittings in your home.

FLAMINGO Foreign travel is indicated.

FLASH To dream of a flash of light, whether from a searchlight or torch, is a sign of important news that will cause your plans to succeed.

FLASK To dream of drinking wine from a flask presages the enjoyment of a fortune; if the flask holds water, you will be happy but not rich; to break a flask indicates losses.

FLATTERY To dream of flattery administered to some person you know means that slander will soon be busy with his or her reputation, but that, however plausible, take no notice for it will be groundless. To dream you are being flattered denotes that before long you will argue with your sweetheart or spouse for paying too much attention to other people.

FLATULENCE You will argue with a friend or colleague.

FLEA To dream you eat fleas signifies problems. To dream of fleas indicates weariness of life; to kill one means success over your enemies.

FLEET To dream you see the naval fleet is a sign that some of your relatives or acquaintances in that branch of the service are about to be promoted. If you dream of seeing a fleet of fishing boats it is a sign of great advancement. You will save money if you are in trade; if you are not in trade, and are married, you will have many healthy children. You will also have great comfort at home, and you will put some schemes into practice which will be financially rewarding in the future.

FLESH To dream you have grown fat indicates that you will gain wealth, according to the quantity of flesh. On the contrary, to dream you have grown thin means you will

lose whatever money you have. To dream your flesh has become spotted or black, means you will deceive your business colleagues or be caught committing adultery, and will split up with your partner. If you dream that your flesh has grown yellow or pale, you will be in danger of falling seriously ill. If you dream your flesh is covered in scabs or corns, you will grow rich proportionately to the number of scabs. If you dream you have eaten the flesh of a man or woman, you will enrich yourself by injuries and reproach. If you dream your flesh is swollen by an ulcer, that indicates wealth.

FLIES To dream that a swarm of flies are pestering you is a sign that you will experience a loss through someone whom you have trusted. If the insects are merely flying around you, however, without landing, the loss will not be so serious, for you will have your suspicions aroused. To dream of killing flies denotes sickness.

FLIGHT For a businessman to dream that some of his creditors have run away without paying their debts is a sign that he need have no cause to doubt the honesty of his trading partners over the last few months.

FLIRTING For either a young woman or a young man to dream of flirting signifies that their present partner is not a stable person and common sense suggests looking elsewhere.

FLOATING To see anything floating on water is a warning that you are taking things too easily and missing opportunities of improving your position. To dream you are floating on water indicates good fortune and speedy success; if you are sinking, look out for reverses of fortune.

FLOCK To dream of a flock of birds is a good sign.

FLOOD This is a bad dream denoting trouble to come. To dream of a flood shows that you will meet with great opposition from rich neighbours, and that a rich rival will attempt to alienate the affections of your lover.

FLOOR To dream that you are lying or sitting on the floor is a good omen of success in most of your undertakings. But you must be careful not to get a swollen head; otherwise you will certainly fail. To dream that you are scrubbing or sweeping a floor which refuses to come clean is indicative of petty worries.

FLOUR To dream that you buy flour is a bad omen and indicates the sickness or death of a close friend.
   If you are cooking with flour, you will have unexpected happiness.

FLOWER To dream of holding or smelling scented flowers in season signifies joy, pleasure and consolation. To dream of seeing and smelling flowers out of season, if they are white, signifies obstruction and failure in business; if yellow, the impediment will not be so considerable; and if they are red, the difficulty and nuisance will be extreme – It usually also signifies death. To dream you are adorned with flowers and posies signifies a short-lived joy and content. To gather sweet-scented flowers signifies happiness and jollity. The person you love best of all truly returns your affection. But should the flowers wither in your hand the other's love will wane before many years have passed. To see flowers growing in profusion is a prediction of a happy future and a well-cared-for life. To plant flowers means you will accomplish good work.

FLUTE   To play or hear someone playing on a wind instrument such as a flute signifies trouble and arguments.

FLYING   To dream you can fly is a good sign. You are destined to succeed in high things, and that every obstacle before you will give way before courage and perseverance. To fly high or a distance means there is much happiness in store for you, as well as success in your undertakings. If while you are flying you suddenly fall, expect disappointments.

To fly very high and without wings signifies fear and danger as does to fly over houses and through streets. To dream that you fly with the birds is a sign that you will keep company with strangers; it also signifies pain and punishment to criminals. It is always good after having flown high to descend low and then to wake up, but it is best of all to fly when you want to and come down when you want to for it is a sign that your home and job are well run. To fly backwards is not bad for sailors, but to anyone else it signifies a lack of work and business. To the sick it foretells death. It is very bad to want to fly and yet be unable to do so or to dream that you fly with your head down. To dream that you fly in a bed or chair or are supported in any way signifies sickness, except to those who want to travel.

FLYING FISH   Deceitful associates and late hours hold especial danger; try to avoid both for some time.

FOAL   You will hear of the birth of a child.

FOAM   Cheerful scenes will soon surround you.

FOG   To dream of wandering in a fog predicts a lingering illness, from which, however, you will recover. To a business person it is sometimes indicative of unsuccessful efforts to improve trade. If you are lost in a fog, you will be tempted to stray from the path of virtue and will need all your courage to keep clear of trouble. Be careful in all your dealings, for you will be tempted to questionable undertakings.

FOGHORN   Your present problems will soon come to an end.

FOLDING   It is a good sign for your love affairs if you dream that you are careful when folding your clothes or house linen.

FOLIAGE If green, a great deal of pleasure is in store for you. If it is dead, your undertakings will not succeed.

FOLLY If you are worried by the thought that you have committed a stupid act, you will be troubled by petty debts contracted through extravagance either on your own part or on that of someone closely connected with you.

FONT To dream that you are beside the font when the ceremony of baptism is performed on a child means that your child, if you have one, is in danger of becoming very ill, and you will be compelled to send for the minister to perform the ceremony at your own house in case the child dies.

FOOD It is generally a fortunate sign to eat food in your dream, provided you are soon satisfied. But it is not a good omen to eat like a glutton.

FOOL To see a fool means someone will deceive you. To dream that you are made a fool is good to anyone who undertakes any business deals in the day following the dream.

FOOT Beware of treachery if someone trips you up with his or her foot.

FOOTBALL To dream that you are watching a game of football may be taken as a sign that you will be forced to stand by and hear a friend slandered without being able to defend him or her.

FOOTMAN To dream that you ride in a wonderful carriage with a footman to attend to you is a sign that you will never become rich and you and your partner will spend everything you earn. You will need to save and try to avoid running into debt.

FOOTPRINT Difficulties which you will soon surmount by your own efforts.

FOOTSTEP You will hear something which will spur you on to greater exertions and success.

FOP For a young woman to dream that a gaily dressed young man seeks her company is a sign that she will meet with a very ordinary and unprepossessing young man who has nothing to recommend him to her notice but his honesty and hard-working nature. He is careful and thoughtful, however, and would make her a good husband if she accepts him.

FORECAST Do not trust to luck but trust in your own good judgement when making decisions.

FOREHEAD If anyone dreams they have a large forehead it signifies an ingenious spirit, and if it is very high it is a sign of solid judgement; it also denotes power and wealth.

To dream that your forehead is brass, copper, marble or iron signifies irreconcilable hate against your enemies.

If a person dreams their forehead is injured, they are in danger of losing money. If someone dreams they have a large and fleshy forehead, that signifies freedom of speech, strength and constancy.

To dream that your brow is hairy is very lucky to everyone, especially to women, but if the brows have no hair it denotes failure and difficulties. To dream that you have the forehead of a lion is good for anyone, especially someone who wants a son.

FOREIGN COUNTRY Your happiness lies at home.

FOREIGNER To dream of foreigners is usually considered very fortunate for your love affairs.

FOREST To dream of wandering in a forest predicts to a single person a happy married life with several children. To a married person it is an omen of a wealthy inheritance. To be lost in a forest indicates uncertainty in love.

FORGE When a blacksmith's forge figures in a dream beware of dispute and dissension.

FORGERY To dream you are guilty of this crime denotes that you will never have a very substantial bank account. If you dream that someone else has forged your signature, however, you may look for the reverse.

FORGET-ME-NOT You are loved and remembered by many.

FORGETFULNESS Be considerate towards those less fortunate than yourself.

FORK To dream of a fork indicates that a false friend will attempt your ruin by flattery.

FORLORN To feel forlorn or miserable is a bad sign, unless in your dream you regain a cheerful state of mind.

FORSAKEN A good omen of the affections of those you dreamed lost.

FORSYTHIA Unless seen out of season, yellow flowers signify a happy love affair.

FORTRESS To see a fortress or castle means hate and sickness.

FORTUNE To dream that you have come into a fortune, or that you have amassed one by your own efforts, is an omen of a period of distress to follow, in which you will contract serious debts. To the tradesman, it forebodes losses in trade, quarrelling with his creditors, and the loss of liberty; to the lover it denotes that your sweetheart does not return your love; to the sailor it indicates storms and ship-wrecks; if you are applying for a job you will not be successful. To dream you are adopting the means of acquiring a fortune is favour-able – it indicates a good legacy and success in love.

If anyone who has lost a lot of money dreams they have regained it, it signifies that good fortune will return.

FORTUNE TELLING If you are having your fortune told, your favourite ambition will be blighted. To dream of telling a friend's fortune indicates that you will have a serious quarrel with a stranger.

FOSSIL You will hear of the sickness of someone you have not met for a long time.

FOUNTAIN If a sick person dreams they see a river or fountain of clear running water, that means they will recover. But if the water is muddy, it signifies the opposite. If anyone thinks that a fountain has dried up, that signifies poverty or death. To fall into a clear fountain signifies honour and gain. To fall into a muddy fountain signifies accusation. To see a fountain spring up in your house signifies honour and profit. To see a fountain means that you will have your eyes opened in a very unpleasant manner to an intrigue between certain of your friends who have taken a dislike to you.

FOUNTAIN PEN Your literary ambitions will succeed.

FOWL To dream of these common domestic birds shows a commonplace and uneventful life, without ups and downs.

FOX   To fight with a fox indicates a disagreement with a wary adversary. If you dream you have a tame fox, the interpretation is the same. If you dream that you have a tame fox at home, you will fall in love with an ill-natured person. To dream that you see a fox in the distance indicates that your confidence will be betrayed, and that this will bring you into trouble with someone in authority. A dead fox is a good omen.

FOXGLOVE   These flowers are an omen of true friendship.

FRAGRANCE   It is a good sign to dream of a pleasant perfume, but the results will not be very serious – some small success is indicated.

FRANTIC   To dream of being frantic means a peaceful holiday after strenuous times.

FRAUD   To dream that you commit a fraud is a sure sign that you will have occasion to do a good turn to a stranger who will handsomely reward you. To dream that you have been defrauded is a sign that you will soon be looking for someone to help you out of your problems. To charge someone with fraud signifies that you will be robbed.

FREEDOM   If you dream of being freed from something, you will find happiness in love.

FREEMASON   To dream you are a Freemason denotes that you will soon make a number of new friends who will prove staunch and true. It also foretells you will take a journey to the East. If you are already a member of the Masons and dream you attend a meeting of the lodge, it portends sickness and heavy loss of property. To dream that you are expelled from the Order shows you will be promoted.

FRENCH   To dream of speaking and hearing foreign languages is a fortunate sign, especially in love affairs.

FRETTING   This brings joyful tidings and explanation of something which has puzzled you.

FRIEND   To see your friends or relations dead signifies joy, or unexpected good news; if you are in love, it indicates a speedy marriage with your lover. If you dream of a friend, your fortune will improve.

FRIGHTENED To dream that you are frightened and yet do not know the cause means you will have no reason to be afraid.

FROG Frogs signify flatterers and indiscreet gossips. To the unmarried, the sight of these creatures in a dream foretells a happy married life after a rather trying courtship. To the married, the dream is indicative of happiness in old age. To catch or kill frogs signifies trouble or the sudden death of someone you know.

FROST If you dream of frost, be on your guard against committing a foolish blunder which will lead to a bad accident. Difficulties, troubles and sorrow are denoted.

FROWN To dream that you see a frown on the face of your father, mother or any of your relatives is a sign that you will have greater pleasure in the society of your family and family connections than ever you have had before. Joy, peace and happiness will be enjoyed by you at all times.

FROZEN If you dream of being frozen, you will have difficulties in your relationships with the opposite sex.

FROZEN FOODS Travel to warmer countries is predicted.

FRUIT To dream you see fruits in season is good, if they are beautiful. To dream of gathering ripe fruit indicates happiness and wealth. If you should be ill when you dream of a collection of fruit, you will quickly recover. If you are already in good health, you will be happy. If anyone dreams that the fruit they have gathered is rotten, that signifies adversity or loss of children.

FRYING PAN To dream that you see a frying pan full of meat is a sign of a quarrel with your cook, if you have one. You will be strong, intelligent and active.

FUCHSIA This can signify ill-health, particularly if you are prone to skin problems.

FUDGE If you are storing the fudge in your dream, you will be frugal and thrifty. If you are eating too much, you will squander your money.

FUGITIVE You will have family problems from which

you will not be able to escape by ignoring them.

FUN To dream that you are having a good time is a sign that you will soon experience problems such as debt or sickness.

FUNERAL To go to the funeral of a relation or friend is a good sign to the dreamer, who will either inherit property or marry into money. To dream of being present at the funeral foretells that the unhappiness which you are at present suffering will soon come to an end, and that you will then enter on the happiest period of your life. If you have children they will be a comfort to you; if you are in love, your affairs will prosper. If you see any particular person attending the funeral either that person or some friend of his will die and leave you something. To dream of a funeral service denotes an inheritance.

FUNGUS If you dream of seeing a fungus growing, be careful that people are not taking you for granted.

FUR After dreaming of fur in any shape or form be careful not to enter into a serious argument for some time to come. If you disregard this, the argument will lead to a quarrel and many of your relatives will be involved.

FURNITURE Happiness always follows a dream of furniture. The person in love will soon marry, and the person in business will make money easily. To dream of buying furniture for a home is also a good omen.

FURY To dream of a furious person denotes a reconciliation; of a furious animal, a friend defends your name.

FUTURE An unusual dream predicting unusual events. You may have the chance to make up an old quarrel or mend an old wrong.

GAG If a man dreams that his mouth is stopped by a gag it denotes that he will soon after be kissed by a pretty girl. To a young girl such a dream predicts that she will meet and perhaps will fall in love with someone.

GAIETY To dream that you are indulging in riotous gaiety is a sign that you will soon be wearing mourning.

GAIN To dream of gain, if acquired honestly, you may hope for wealth; if by injustice, you will lose your money.

GAITER To dream you see a man wearing gaiters is a sign that you will marry soon.

GALA A change of residence, many employees and a parting from relations is indicated.

GALE Better times to come, do not take present vexations too seriously, especially quarrels.

GALL To dream that you have problems with your gall bladder signifies that you will argue, perhaps violently, with an employee. If you are married, you will have an argument with your partner; and will also be in danger of losing your money by gambling or robbery.

GALLEON To dream of a galleon in full sail indicates that you will have a period of prosperity and will leave your troubles behind you.

GALLERY Worries will soon pass unless you should dream of falling from the gallery.

GALLOP An easy gallop on a straight road portends success to your plans; up a steep path warns the dreamer to think well before acting.

GALLOWS To dream of the gallows is fortunate; it shows that the dreamer will become rich, and be well respected. To the lover it shows the consummation of his deepest wishes; for a pregnant woman to dream of the gallows signifies that she is carrying a son, the birth will be straightforward and the child will become rich.

GAMBLING Do not act on the ideas of others or you will incur loss.

GAMES To play at any party games signifies prosperity, joy, pleasure, and health and concord among friends and relations. To dream you play ball or spinning top signifies hard work and pain. To leap, run or dance signifies prosperity in affairs, but to dance without music foretells a shortage of money. To dream you play at dice or at cards signifies noise and debate for money. However, it is always good to dream you win, no matter what the game. To see a child play games is good.

GAMEKEEPER You will reassess your lifestyle to your advantage.

GANG To dream you are a member of a gang indicates that you should take control of your own life, not be led by others. To be attacked by a gang indicates a difficult period ahead.

GANGWAY Should you cross it you have aroused the hostility of a rival. Take care

not to lose what is now your own through over-confidence.

GAOL To dream you are locked in a gaol is a sign that in a short time you will be offered a job as a commercial traveller, and you will have offers of promotion if you go to another part of the country to work. You will do well by the move.

GARDEN To dream that you are walking in a garden of flowers and among trees shows much pleasure and delight to come from conversation. It indicates increased wealth and position. To dream of a curious garden, enclosing delightful fountains, pleasant groves and fruitful orchards is a sign you will marry and have many lovely children. You will gain a great deal of pleasure from simple and healthy pursuits and by carefully making sure you spend only what you earn. Your lover will always be faithful and loving.

GARDENING To dream you are working in a garden signifies melancholy to those who are normally cheerful; and to labourers it signifies gain and a plentiful crop.

GARLAND The young lady who dreams that she is wearing a garland of flowers should be extra careful how she conducts herself for some time to come. Some evil people are watching and waiting for an opportunity to take away her good character.

GARLIC To eat or smell garlic signifies a discovery of hidden secrets and domestic quarrels.

GARMENTS To dream you are wearing a new suit which you like signifies joy, profit and success in business. If a woman dreams she is dressed in a hood, that indicates damage and dishonour. If someone dreams they are expensively dressed, that signifies honour to the dreamer and their partner. If a man or woman dreams they are dressed in rags, it signifies trouble and sadness. To dream you have a red garment on signifies blood or bleeding.

GARNET To dream of wearing garnets means that you will work hard for little reward. If others are wearing them, remember to spend your time thinking of the future, not the past.

GARRETT An advancement in position will soon be on its way.

GARROTER To dream that you meet a person who tries to murder you by the brutal practice of garroting you is a sign that you will be overcome in your judgement by a person you know well; you will lose money by buying inferior goods; or will be induced to lend money to a friend which you will never be able to recover.

GARTER If a man ties on a girl's garter, it denotes a speedy marriage.

GAS To dream of an escape of gas means that you are about to become engaged, but you will quarrel with your fiancé within a week. Your too light-hearted behaviour will, in the end, so excite the fears of your present sensible lover that he or she will leave you for- ever. If you dream of bright and pleasant gas lights it shows success in love. If the gas is dim and looks unnatural your sweetheart will either leave you or die.

GAS MASK If you see someone wearing a gas mask, trouble will come from an unexpected source. If you are wearing the mask, you will not be able to avoid the coming trouble.

GATE To see gates consumed by fire can signify death to a close female relative.

GATHER To dream of picking up money, is a fortunate sign; if you are gathering fruit, it refers to pleasure or enjoyment. Flowers concern love affairs.

GAUZE To dream of gauze signifies concealed feelings.

GAVOTTE To dream of dancing a gavotte signifies a calm and happy future.

GAZELLE To dream of this gentle-eyed animal means to a girl a rough wooer but a true husband.

GEM To dream of handling gems of a great brilliance is a sign that you will be blinded by flattery to the evil designs of a person of the opposite sex.

To dream that you wear a costly gem in the shape of some precious stone or jewel of some kind is a sign of a falling off of your financial resources; your prosperity in business will not be so good in the future as it has been in the past. It will be better for you to husband your

resources and prepare for problems ahead.

GERANIUM For a young woman to dream she sees a large quantity of geraniums in flower is a sign that she will become more beautiful in personal appearance in the future. Very many eligible offers will be made to her by men of different positions in life. Her perplexity will be increased by the host of admirers who vow their attachment to her. She must guard against those who admire her for her beauty alone, and only listen to those who do not flatter above her merit.

GEOGRAPHY For a young person to dream of geography lessons is a sign that they will become a better scholar in grammar or arithmetic than in geography.

GERM To examine germs under a microscope means that you will enjoy the things closest to you.

GERMANY You will have plenty and prosper.

GHOST To dream of ghosts and spectres of people you have known shows good news from abroad. If you dream that you are frightened by a ghost it signifies that you will encounter great difficulties; if you are unafraid it signifies good fortune.

GIANT To dream you see a giant or a very tall person is a very good sign. If you are in trade you will have a great increase of business from abroad.

GIBBET To dream you see someone hanging on the gibbet signifies damage and great distress.

GIDDY To dream that you grow giddy in a dance is a sign that you will lose your present good health. Illness from exposure to cold will shortly overtake you.

GIFT To dream that you have something given to you is a sign that some good is about to happen to you; it also denotes that a speedy marriage will take place between you and your sweetheart. To dream you have given anything away is the forerunner of adversity, and in love denotes sickness and inconstancy in your partner.

GIN To dream of drinking gin indicates a short life and many changes.

GINGER Your passionate love affair may not be all you hoped for.

GIPSY To dream that you are talking to a gipsy denotes a wandering nature. You will probably live abroad for some time, but will return to your home when you are approaching old age. Be careful in all your actions for it looks as if some carelessness of yours will bring you trouble.

GIRDLE To dream you are wearing an old girdle signifies labour and pain. To have a new girdle signifies honour.

GIRL To dream you see a handsome girl in bed is a sign of good fortune. For a man to dream of a girl means that he is engaged, or shortly to be engaged, in paying attentions which may or may not lead to matrimony. It is important to notice whether the girl seen in the dream holds anything in her hand. If she has a bag that looks like a money bag, it signifies that you are to marry someone who will always be arguing over money. Should the girl hold a notebook in her hand it means that you will end in separating from your lover, but you will easily console yourself.

GLACIER Foreign travel to exciting places.

GLADIATOR   Something will happen which will cause you sorrow and anguish.

GLASS   To dream you are given a glass full of water signifies speedy marriage and children, for anything glass in a dream is applicable to the wife and water signifies abundance and fruitfulness. If the glass seems to be broken and the water unspilt that signifies the death of the wife, but the life of the child, or vice versa. To dream of a glass being broken shows shipwreck to mariners, and bad luck to anyone in business. To dream of a glass is a warning sign that you are inclined to be too trusting, and you are not doing yourself any good by talking about your private affairs to everyone you meet. To dream of a broken glass foretells a sudden end of something you have been in the habit of doing for a long time.

GLASSES   Good news and an improvement in your position.

GLEAN   To dream that you are gleaning, or that you see gleaners at work, foretells good luck to you and your family.

GLIDER   If you dream of being in a glider, you will be able to overcome your present professional difficulties with help from a colleague.

GLOBE   To see a globe indicates that you will have friends in several different foreign countries.

GLOOM   To dream that you see the sky cloudy and gloomy should give you courage, for by great perseverance you will make a success of your life.

GLOVES   To dream you are wearing gloves signifies honour. To put on a glove and keep it on indicates marriage. If you dream you have trouble in getting a pair of gloves to fit, you may expect a proposal of marriage at an early date. To dream that you receive a present of a pair of gloves indicates that you will have rival lovers, and have some difficulty in making your choice between them.

GLOW   An improvement in your fortunes is about to happen, should you dream of a brilliant glowing scene.

GLOW-WORM   You will have the chance of doing a great kindness which will well repay you later.

GLUE This portends faithful friendship from one whom you trust.

GLUTTON You are in danger of poverty; make every effort in your power against it while there is yet time.

GNAT Back-biters will cause you loss and trouble.

GNOME The sooner you face up to your problems, the sooner you will be able to overcome them.

GOAT To dream of goats is both a good and bad omen. You will have petty enemies to worry you but, in spite of their actions, you will become rich and the mainstay of your family. White goats are fortunate; black goats indicate illness; goats on high places mean riches; badly kept animals signify misfortune.

GOBLET To drink out of a goblet indicates that good times are coming, and you will be happy.

GOD To dream you see God's face, and that he seems to stretch out his arms while you pray signifies joy, comfort, grace, the blessing of God and success in business. To dream you see the body of our Lord signifies respect. To hear his voice, or to dream that he speaks to you means happiness and joy.

GOLD To dream of gold signifies that you will be surrounded by great wealth which you will be unable to enjoy because of disappointment and unhappiness. To dream you handle or chew gold signifies anger. If you receive sovereigns or any other gold coin, your affairs will prosper, and your sweetheart will be true and marry you.

GOLD MINE To dream of a gold mine foretells that an attempt will soon be made to get you to lend money to advance a hazardous speculation, and that if you yield there is small chance of your ever seeing it again. To imagine yourself working in or exploring a gold mine indicates a spendthrift nature, which will prevent you from accumulating wealth, although a good deal may come your way.

GOLDFISH Trouble in business.

GOLF To dream of watching a game of golf, or of taking part in one, means that your health is likely to suffer from too close attention to business; that it is unwise to neglect the enjoyment of the present; and that to a certain extent the future may be left to take care of itself.

GONDOLA To dream that you are travelling in a gondola signifies an easy existence and independence through another's exertions. To the young, it also foreshadows an early engagement.

GONG An exciting event in family life. Avoid trifling with important matters.

GOOD To dream that you do good signifies jollity and pleasure, and to dream that others do good to you means profit and gain.

GOOSE To dream you cut off the head of a green goose signifies joy and recreation. To hear geese cry signifies profit, and assurance of the completion of business. The goose may be taken as an emblem of sincerity when seen alive. To dream that you are eating goose predicts a wish granted.

GOOSE PIMPLES To dream of having goose pimples indicates that you will soon fall in love with someone who may not be trustworthy.

GOOSEBERRY To dream of gooseberries indicates many children, chiefly sons, and an accomplishment of your present activities. To see the fruit growing is an omen first of lack of work, and afterwards more work than you can do. To dream that you are eating gooseberries predicts trouble, but it will not be of a very serious nature.

GORILLA To dream of a gorilla means that your reputation will be attacked by others.

GORSE Good fortune will come your way; try to grasp it.

GOSPEL You will help others with no thought for reward.

GOSSIP You will become too involved with other people's problems.

GOUT To dream you have gout signifies fear to the young, and potential physical injury; and to the old, it denotes poverty and lack of energy.

GOVERNMENT To dream that you are employed by the government means that you will have to work hard all your life, and that you will probably have someone else depending upon your exertions.

GOWN For a woman to dream she sees a new gown brought home for her is a sign that some retrenchment will be needed in the expenses of her family; the prevailing fashions are expensive and very much above the income of the family, of which she is constantly reminded by her husband, who will often get cross and bad-tempered about the large amount he will have to pay for her clothes. If a woman has this dream more than once it proves her to be vain and extravagant. For a woman to dream that her gown is torn and mended in several places is a good sign; her husband will make progress in business.

GRAIN To dream you see any kind of grain and gather it signifies profit and gain.

GRAMOPHONE Pleasant tidings from a distance. An unexpected discovery will be made.

GRANDCHILD To dream that you see grandchildren is a sign that you will remember some of the old

pleasures of youth, and will recount stories about the past to your children.

GRANDPARENT To dream that you are a grandparent, or that your grandchildren are present, is a very favourable sign.

GRAPE To dream of eating ripe grapes signifies cheerfulness and profit. To dream you gather black grapes signifies damage. To gather white grapes signifies gain. To dream you tread grapes signifies the overthrow of your enemies.

GRAPEFRUIT The course of your life may have some bitter-sweet moments.

GRASS You have to fear deceit.

GRASSHOPPER All sorts of grasshoppers signify impertinent gossips and bad musicians. If a sick person dreams of grasshoppers, it means bad luck.

GRATER To dream that you see a nutmeg grater is a sign that you will form a friendship with someone who will prepare many delicious meals for you.

GRATITUDE Surprising events will happen to you

should you dream of being exceedingly grateful to someone. But should you dream of another expressing gratitude to you, the events will happen to someone dear to you.

GRAVE If it seems that you are put in a grave and buried, that indicates that you will die poor. Some believe that to dream you are dead and buried means that you will inherit money or property, according to the amount of earth that is laid on you. To dream you go into a grave shows you will lose property. If you come out of the grave, it denotes success in your undertakings, and that you will rise in the world.

To see a grave foretells sickness and disappointment; if you are in love, you will never marry your present sweetheart.

To dream of taking another out of the grave signifies that you will be the means of saving the life of a person who will be a very great friend to you.

GRAVEL WALK To dream that you see a smooth gravel walk is a sign that your path of life will be made somewhat rugged by difficulties. You will have to fight with obstacles of a new

kind; some of your intimate friends whom you thought would assist you will be shy and reserved towards you, and will refuse you that financial help which would tide you over your present commercial difficulties.

GRAVY This indicates good luck in a dream. But if you are passing the gravy to someone else, do not let your luck pass you by.

GREEN Indicates a journey, or transacting business with people at a distance.

GREENFINCH Warns you to stick to your work and undertakings if you want to avoid making a loss.

GREENHOUSE You will work hard, but your plans and dreams will flourish.

GRENADIER For a young woman to dream that she meets with a Grenadier guardsman is a sign that a member of one of the horse regiments will soon want to take her out.

GREY HAIRS To dream that your hair is sprinkled with grey at an early age is a sign that you will carry age very well; you will look younger than you really are.

GREYHOUND To dream of these dogs racing is good, signifying action and jobs.

GRIEF This indicates joy and merry times.

GRINDING Grinding corn indicates good fortune; grinding coffee means trouble at home; grinding pepper signifies sickness and sorrow.

GRINDSTONE To dream of seeing a grindstone is a sign that you will always be in a comfortable position in life, but it will be by your own hard work as you will never receive money from a friend or relation. To dream that you are working at a grindstone means that you will have many debts to pay; but you will meet all your liabilities, and come off with a small income from your work in your old age.

GRIT To dream of eating grit in your food foretells that you will have to reassess your opinion of someone close to you.

GROAN It is not fortunate to hear people groaning in your dreams, unless you assist them.

GROOM Legal affairs will be made known to you probably to your advantage.

GROPING To dream that you are groping your way in the dark means that you and your partner are not made for each other, and that after marriage you are certain to have continual friction.

GROTTO Your business will improve. To be transported into one indicates a perilous journey.

GROUND To dream that you are stretched out on the ground signifies a humble status for some time to come.

GROVE To dream you own good lands with pleasant groves and orchards adjoining them signifies you will marry a sensible and attractive partner and will have very handsome children.

GRUEL If you dream of eating gruel, do not put yourself in the power of anyone who is addicted to strong liquors, or you may have cause to regret it.

GUARD To dream of keeping watch against peril of some kind is a warning to avoid ill-considered speech which may put you in a difficult position.

GUEST To dream that you are embarrassed by receiving

a great number of guests predicts that you will be parted from your friends for some time and be forgotten by many.

GUIDE   To be guiding someone else in a dream signifies kindly assistance in your own difficulties from good friends.

GUILLOTINE   Illness will befall you if you dream of being guillotined. If you are watching someone else, you will quarrel with a friend.

GUITAR   To hear the guitar played is for the young a sign that their thoughts will constantly be occupied by their lover and their marriage will be happy and successful. To dream of playing the guitar means that you should look to it that you are not a flirt, for if you trifle with the affections of the opposite sex you will suffer for it.

GUM   Someone will 'stick to you' in an emergency. Financial delays are indicated.

GULF   A sign of a parting which will sadden you. Avoid it if you can.

GULL   A soaring gull indicates an exciting sexual adventure.

GUN   To dream you see people firing guns or cannons denotes that the dreamer will experience many problems. To hear the report of a gun is a sign that you will be the cause of a serious quarrel, and will lose the regard of someone you love. To dream that you are handling a gun is a bad sign. You will do something which you will regret for the rest of your life. If you dream you are firing a gun, it foretells that you will be involved in a lawsuit.

GUNPOWDER   Seeing or smelling gunpowder indicates an alliance of one kind or another with someone involved with the Forces.

GUTTER   To dream of being in the gutter yourself, denotes hard times to come. Should you find anything valuable in a gutter, financial reward will come later for hard work done now.

GYMNASTICS   To dream that you take part in some gymnastic exercises is a sign that you will shortly have to give up work through illness. To dream that you see some other people taking this exercise is indicative of some fatal accident to either a friend or an acquaintance.

HABIT To dream of putting on or wearing a riding habit indicates a great effort which you will have to make to escape from some unhappy position. Be brave, as you have more friends than you think you have.

HADDOCK To dream of this fish indicates that you have a contented mind which will prevent you from stirring yourself to achieve great things. You will always be in flourishing circumstances.

HAG Gossip and scandal about women friends.

HAIL To dream that you are caught in a hailstorm foretells that you will form a subject for envious remarks on the part of many who have not been so successful in the world as yourself, and whether these remarks are to prove injurious or not may be judged by the severity of the storm. Persevere with whatever you have in hand, no matter how many obstacles may stand in the way of success, and you will be rewarded sooner or later.

HAIR If you imagine you see a strange woman with long and beautiful hair, it is a very good sign as it denotes friendship, joy and prosperity. If a man dreams his hair is long, like a woman's, that signifies cowardice and effeminacy, and that he will be deceived by a woman. To see a woman without hair signifies famine, poverty and sickness. To see a bald man signifies the opposite. To see plaited hair signifies annoyance and grief, and sometimes injuries and quarrels. To see black hair, short and curled, signifies sadness and loss. To see well-combed hair signifies friendship. If your hair seems to be longer and blacker than usual, your wealth and reputation will increase. If anyone dreams that their hair has grown thinner than it was before, it is a sign of affliction and poverty. If you dream you perfume your hair, that signifies vanity and conceit. If a woman dreams this, she will deceive her husband, and 'wear the trousers' at home. If you dream your hair is permed, it signifies that you are in some danger either from sickness or injury. To dream you have long, tidy hair is good for a woman, but if the hair is untidy it indicates anger and sullenness. To dream you have a thick beard and some boys pull it off shows you must take care against danger.

To dream that your hair is long is good; if it is untidy, long and brittle, it shows disturbance and trouble. To dream a man has no hair on his face denotes shamefacedness. Dreaming of losing hair means you will lose something – either friends, property, a lawsuit, or perhaps even your reputation. Something is wrong with your love affairs or domestic arrangements. Try to find out what it is, and put it right before it is too late. A girl who dreams of combing her hair may expect a proposal of marriage; a married woman a present from her husband. To dream that your hair is growing rapidly is a sign of fickleness. To dream you plait or curl your hair is only good for a woman; to others it signifies debt and impeachment for money and sometimes imprisonment. If you dream you have fair, long hair and you seem to take a pride in it, it is a good sign especially to a woman or a man who normally wears his hair long. To dream you have wool instead of hair foretells a long sickness.

HAIRDRESSER Avoid repeating gossip or you will find others gossiping about you.

HAIRPIN A visit to a place of amusement of a novel kind or to see something which is quite new to you is indicated.

HALIBUT To dream of this fish betokens a meal in public, held in your honour.

HALITOSIS If you dream of having bad breath, try not to be too pushy. If you dream of someone else's bad breath, a business obstacle will arise in your path.

HALL To dream of a great hall in a strange place means important decisions to be made shortly.

HALLMARK A double-faced companion is trying to injure your reputation.

HALLOWEEN A light-hearted comment will lead to a serious and productive opportunity.

HALTER A former playmate will become your marriage partner.

HAM To dream of ham implies cruel enemies. Be on your guard against them. To dream of eating ham is a sign of discontent in later life.

HAMLET To dream of a small village or hamlet indicates a removal to a crowded city.

HAMMER To dream that you are using a hammer denotes that one of your wishes will be realised. To hear the clang of a hammer foretells unpleasantness.

HAMMOCK This is a sign of a loss, and also of a gain of more value than the loss, probably to do with a lover.

HAMPER A pleasant visit is to be paid. Be careful of travelling at a late hour.

HAND To dream your hands are more attractive and stronger than usual signifies that you will be employed in some important affair, which you will bring to a happy conclusion, and gain reputation and advantage from it; and your employees will work for you cheerfully and loyally. To dream that your hand is cut off, that it has become thin and dry or that it has been burned means that you will lose your most faithful employee. If you have none, you will not be able to work but will become poor. If you dream of working with your right hand, that is a sign of good fortune to you and your family; if with the left, that denotes bad luck. Some also attribute the arm and the right hand to the father, son, brother and friend, and the success that may happen to them; and the left arm or hand signifies the mother, daughter, wife or employees. To dream your hand is hairy signifies trouble and imprisonment. To dream that you have clear and white hands signifies friendship if you are rich or idleness and necessity if you are poor. To dream you have many hands signifies good luck, strength and wealth. To dream you look at your hands signifies sickness. To dream you wash your hands signifies anxiety and vexation. To dream that you have hurt your hand signifies that you will soon be receiving a present of money as a reward for some good action. To dream you have hair on the backs of your hands signifies captivity, but if it comes on the palm it denotes idleness.

HANDBAG A mystery will be revealed.

HANDCUFFS To dream that you are handcuffed is a sign that you will become connected with someone to do with the law – either by marriage or because you need legal advice. To see another person handcuffed is an indication that one of your friends will shortly find themselves in serious trouble, in which you will be involved.

HANDKERCHIEF Someone has a gift for you.

HANDWRITING To see the handwriting of a dead friend is a warning to stop indulging in your accustomed bad habits or there will be dreadful consequences. To dream that you see the handwriting of your lover is a sign that they may soon experience some accident or injury. They may fall out of a boat, be accidentally shot with a firearm, or fall from a rock or a tree and be seriously injured. It could also mean that they are seeing someone else behind your back.

HANDYMAN You will have problems around the home.

HANGAR Your fortunes will change if you dream of an aircraft hangar, but it will be for the worse if the hangar is empty.

HANGING If you dream you have condemned someone to be hanged, it signifies you will be angry with that person for a short time but will be reconciled with them. If you dream that you were taken to the bottom of the gibbet to be hanged, you will lose your property and dignity.

To dream of seeing people hanged is a sign you will rise above your present condition; or you will be asked a favour by someone in need.

HANGMAN Problems ahead.

HANGOVER If you dream of having a hangover, you will have worries regarding your financial or love life.

HAPPINESS To dream of being extremely happy signifies that in your waking hours you are, perhaps quite unconsciously, walking the brink of a precipice, and that you should therefore exercise the greatest caution in all you do. If during a period of distress you dream that you are very happy, your problems will increase for a short time but then everything will come right. But you must meet your troubles head on and sort them out.

HARBOUR To see a harbour signifies that you will have joy, profit and good news.

HARE To dream you see a hare running signifies great wealth gained by application and intelligence. To dream of hunting a hare which escapes shows losses.

Should you see two or more hares in company, the dream indicates that you will shortly make a pleasant excursion to a popular rural haunt.

HAREBELL To dream of gathering harebells, bluebells or any blue wildflowers is an omen of finding a true lover.

HAREM Truth will out. Things you believe unknown are the subject of much gossip, but you will triumph in the end.

HARMONIUM To hear this played or play it in a dream signifies a happy but solemn occasion, probably a friend's wedding to which you will be invited.

HARMONY All pleasant music is a fortunate omen, but there must not be any sudden stoppage.

HARNESS A pleasant evening and an introduction which will lead to friendship.

HARP To dream of playing the harp denotes that through envy you will make an enemy. To hear the music of the harp is significant of a nervous breakdown.

HARPY To dream you see a harpy, the legendary half-woman and half-bird, signifies troubles and pain caused by envious and treacherous people.

HARROW To dream of implements is fortunate only if they are those used in your own work, otherwise they indicate dangerous rivals.

HARVEST To dream that you see the workers busy on the harvest is a most favourable dream – nature favours you. It is very fortunate for those in love.

HASSOCK To dream of a hassock betokens disappointment if you kneel upon one, and triumph over rivals if you have your feet upon one.

HAT If you dream you have a hat on which you like, that signifies joy, profit and success in business. To dream your hat is torn or dirty signifies damage and dishonour.

HATBOX To dream of opening one denotes a gay occasion unless you find it empty, in which case it means disappointment about a festivity to which you will not be invited.

HATCHET You will be in danger soon. Anxiety and trouble are looming.

HATCHING Turn your mind from all unhappy thoughts and look ahead to brighter times among friends.

HATE It is a good dream that someone hates you, for it is a sure sign of success. On the contrary, to dream of someone you hate is unlucky, and brings sorrow.

HAWK To dream you see birds of prey or falconry signifies increase of wealth to the rich, but the opposite to the poor. After dreaming of a hawk beware of a dark man, who will endeavour to harm you. Keep a tight hold on your money. Someone will be jealous of you.

HAWKER A new influence is about to enter your life; be reserved with present associates.

HAWTHORN For a young woman to dream that a young man presents her with a piece of hawthorn blossom is a sign that she is highly respected by a young man living nearby who is too shy to speak to her.

HAY The man who dreams of working in the hay will become famous throughout the country. To dream of hay signifies happiness and success; to mow it denotes sorrow.

HAY FEVER If you dream of suffering from hay fever, you should take care to look after your health.

HAY CART Through diligence you will succeed in your undertaking.

HAYMAKING You have a good character and are respected by your friends.

HAYSTACK Strive on, you have laid the foundation for a prosperous future.

HAZEL NUT To see and eat hazel nuts signifies difficulties and trouble.

HEAD If anyone dreams their head is bigger than usual, that signifies that they will be promoted to a powerful job. It sometimes also indicates victory over enemies and overthrowing adversaries at law; and to merchants and bankers, collecting money or recovering treasure. If a sick person dreams this, it indicates a serious and violent fever. To dream you have a small, light or sharp head signifies lack of spirit and disgrace. To dream you have three heads on one neck signifies authority, power and reputation. To dream that you have the head of a lion, wolf or some other wild animal, is a good sign; you will accomplish your intentions, will overcome problems and be respected by friends and colleagues. To dream you are holding your head in your hands signifies the loss of your wife and children. If you are not married, it means good luck; and if you comb your hair and put on a hat, your business will succeed. To dream you have two heads signifies company. To dream you wash your head signifies escape from danger. To dream your head is turned back to front is a warning to leave the country, otherwise there will be dire

consequences. To dream that your head is very large signifies good fortune.

HEAD HUNTER If you are captured by savages, you should be careful whom you offend at work.

HEADACHE To dream of having a headache foretells that you are about to be tempted to do wrong. But the temptation must be resisted at any cost; for if you yield, your conscience will trouble you continually.

HEALTH Dreaming about your health indicates happiness.

HEARSE To dream of a hearse ornamented with feathers signifies that you will marry a rich person or help at a relation's wedding, who will marry well and be a friend to you.

HEART If anyone dreams they have a pain in the heart it is a sign of illness approaching, its seriousness being shown by the level of pain. If anyone dreams they have lost their heart it is a sign that they will fall completely under the power of their most bitter enemies. To dream your heart is more lively, large and vigorous than usual is a sign of long life, that you will overcome your enemies and be prosperous in your enterprises. In the opinion of some, the heart in dreams signifies man, and chiefly the husband. So that if a woman dreams she has pains in her heart, the evil indicated will happen to her husband; if it is a girl the evil will happen to her father.

HEARTH To be cooking over a fire means you will successfully carve out your own fortunes.

HEAT To dream you feel very hot signifies grief.

HEATHEN To have any dealings with heathens, or to dream of them in any way, is a warning of treachery in a person you would suspect least of anyone you know. Be careful whom you trust until you have found the guilty party.

HEATHER Good fortune and a pleasant journey follow a dream of heather. It indicates hope; although if it is withered, your hopes are vain.

HEAVEN To dream you ascend up to heaven signifies authority and power. To dream of heaven is an assurance that you will have

no cause to complain of lack of comfort in your married life.

HEDGE To dream of a high hedge indicates that you will have to fight hard to gain success in something you have undertaken, and unless you put your best efforts into it you will be overwhelmed by the opposition you will encounter. If the hedge is green, it indicates prosperity and success.

HEDGEHOG To dream of a hedgehog signifies that your kindness will be taken advantage of.

HEEL If wounded or in pain in your heel, it indicates innumerable troubles.

HEIRLOOM An answer you needed has been postponed. Do not be dominated by a friend.

HELL To dream you see hell as it is described, and hear the damned souls groan and complain of the extremity of their torments, is an indication from God that you must improve your morals and way of life. To dream you see the damned plunged in the fire and flames, and suffer great torture, signifies sadness, repentance, grief and a melancholy. To dream you have descended into hell and returned signifies misfortunes to the rich and powerful, but it is a good sign to the poor or weak.

HELMET Pleasant visitors will come to see you. Avoid extravagance; you will need all your savings.

HELP If you are calling for help in a dream, you will soon need the assistance that will be offered to you. If you respond to a call for help, you will be well liked by your colleagues.

HEMP Fortune favours you. A dream of hemp indicates luck.

HEN To dream of hens is very unfavourable; it indicates loss of property, friends and reputation; in love it denotes misery and disappointment. After such a dream I would advise the dreamer to change residence.

To dream that a capon or hen crows signifies sadness and trouble. To dream you hear hens cackle, or geese honk, signifies profit and assurance of the completion of a business project. But to dream you catch hens signifies joy.

HERB To dream you eat any herb indicates good health

and long life. To be hunting for herbs means gain in business or your profession. To dream of smelling herbs such as marjoram, hyssop, rosemary, sage, etc. signifies hard work, trouble, sadness and weakness to anyone but a doctor to whom such dreams are propitious.

HERMIT To have dealings with a hermit is a sign of a loveless marriage.

HERO A change of heart in someone who has hitherto been cool to you, especially should you dream of some great hero of historic times.

HERON Your business career will take off and you will gain while others lose.

HERRING To dream of herrings, whether of catching them or eating them, is a dream for the economical and signifies that by frugal living they will soon become the owners of a vast amount of property.

HICCOUGH To dream you have a fit of hiccoughing predicts travel; to dream a friend has it means a parting.

HIDING To dream you are hiding denotes obscurity and blighted hopes. Bad news will soon reach you.

HIEROGLYPHICS You will make a discovery which will prove important both to you and others.

HIGHLANDER To dream that you see a Highlander in full Scottish costume is a sign that you will be a cool and calculating trader and a careful and plodding contriver in all your business transactions.

HIGHWAYMAN Astonishing information which will be to your advantage will soon come your way from a surprising quarter.

HILL To dream of travelling over steep hills shows that you will encounter many difficulties, and enter upon some arduous undertaking. If you descend the hill easily, you will get the better of all your problems and become rich. To dream you climb a steep hill and never get to the top signifies your life will be one of difficulties and troubles.

HIPPOPOTAMUS If you dream of a hippopotamus, you will have to be agile to escape danger. If the animal is in a zoo, you will not escape being bored by family or friends.

HIPS To dream your hips have grown larger and stronger than usual indicates that you will be very happy and healthy and will have lovely children. To dream your hips are broken, and that you cannot walk, denotes affliction, sickness and loss of children. If you dream that your hips are black and blue with whipping, or blows with a stick or sword, that means a severe crisis, or at least that you will hate your wife and have several grievances. If you dream your hips are cut half through, your hopes in your wife and relations will be utterly lost.

HIPS and HAWS This indicates poverty or loss of money, especially if you are eating them in your dream.

HITCH-HIKING Try to avoid depending on others to such an extent. Make your own plans and follow them through.

HIVE Dangerous undertakings will need to be completed which you will bring to a successful conclusion.

HOARDING Be on guard against misfortunes through deceitful companions. Your affairs will improve before long.

HOARSENESS A chance of advancement but to an insecure position. Think well before deciding.

HOAX To trick someone in a dream is a sign that your actions will not be appreciated by others and you will have to explain yourself.

HOBBY To dream of practising your favourite hobby predicts gains through your own brainwork and efforts.

HOBBYHORSE Riding a hobbyhorse in a dream means that you will make great strides in following your favourite themes.

HOE To dream that you see this agricultural implement is a sign that you will have good health and spirits for a long time.

HOG A well-fed hog indicates prosperity; thin hogs denote bad times to come.

HOG'S BRISTLES To dream of these signifies great and violent dangers.

HOLE To dream you creep into or fall into a hole means you will come in contact with undesirable people.

HOLIDAY This dream indicates that you will have to work very hard in life, but your efforts will be rewarded.

HOLLY To dream of holly signifies vexations and disagreements.

HOLLYHOCK This flower in a dream signifies that your present difficulties will be overcome.

HOME Your life will be contented and happy with the ones you love.

HOMESICK If you are away from home and dream of those you love and have left there, and have intense feelings of homesickness, it is a sign of great wealth coming to you from an unexpected source. Someone who has no family has taken a fancy to you and will leave you the largest portion of his fortune.

HOMICIDE Misfortune and heavy loss are not far away.

HONEY This signifies prosperity, profitable enterprises, honour and renown. But be careful to be honest in all your dealings. If, however, the honey is surrounded by bees, beware of jealous people who will attempt to snatch away your success.

HONEYMOON Changes, journeys and disappointments may all be coming to you.

HONEYSUCKLE If in flower you will soon change your residence for a fairer scene.

HONOUR To dream that you have been the recipient of some special honour is a sign that you will be humiliated in the presence of someone who will be pleased to see you embarrassed.

HOOD If you dream of wearing a hood, your trust has been misplaced.

HOOK A present will soon be given you which you will value greatly.

HOOP To dream of a hoop foretells a pleasant surprise or a visit from two friends whom you had almost forgotten.

HOPS Picking hops signifies that your love will be passionate but short-lived.

HORIZON Your love-life will be successful.

HORNET To dream of hornets attacking you is an omen that you will shortly meet a person of the opposite sex who will fascinate you.

HORN If you dream you have horns on your head, it signifies dominion, grandeur and royalty; nevertheless some authors say that to dream you have the horns of an ox, or any other potentially dangerous creature, denotes anger, pride and violent death by the hand of justice. To dream you see a man with horns on his head signifies he is in danger both of the loss of his life and property.
  To hear a horn blowing is a sign that your help is wanted by someone living a long distance away. To see the horns of a bull or any other animal indicates that you have vicious enemies.

HOROSCOPE To dream of a chart of your starry influences is a sign that a stronger mind than yours will dominate you, unless you resist with all your might.

HORSE To dream you see many horses signifies wealth and plenty. The horse is a good sign, for if anyone dreams they see, take or mount a horse, that is a happy omen to the dreamer. If anyone dreams that they are mounted on a stately horse, nimble, full of metal and well harnessed, they will have a handsome, noble and rich lover, provided the horse is their own; if it belongs to someone else, they will receive comfort, property and honour through a stranger. If you dream that you are riding and you pass a place without making your horse rest by dismounting, you will gain honour, dignity and fame. If you dream of riding a horse with a long tail, it is a sign you will find many friends to assist you in your undertakings. If the horse stops, you will meet with obstruction in your designs. If you dream that another rides your horse without your consent, it signifies that some person will commit adultery with your partner. Some authors are of the opinion that if you dream you are mounted on a nimble, sprightly, active and well-managed horse, you will be honoured by everyone. If you dream you spurred the horse too violently and forced him to what he did, you will be advanced to a position of authority.

For a man to dream he has a young, well-harnessed mare, it is a sign he will soon be married to a beautiful, young and rich woman, and will be very happy. If it is a poorly-formed mare without a saddle, that denotes his wife will have no money of her own. To dream that you ride on a white, grey or dappled horse signifies prosperity. To dream you see white horses signifies joy; black horses signify sadness. To see horses pace signifies mirth. To see horses of several colours signifies success in business. To see red or roan-coloured horses signifies prosperity. To see a gelding signifies accusation. To see a horse mount signifies prosperity. To dream you are on horseback, and the horse runs away with you shows you will be called away on something contrary to your liking. To dream of riding a horse indicates a change of scene, change of friends, new lovers, new rivals – in fact quite a sensational upsetting of everything in your life.

To dream that you are dealing in horses denotes that good luck awaits you in connection with a favourite project. To dream of a horse kicking is an indication that someone you love will be taken with a sudden illness. A horse-shoe means good news. To dream you see a horse running signifies prosperity. To dream of riding on a tired horse shows that you will fall desperately in love. To dream you see a horse dead is a sign that stagnation will take place on your business with some losses.

HORSE CHESTNUT To dream of this tree or its fruit means that you must be careful of your health.

HORSEHAIR To dream of horsehair is a sign of servitude and misery.

HORSEMAN To dream of a horseman signifies a dangerous journey.

HORSERADISH You will doubt the honesty of your friends.

HORSESHOE To find one indicates a legacy. To see one means you will travel over land and water.

HOSPITAL To be in a hospital indicates you will suffer a long illness.

HOST If you are the host or hostess of an occasion, your financial affairs are in good order.

HOTEL To dream of living in an hotel signifies to a man that he will shortly be compelled by an accident to reside for a time in an hotel

in a strange town, and that he will end by marrying the best girl in the neighbourhood. A girl dreaming of hotel life may conclude that she will marry a husband who will be of a roving disposition.

HOTHOUSE Anyone who dreams of a hothouse may look for a rapid improvement in financial affairs.

HOUNDS These do not form a favourable dream, but show that any success will only come after much struggle and hard work.

HOUR GLASS Forewarns that whatever your health or your state, you have arrived at a decisive moment in your life and must act wisely or you will suffer the consequences.

HOUSE To dream of building a house means that single people will marry, but those who are already married will encounter trouble and anxiety. A dream of a house falling down denotes to the businessman that he ought to look into his affairs; the balancing of his books has been too long neglected. If you dream of your own house, domestic happiness will be yours. But should the house be in a dilapidated state, illness will occur in the family. To dream that you are building or buying a house generally means that you will have to cut down expenses by moving to a cheaper residence.

HOUSEBOAT   Your love-life will suffer many ups and downs.

HUG   A friendly hug signifies a happy and contented future. A passionate hug signifies that your love affairs may be stifling.

HUMMING BIRD   You will travel to a foreign clime and do successful business there.

HUNCHBACK   A period of many trials and changes is to come, followed by a happy love affair.

HUNGER   If you dream you are extraordinarily hungry you will be ingenious, hard-working and eager to advance in your job in proportion to the greatness of your hunger. To the lover it denotes that your sweetheart will under-take a journey before you marry.

HUNTING   To dream you go hunting signifies an accusation. To dream you are hunting and that the game is

killed shows much trouble. To dream you are hunting a fox and that he is killed shows much trouble through the pretentions of false friends, but that nevertheless you will discover them and overcome all their deceits. To dream that you are hunting a hare is indicative of failure and that you will be disappointed in your favourite object, whatever it may be. To dream, however, that you are hunting a stag is good if he is caught alive; you will be successful in all your present undertakings.

HURDLE   Injustice and wrong accusations will upset you; you must clear yourself of false suspicions. You will hear of an old acquaintance again.

HURRICANE   Be on your guard, otherwise you will be led into a serious quarrel that will end in the law courts. The quarrel will not concern you personally, but the contending parties will do their best to include you in the mutual recriminations, and you will have to take a firm stand.

HURT   A dream of warning; the result depends on the nature of the accident and whether you recover from it.

HURRY Danger of fire or accident which can be averted with care.

HUSBAND For a wife to dream of her husband is a sign of growing affection. A widow dreaming of her deceased husband may safely anticipate receiving a proposal. For a wife to dream of an absent husband is a sign that he is well and will soon return to her. The girl who dreams she sees the man she is destined to marry will not find a partner until late in life.

HUSSAR For a young unmarried woman to dream that she meets a hussar is a sign that she will fall desperately in love with a soldier who has never shown any attachment towards her but who has known her for a long time. She will do her best to gain his attention, for in her case 'love is blind', but she will not be able to win his love, and the consequence will be that she will spend many days in a gloomy love-sick state of mind.

HYACINTH You will hear of the misfortune of others, probably through sickness.

HYDROPHOBIA Robbery and losses are indicated; guard your treasures.

HYMNS To dream that you are singing hymns means your plans will be successful after some problems.

HYPNOTISM To dream that you have been hypnotised indicates that you will reveal some secrets that will cause unpleasantness to some of your friends.

HYPOCRITE If you are acting hypocritically in a dream, do not work too hard or you will suffer ill health. If someone else is acting in this way, be careful of jumping to conclusions about those around you.

HYSSOP To dream that you smell of hyssop signifies hard work, trouble, sadness and weakness, unless you are a doctor in which case the dream is propitious.

HYSTERICS Be firm and do not allow yourself to be dominated by others if you want to achieve success.

ICE   When you dream of ice and snow in winter, that has no particular meaning for you are thinking about the cold of the preceding day. But if it is in another season, that denotes a good harvest to farmers; to merchants and other businessmen it signifies hindrance in their negotiations and voyages; and to soldiers that their designs will be frustrated.

To dream you are sliding or skating on ice denotes that you will pursue some unprofitable concern, and lose out; in love, it shows that your sweetheart is fickle and deceiving, and that you will never marry your present one.

To see a sheet of thin ice is a sign that you will make and break a promise on the same day, which will lead to a coolness between yourself and your sweetheart. Should the ice be thick, however, and you see people skating on it, you will have a desire to travel but will not be able to gratify it.

ICE CREAM   After dreaming this, children will figure prominently in your future.

ICEBERG   Denotes an enemy who will take advantage of your superior position to do you harm.

ICICLES   To dream of icicles denotes good luck, happiness and success in love.

IDIOT   To dream you have become an idiot, or mad, and are guilty of stupid behaviour in public, signifies that you will live long and be popular.

IDLE   To dream that you are idle in your character and habits is a sign of having great profits, both in money and intelligence, from your industry. You will only need to persevere in your daily hard work at your job to gain a position of influence.

IDOL   Your eyes are about to be opened; do not show your feelings too plainly.

IGNORANCE   To dream that you are ignorant, or cannot understand some matter, is an omen of contrary.

Success will crown your efforts.

ILLEGITIMACY You will receive wealth and find fame.

ILLITERACY Your responsibilities at work will increase.

ILLNESS To dream you are ill and in pain indicates misery and unhappiness. To tend or visit the sick means joy and happiness. To dream you have a lingering illness signifies that you will become rich.

ILLUMINATION It is a certain sign of war when a person dreams of seeing a city illuminated. To dream your own house is illuminated means much quarrelling among relatives.

ILLUSION To dream of seeing an illusion foretells the discovery of valuable secrets.

ILLUSTRATION To dream of illustrations in a book indicates happiness in love.

IMAGE Not a fortunate dream; postpone important decisions, until you have all the facts at your disposal.

IMP Grief and disappointment.

IMPALEMENT To dream one of your relatives or friends falls from a window or the top of the house and is impaled upon the rails beneath is a sign that something will fall from a housetop and injure your head.

IMPOSTER If you are deceived by an imposter, expect problems at work. If you are the imposter in the dream, you will have to be tactful to obtain your just rewards.

IMPRISONMENT To dream you are imprisoned signifies enjoyment and happiness.

INCENSE It is considered a favourable omen if the incense is pleasant to your senses, as in the case of all perfumes. But incense is so closely associated with the interior of a church that we are inclined to treat it doubtfully ourselves, and suggest that success will only come after effort and anxiety.

INCEST For a man to dream he is in bed with his mother means he should make haste to complete his business arrangements.

INCOME To dream that you possess a comfortable income is an unfavourable omen.

INCOME TAX Financial losses will trouble you, probably through assisting a friend.

INCUBATOR To see a baby in an incubator foretells good health for yourself and your family.

INDIA To dream of India signifies strange happenings; a message from an unfriendly woman will upset you.

INDIGENCE This dream is often the forerunner of good fortune; you will inherit or earn wealth.

INDIGESTION If you are suffering from indigestion in your dream, be less exuberant in your lifestyle.

INDIGO A journey over water as blue as this dye, and perhaps a long time before you return.

INFANT If an unmarried woman dreams of an infant, it means that she will go through some trouble.

INFANTRY Infantry on the march indicate passing troubles and short-lived love affairs.

INFIRM It is a dream of contrary if you imagine yourself aged and infirm.

Old age is a good omen.

INFIRMARY A sign of some coming misfortune, if you dream that you are in a hospital. If you recover and leave, you will overcome your difficulties.

INHERITANCE To dream of receiving an inheritance is often the augury of a real inheritance.

INJECTION Do not be too sensitive to outside pressures.

INJURY To dream you receive an injury warns you to beware of enemies. If in business, you will meet with overwhelming competition.

INK To dream of ink being spilt, or of your being soiled with ink, means that someone is harbouring evil against you, and that you will shortly receive an anonymous letter of which it would be unwise to take any notice.

INN To dream of being in an inn is a very unfavourable sign; it denotes poverty and failure. Expect yourself or one of your family to be committed to prison. If you are sick, you will never recover. To the tradesman, it indicates loss of credit and bad employees. If you are in love, you will be disappointed.

INNOCENCE   If you take advantage of the innocence of others, you will fail in everything you undertake.

INQUEST   To dream of being at an inquest denotes prosperity.

INSANITY   To dream that you are insane is an omen of good fortune.
    To dream that you are watching another person who has lost their senses indicates coming mild sickness in your family.

INSECT   To dream of insects crawling over you is a good omen of prosperity. To see them running away from you predicts disappointment.

INSTRUMENT   To dream of musical instruments, or to see one instrument alone being played, or to play one yourself, indicates mourning and sorrow.

INSULT   To dream that you have been insulted is a sure sign that someone will be flattering you before long, and by that means trying to make you commit a foolish indiscretion.
    Be careful of the person, and have as little as possible to do with them.

INTESTINES   To dream of intestines signifies sickness and anxiety.

INTRIGUE   Others will discuss you behind your back.

INVALID   To dream you comfort invalids and prescribe remedies and medicines for them signifies profit and good luck. To dream you are an invalid and unable to leave your bed is a really good omen. For although you may expect a bad illness soon, it will pass quickly and you will afterwards enjoy a long spell of good health. To dream that someone you know is an invalid foretells bad news concerning a brother or sister.

INVITATION   The person who dreams of receiving an invitation to a party or social function may expect to lose someone close to them.

IRON   To dream you buy and sell iron goods with a stranger signifies loss and misfortune. To dream you see yourself hurt with iron signifies damage.

ISLAND   To dream you are on an island signifies that you will lose the friendship of someone.

ITCH To dream you itch signifies that your fears and anxieties are groundless.

IVORY To dream of ivory signifies riches, success, abundance, prosperity; this is a very good dream.

IVY Dreaming of ivy means that your present lover will soon have to take a back seat, and that your next partner will be the one with whom you will form a lasting and serious relationship. Should you dream that your lover is picking ivy for you, you will marry a faithful husband. Your friends and everyone you love will cling to you. It also signifies good health and happiness.

JACK To dream of playing cards and holding the Jack of Clubs signifies a good friend; of Diamonds, a false friend; of Hearts, a true lover; of Spades, an enemy.

JACKAL To dream of this bird signifies that some enemy will talk about you behind your back and cause you trouble.

JACKASS For a young person to dream that they see a jackass is indicative of their meeting with a young person who is patient in character and dull in intelligence, but who will be true to their vows of attachment. They will prefer meeting in private because they will be reserved and shy. It is possible to meet with a worse match than a marriage with this suitor would prove.

JACKDAW The person who dreams of a jackdaw must be wary of a jealous enemy who will not rest until he has done that person an injury. To dream you catch one signifies you have enemies, but you will overcome them.

JACKET Hard work and little reward will be your lot. Be patient, but take the first opportunity of a change.

JACKPOT If you win a jackpot in your dream, you may do well to place a bet on an outsider.

JACOBEAN To dream of Jacobean furnishings presages a quiet time with elderly people whose ways are not so modern as yours, but you will gain by the experience.

JADE To dream of jade ornaments is a fortunate omen, though the colour, green, indicates hard work in front of you if you wish to succeed.

JAGUAR Guard against slander.

JAIL This is generally considered an unfortunate dream, unless you are released in due time.

JAM To dream of eating jam foretells a short illness. To dream that you are making jam is an omen of prosperity.

JAPAN An unusual experience will soon occur.

JAR To dream of receiving the present of an ornamental jar means that you are in danger of a close relative causing arguments in your family.

To dream that a house is jarred or shaken by an earthquake, an explosion, or anything that may occur outside is a sign that the head of the family in that house will be ill.

JASMINE This foretells good luck. Lovers will soon marry.

JAUNDICE To dream of this complaint signifies sickness and poverty.

JAVELIN Throwing the javelin signifies that you should extend your career ambitions.

JAW The jaws represent cellars, shops and places used to store goods.

JAY Difficulties which it will take your utmost efforts to surmount.

JAZZ Your lively lifestyle will cost you more than you think.

JEALOUSY Signifies trouble and anxiety.

JEER To dream of being jeered at by companions foretells triumph over enemies.

JELLY To dream that you are eating jelly is a sign of approaching physical weakness, but not severe illness. Give careful attention to your children, as one of them will have weak ankles. For a young man to have this dream is a sign that his special object will not be so easily attained. Difficulties will be presented which will require great patience and perseverance to be exercised by him.

JELLYFISH A scheme is on foot to injure you; be on your guard.

JEOPARDY If you dream you are in jeopardy, it will be fortunate for you.

JERUSALEM Misery and loneliness.

JESSAMINE It is great good fortune to dream of this beautiful and welcome blossom.

JESUS Calm and contentment.

JET This black ornament carries no good fortune, and must be judged by its colour alone.

JETTY You will travel shortly to another country.

**JEWEL and
JEWELLERY** Chains, pearls or precious stones and jewellery for the heads and necks of women are good dreams for women. To widows and girls they signify marriage; to those without children, that they will have a child; to those who are married with children, purchases and riches.

To dream that you are the owner of many valuable jewels is a sign of joy to come. Should there be many emeralds, however, your jubilation will be tempered with bad news which will bring many tears.

To dream of looking at, but not possessing, a rare jewel means that you will shortly meet someone whose worth you will at first fail to recognise, and whose friendship you will reject, and that the rejected friendship can never afterwards be yours.

JEW'S HARP To dream you see one indicates good news of a reconciliation. If you play one, the news will affect business relations with an important personage.

JIG To dream you are dancing portends at least one lover; be careful not to cause jealousy.

JILTED The girl who dreams she has been jilted may rest assured that her lover is very faithful to her. But she must not trifle with his affections, otherwise his love will turn to hatred.

JINGLE To hear the jingle of small bells, either cattle bells, dog bells or sleigh bells, foretells innocent flirtations and amusements.

JOCKEY For a girl to dream that she is in love with a jockey is an omen of a gay life for some time, then poverty. If a woman dreams she sees a jockey riding at full speed, she will have an offer of marriage made to her very unexpectedly.

JOINT A good omen if you cook a joint of meat for your family, but threatened poverty if you eat it yourself.

JOKER Light company will bring you no good; seek your equals.

JOLLITY To dream of jollity, feasts and celebrations is a good sign and a prosperous dream.

JOURNEY To dream of going on a journey, by

whatever form of transport, means that you are about to have a change in your circumstances. To ascertain whether it will be for the better or for the worse, recall the style in which you were travelling. To dream that you are forced to undertake a journey gives promise of an invitation to a social function where the dreamer will meet someone who will be very useful later in life.

JOY A dream of being overjoyed about anything is in many instances, but not always, a bad omen, denoting the approach of grief. To dream you are taking part in some joyous festivity, or that you have cause for feeling particularly happy, is a bad omen; minor troubles are sure to arise.

JUBILEE To dream you are at a jubilee is a sure sign that you will have a fortune left you by some rich relatives.

JUDAS Be careful of trusting others.

JUDGE To dream of seeing a judge on the bench means that you will shortly find yourself engaged in a lawsuit, in which if the judge sits with the window of the court to the right you will be successful, if to the left you

will come off second best. Should the court be lighted from the roof the jury in your case will be unable to agree. To dream of a judge is a sign that you will be likely to grow discontented with your lot, and in trying to improve matters you will go from bad to worse.

JUG The person who breaks a jug will receive a great surprise. To dream of drinking out of a jug is a sign of going on a journey. If the jug is large, the journey will be long; if small, the journey will be short.

JUGGLER An advancement in position will come within your grasp. Do not hesitate to grasp the opportunity.

JUMPER This dream signifies that someone will speak evil of you, and warns you to be circumspect in all your dealings.

JUMPING To dream that you are jumping from a high position or over obstacles is a sign that you will meet with lasting success if only you will put your heart and soul into your work.

JUNGLE If you dream of being lost in a jungle be careful to whom you speak, for someone will be trying to lead you astray. Should you meet a wild animal when you are lost you will be pestered by this person for some time.

JUNIPER   Someone will speak evil of you. This dream warns you to be circumspect in all your dealings.

JUNK   You will find your next decision hard to make. Get to the heart of the problem before committing yourself.

JURY   You are about to suffer a good deal of annoyance from the unreasonable conduct of one of your neighbours, and it will only come to an end by your instituting legal proceedings. For a man to dream that he has been summoned to serve on a jury is a sign that he will have trouble with his fellow workmen, which will lead to grave charges being levelled against him.

JUSTICE   To be brought to justice signifies happiness. To be condemned by a judge signifies a love affair.

KALEIDOSCOPE Indicates frivolity. Do not take things too lightly or you may regret it.

KANGAROO The hostility of someone influential will cause you great anxiety.

KEEL To dream of the heavier parts of a ship, such as the keel, or deck, signifies news of a lover at sea.

KEEPER To dream of a gamekeeper or park keeper means danger in love matters; a rival will take your place in your sweetheart's affections.

KEEPSAKE A dream of good fortune. But if a friend asks for a keepsake or a gift and you fail to respond, then your difficulties will be severe.

KEG To dream you see a keg of whisky is a sign of your children being placed in danger in the streets; some kind friend will rescue them from being run over by a lorry. To see a keg of gunpowder is a sign of your having false friends. Your conduct will be the subject of ridicule in the company of your friends.

KENNEL You will be invited to the house of a man you know well. Do not go alone, and avoid quarrels.

KERB It is unfortunate to step off the kerbstone in your dream. Beware of quarrels with friends and relatives.

KETTLE To dream that you see a bright copper kettle is a sign of great domestic comfort. You will have much peace and joy in everyday life. Your partner will strive to make your home attractive by their winning ways and cheerful smiles. Your children will welcome you home with shouts of joy and happiness and they will chatter about what they have been doing all day. At home you will be exceptionally happy. If a young man has this dream it means that his intended will be neat, tidy and a good housekeeper.

KETTLEDRUM Trouble and anxiety.

KEY To dream you lose your keys signifies anger. To dream you find a key denotes admission to a position of trust. To dream of carrying about a bunch of keys means that you will shortly be placed in a situation of great responsibility, leading to proposals which will greatly influence your future fortunes.

KEYHOLE To dream that you see a person looking through the keyhole of your door is a sign that your house will be burgled, but the thieves will be frightened away before they can force an entrance.

KHAKI If you see a khaki uniform or imagine you are ordering a suit of that material or colour, be sure that you will shortly be mixed up in a serious quarrel which will make you very unhappy. Should you already be dressed in khaki, however, expect good news – possibly of an improvement in your affairs.

KICK It is a bad omen to be kicked in your dream, for you will have many powerful adversaries. But it is a good omen if you kick some other person.

KID An addition to the family is indicated, who will in time bring happiness to the home.

KIDNAPPING Your circumstances are about to improve and many of your worries are needless.

KILLING To dream you kill a man signifies success in business. To dream you kill your father is a very bad sign. To kill a stranger signifies loss. To dream you are killed denotes loss to the person who has killed you.

KILT Long-distance travel is forecast.

KIMONO To dream of women wearing kimonos indicates that you will find your heart's desire at a celebration.

KINDLING Be careful with tools; you are in danger of accidents. Your love affair will end happily.

KING To dream you are talking with a king signifies good reputation. To dream that you receive an audience of a king signifies gain. To receive a gift from a king signifies great joy. To see a king signifies honour and joy. To dream you see or speak to a king signifies that you will rise to honour and will acquire riches. Your business will improve.

KINGFISHER To dream of the flash of a blue bird across water signifies a change of luck. If fate has seemed against you, good fortune will befall.

KISS To dream of kissing a father or mother denotes a good friend. To dream of one woman kissing another denotes disappointments in love; if she has a crying child in her arms it shows affection through loss of her parents. To kiss without power of speech signifies the dreamer will fall in love, but not possess the lover.

To dream you are kissing a pretty girl is good as it denotes that a friend will do you an unexpected favour. To dream of kissing a married woman is a sign of poverty, and that you will fail in your present undertakings – but it usually means deceit, and the day will not pass without quarrels. To dream of kissing may be pleasant enough while it lasts, but it indicates that in waking hours there will be arguments, and that words will run more or less high in proportion to the warmth and enthusiasm recognised in the dream. To dream that you kiss the dead is a bad sign for anyone who

is ill. To anyone who is healthy, it means he should not tell anyone about his business dealings, unless the dead person was a particular friend.

KITCHEN To dream of a kitchen signifies that you will receive a visit from relatives. If you dream that the kitchen is on fire, that denotes death to whoever does the cooking.

KITE Dreaming of flying a kite indicates advancement in business and ultimate prosperity. To watch kites flying is a sign that you will meet with many bad debts, and experience all the bad fortune that results from trusting customers without making proper inquiries.

KITTEN A favourable dream, unless you hurt the young creature.

KNAPSACK An obstacle dream, unless you feel no strain from carrying it on your shoulders. But at best, it means difficulties ahead for a time.

KNAVE To dream of the Knave of Hearts indicates a lover; the Knave of Spades, widowhood; the Knave of Clubs, business.

KNEE The knee denotes hard work, therefore if anyone dreams that they themselves, or any other person has hurt their knee, they will be prevented from working efficiently by malicious and envious people. If anyone dreams that their knees are cut and they cannot walk, they will be reduced to poverty and be unable to work. If their knees heal and they recover their strength, the bad luck will alter, and they will grow rich and live happily. If anyone dreams they can run swiftly, they will be happy in all their undertakings. If a man dreams his knees are weary, that signifies sickness. If anyone dreams that they are kneeling, that denotes devotion and humility, and sometimes vexation and trouble in business. To dream the knee is swollen and painful signifies sickness, pain, loss and bad business, or problems in business.

KNEEL To dream you kneel signifies anxiety in your affairs.

KNELL Bright and joyful times are in store for you.

KNICK-KNACKS To a woman a dream of knick-knacks portends domestic worries, but should she be arranging them in a room and have trouble over the task, the worries will be slight. To a man the dream foretells bickering and arguments.

KNIFE To dream you give someone a knife signifies injustice and contention. To dream of knives and forks denotes great contention. To dream of receiving a present of a knife is a bad omen, for it signifies that many ties in which you take pleasure are about to be cut, and that death and indifference and misunderstandings will cause havoc in the circle of your friends. It is a bad omen to dream of giving a knife as a present. To dream that you are using a knife for any purpose denotes deceit and tears. If you cut yourself, be prepared for sickness.

KNIGHT To dream of a knight is an omen of success in love and domestic affairs.

KNIT To dream you are knitting signifies that your undertaking will be successful. To see someone knitting signifies that you will be deceived.

KNOCKING Guard your tongue and you are well on the way to happiness.

KNOT To dream of knots signifies that you will meet with much to cause you anxiety.

KNUCKLE Should you dream you knock your knuckles, it indicates unrequited affections.

KU-KLUX-KLAN Do not act badly towards your friends, even if it would be to your advantage.

LABEL Fixing a label on a box or trunk shows that you may expect a surprise.

LABORATORY To dream of a laboratory signifies danger and sickness.

LABOURER To dream of a labourer signifies that you will have increased wealth.

LABURNUM Ill-natured gossip about you caused by jealousy will upset you for a time.

LABYRINTH To dream you are in a labyrinth signifies that you will unravel a mystery.

LACE To dream of lace signifies extravagance. If you dream you are buying lace you will need in future to be more careful with your money. You are probably a spendthrift and will live to regret it.

To dream of bootlaces is a sign that you will rise much higher than your present position, though the change will not come until you are older.

LACERATION If you are painfully cut in your dream, prepare for difficult circumstances.

LACKEY Unexpected joy lies before you.

LADDER A ladder is a sign of good luck, and to dream that you are climbing one predicts that if you keep plodding along you will reach your goal. Should you dream of descending a ladder, however, you will have several ups and downs before success ultimately comes to you.

LADLE Using a ladle in your dream indicates news from an absent friend.

LADY If you dream of meeting a titled lady who acts perfectly, then you will have good luck. If she behaves badly, expect difficulties.

LADYBIRD Good luck in a small venture.

LAGOON If you dream of sailing alone in a lagoon, your life will be tranquil but lonely.

LAKE To dream of a lake of clear water is an omen that life will hold more joys than sorrows for you; and should you be in a boat on the lake, your lover will be successful. To sail on a smooth lake signifies comfort, happiness and success in business. If the water is rough, you will have a serious illness, but it will not permanently affect your good fortune. If the water is dirty or muddy it foretells trouble and loss.

LAMB To dream of a lamb is a sign that your worst enemy is a person whom you trust more than any of your friends, chiefly because that person is forever boasting of their faithfulness. If you can, discover the false one, obtain good proof of the deceit, and then have nothing more to do with him or her. To dream of watching lambs feeding or playing about means approaching grief and pain from a quite unexpected quarter.

LAME To dream of a lame man means you will have business problems.

To dream that you have become lame denotes disgrace; or if you are a prisoner, it foretells the punishment of your faults.

LAMENT This is a dream of contrary. You will hear good news or carry out some favourable business transaction. It does not matter whether you yourself lament, or whether you dream that someone else is sorrowing.

LAMP To dream of a brass lamp signifies either great goods or great evils, according to the disposition of the light.

LAMPPOST Leaning against a lamppost signifies that you will need the support of your family to get you through a rough patch.

LANCE To dream of a lance signifies hatred.

LAND If you dream of owning considerable lands, enclosed with pastures, it signifies that you will have a good-looking spouse.

LANDING To dream of landing from a boat portends ill-luck from one associated with the sea.

LANDLADY If a man dreams of the landlady of a public house it is a sign that he will not care for his wife. He will give his attention to anything but his home, and will carry misery with him wherever he goes.

**LANDSLIP or
LANDSLIDE** A short and pleasant visit payed to places once well known to you.

LANDSCAPE To dream of a landscape signifies great good fortune.

LANTERN To see a clear, shining lantern on a table or cabinet is a good sign to the sick since it denotes recovery and health. A single person who dreams of a lamp will soon marry, will be successful and prosper in his undertakings. If anyone sees a lantern with a light in it extinguished, that signifies sadness, sickness and poverty.

LAP Sitting on the lap of someone of the opposite sex predicts passionate love affairs.

LAPDOGS To dream of little dogs signifies delight and enjoyable pastimes.

LAPIS LAZULI An indication of contentment.

LARD To dream of lard signifies that you will triumph over your enemies.

LARDER To dream of a larder foretells that you may expect happiness and a joyful time.

LARKS To dream of larks signifies that you will soon be richer than you are.

LARYNGITIS You will be unlucky in gambling.

LASH To dream that you see a criminal being flogged is a sign that someone you love will be punished because they have fallen into bad company, and been present when others have broken the law by committing a felony or an assault.

LATE To dream of being late means that your opinions will be asked.

LAUGHTER To dream of laughter brings tears, grief and pain.

LAUNCH Profitable adventures are in store.

LAUREL If a woman sees or smells laurels, it means she will have children; she will be married suddenly or will be happy, successful and prosperous. To dream you see a laurel tree is a token of victory and pleasure; and if you are married, it denotes the inheritance of possessions by your spouse.

LAUNDRY A sign of a quarrel, parting or loss.

LAVA You will lose your job unless you work harder.

LAVATORY You will have a disagreement with someone working for you.

LAVENDER An omen as pleasant as it smells.

LAWSUIT To dream you have a lawsuit signifies that you will have occasion to fight for your rights, but there will be joy, consolation and good news.

LAWN To dream you see a smooth, green lawn portends prosperity and well-being. But should you walk on it, the meaning is anxiety.

LAWN TENNIS You will find work in which you will take the utmost interest.

LAWYER To dream of meeting a lawyer brings bad news; if you speak to him you will lose some property; if you hear someone speaking in his favour you will meet with misfortunes. To dream of being a lawyer foretells the marriage of a friend.

LAXATIVE You have underestimated the generosity of someone close to you.

LAZY To dream of idling denotes trouble to those near to you affecting you indirectly. A legal matter will end in marriage.

LEAD To dream you trade in lead signifies sickness.
To dream of handling lead is a bad dream, and signifies death. In all probability a succeeding dream will indicate whether the death will occur within your own family, or of a friend or acquaintance. The person who dreams of lead in any shape or form will hear of someone afflicted with illness, mental or physical. To an engaged person such a dream foretells broken promises and deceit. To a business person it indicates a down-turn in affairs.

LEAF To see trees in full leaf in your dream is a very happy omen. Your affairs will prosper; nature is favourable. It is a very good dream for lovers, especially if blossom is seen in addition to the leaf. With fruit, it is a sign of a happy marriage. But if the leaves are withered, or are falling, as in autumn, it shows loss in business, disappoint- ment in love and in domestic affairs, or quarrels with friends.

LEAKAGE You are wasting your time; find a wider scope for your activities.

LEANNESS If anyone dreams they have grown very thin they will either become ill or lose money or property.

LEAPING To dream you are leaping over walls, bars or gates is a sign that you will encounter many difficulties in your present occupation, and that your lover will not marry you.

LEAP YEAR You act with frivolity in matters that should be taken seriously.

LEARNING To learn a lesson of any kind denotes that you will not make a great success of your life. You should better yourself and try to get out of the rut into which you have fallen.

LEASE The person who dreams that he or she has taken over the lease of some premises will shortly have occasion to move into another area.

LEATHER To see a quantity of leather or any article made of leather is a sign that you will have to suffer many insults without being able to avenge them.

LECTURE You will soon be in handsome surroundings for a time, but your plans will not wholly succeed.

LEDGER All written documents or books are unfavourable omens in a dream – this includes bookkeeping, or the use of ledgers or cash books.

LEECH To dream of a leech signifies fortunate friends and happiness awaits you.

LEEK To dream that you eat or smell roots that have a strong smell like leeks signifies a discovery of hidden secrets and domestic arguments at home. To dream of leeks signifies that perseverance in your project will bring its reward in due course.

LEFT-HANDEDNESS A dream portending triumph to all those who are naturally left-handed.

LEG To dream your legs are scabby or itchy signifies pointless worry and care. To dream that your legs are perfectly well signifies joy and good fortune, that you will be prosperous in your business. To dream that your legs are swollen or cut off signifies the loss or damage of employees and of best friends, who will either fall sick or die. To dream that your leg is dislocated or broken signifies that an employee will be injured or die. To dream you have a wooden leg signifies the alteration of your condition; from good to bad, and from bad to worse.

LEGACY   It is always a fortunate sign to dream that you receive a legacy or a gift, but naturally the extent of the good fortune will depend entirely upon the nature of the legacy.

LEMON   To dream of lemons denotes bitter arguments in your family.

LEMONADE   Making lemonade indicates that you will make new friends who will be faithful.

LENDING   A dream of contrary. If you appear to be lending money or other articles, it foretells that you will want before long. It is an omen of loss and poverty.

LENTIL   Lentils signify corruption.

LEOPARD   Dreams of leopards have the same interpretation as those of lions, only they are more subtle and malicious than the lion (who is always generous).

LEPROSY   If anyone dreams of being a leper, that denotes profit and wealth with notoriety.

LESSON   A sign of good fortune of every kind.

LETTER   To dream of receiving letters is demonstrative of your being loved by a person of the opposite sex, who is very much your friend and will do all in their power to make you happy. To dream of writing letters shows success in enterprises, and that you will receive some very pleasant news. If you are at present in doubt as to what course of action to follow, the first words spoken by the first person you meet on the following morning will indicate what you should do.

LETTUCE   To dream you eat raw salad, such as lettuce, signifies trouble and difficulty in the management of affairs.

LIAR   If you dream of being called a liar, you can expect a serious quarrel with someone. If you call someone else a liar, you will be slandered.

LIBEL   To dream that a person has libelled you means that your character is above suspicion, but you will be single-minded in political controversy, rash in your expressions when in debate, and full of eccentricities. The religious sect which you might join will be small in number, but very dogmatic in their teachings. To dream that you have libelled a person is a sign that you will express your opinion quietly on any subject. You will be mild, gentle and peaceful in your behaviour.

LIBRARY   To dream of sitting in the library means that you have abilities which, rightly cultivated, would enable you to attain literary distinction.

LICE   To dream of killing a few lice shows you will have no worries, but to kill a large number foretells long sickness.

LICENCE   To dream that you take out a licence to sell any article is a sign that you will be very desirous of getting a livelihood by some other occupation than your present one.

LIE   It is a bad omen to dream that you are telling lies, as your coming troubles will be due to your own misconduct.

LIFE INSURANCE
   Dreaming of being refused life insurance on health grounds indicates a long and happy life.

LIFEBOAT   To dream you see a lifeboat means that you will be connected in one way or another with a seafaring person – either relation, friend or lover – who will have to return to sea for a long voyage.

LIFEGUARD   If you dream of being rescued by a lifeguard, you will soon meet a responsible and companionable partner.

LIFT   Uncertainty. To dream that you are ascending in the lift, your success is probable; if descending, it is doubtful.

LIGHT   To dream you see a great light is a happy omen which denotes that you will become powerful and rich; in love, it shows a sweetheart of an amiable disposition, and that you will marry well, have children, and be very happy. If the light disappears all of a sudden, it means a great change in your present situation, much for the worse; it portends imprisonment and loss of goods, with unexpected misfortunes. You are about to lose sight of a friend, who will disappear as effectually as if the ground had opened and swallowed them up. To dream of a light gradually increasing means that you will marry someone of limited education, but that by self-teaching they will become as valuable in your business as they have always been a sympathetic partner.

LIGHTHOUSE To dream of a lighthouse is an indication that you will be forced, much against your will, to take a journey by water.

LIGHTNING To see lightning in a dream means much the same as hearing thunder, except that what is to happen will come sooner (light travels much faster than sound).

LILAC Conceit. Do not think too much of appearances, either in yourself or in others.

LILY To see, hold or smell lilies out of season signifies your hopes of obtaining something will be frustrated.

LILY of the VALLEY To dream of lily of the valley indicates that your matrimonial choice is a wise one, and you will be happily married. Your partner may never distinguish themselves in anything, but may be trusted to go through the world quietly and respectably.

LIME To dream that you see a quantity of lime is a sign that you will have some property left you; a few old houses in a dilapidated condition will be your inheritance in the will of a wealthy relative.

LIMPING To dream that you limp is a sign that you will have to take a long journey on foot.

LINEN To dream you are dressed in clean linen denotes that you will shortly receive some good news, that your lover is faithful, and will marry you; that you will be successful in all your present undertakings; and that you will receive a handsome present from an agreeable young man. If your linen is checkered, you will get a legacy from a friend, and marry a very industrious person; if it is dirty, then it denotes poverty, a prison and disappointment in love, with the loss of something valuable.

LINER A portent of adventure or new lovers.

LINGERIE You should be more circumspect when talking to the opposite sex.

LINSEED If you dream that you have a poultice of linseed put on any part of your body it is a sign that you will have an attack of inflammation of the lungs or chest.

LINT To dream of binding up a wound with lint is a warning not to be unforgiving or you will regret it.

LINTEL A sign of a move to a larger home.

LION If you dream you see a lion, that signifies a meeting with someone in authority. If anyone dreams they fight with a lion, that signifies a quarrel with a strong opponent; if they won in the dream, they will win the argument. To ride on the back of a lion signifies protection from someone in authority. To be afraid of a lion signifies you will feel the anger of someone in authority. If anyone dreams that they have eaten lion's flesh, they will grow rich through the means of a king or someone powerful. If anyone dreams that they have found the skin, liver or bones of a lion, they will suddenly grow rich. To dream you have the ears of a lion signifies treachery or deceit from your enemies and those that envy you. To dream you have the head of a lion is a good sign as the dreamer will accomplish his ambitions. To dream of a lion

fawning on you denotes the favour of a noble person.

LION CUB To dream of a lion cub foretells protection and friendship.

LIONESS Dreaming of seeing a lioness indicates good fortune, for she is an excellent hunter and protects and cares for her family.

LIPS To dream that you have beautiful lips is a sign that your friends are healthy; and to have them dry and chapped, the opposite. To dream that your lips have grown larger signifies that you will have fine children.

LIQUEUR To dream of liqueur warns you to beware of flattery.

LISPING Be warned against insincerity in a friend.

LITTER For a newly married woman to dream that she sees a litter of pigs is a sign that she will have a large good-looking family. She will have twins once or twice and her children will grow up to be attractive and respected.

LIVER If anyone dreams that they have a liver complaint, their money will be wasted and they are also in danger of falling ill. If anyone dreams they have seen or found the liver of any of their enemies, and carried it away, they will defeat those who wish them ill.

LIVERY Seeing someone dressed in livery foretells annoyance.

LIZARD To dream of lizards signifies bad luck and misfortune caused by unknown enemies. It indicates great change in your business and affairs.

LLAMA If you dream of a llama carrying a pack, you will be successful in your merchandising business.

LOAD To dream you are loaded down signifies that your business will soon come to an end.

LOBSTER A favourable omen for love and domestic happiness.

LOCK To dream of a lock foretells difficulties. If you can open the lock, you will succeed in life.

LOCKET If the locket carries a picture, expect a passionate love affair.

LOCKJAW To dream that your spouse has lockjaw means that they will get you

into trouble by talking too much.

LOCOMOTIVE To dream of a railway engine is a certain sign of travel, or the arrival of some friend – this depends upon whether the engine is travelling from you or towards you. If you find yourself burdened with luggage, it becomes an obstacle dream; if your baggage is light and easy to handle, then your difficulties will be overcome easily.

LOCUST A locust signifies that you will be short-lived.

LODGINGS To dream of looking for lodgings means that your present ideas on the choice of an occupation for life are wrong. If the lodgings you are inspecting are on the ground floor, it may be taken as a sign that you would succeed in one of the professions. The floor above that indicates a prosperous career in mercantile life. The top floor points to distinction as an author, artist or musician.

LOG To dream that you are chopping logs is a sign that strangers will come to your house.

LONELY To dream that you are meditating in a lonely

place is a sign that you will become a proficient scholar in languages and theology; you will be fond of solitude, and study much by moonlight.

LOOM Weaving at a loom indicates a peaceful and contented life, although not without its hard work.

LORD To talk to a lord or that you go anywhere with him signifies honour.

LORRY Guard your speech or you will lose by it. A chance meeting will bring fortunate results.

LOSS To dream that you have lost something of value predicts a find.

LOTTERY To dream of a lottery signifies heavy loss.

LOVE It is a bad omen for a girl to dream that she is in love before she actually is in love. She will in all probability die unmarried. To dream that you are loved by someone whom you dislike is a warning that you will one day need a friend and will not know where to turn for one.

LOVE LETTER Unpleasant explanations have to be made, and a great deal will rest upon your decision.

Remember that frankness is an admirable quality.

LOVE TOKEN A love affair in which you will be greatly interested is on the horizon. Several others know more about it than you think; be circumspect.

LUCK To dream that you have experienced a stroke of good luck is a sign that you are inclined to leave too much to chance. You should rely more upon your own judgement. It can mean that you will be disappointed.

LUGGAGE To dream of luggage signifies trials, difficulties and danger.

LUNATIC Surprising news which will lead you to different surroundings.

LUNGS If anyone dreams they have the lungs of a bull, goat, ram or any other horned animal, they will become the heir of a wealthy and distinguished person. If anyone dreams that some-body has taken out their lungs, or that they are injured or ill, their designs will be frustrated, and they will run the risk of a great danger.

LUST Unless you stop giving way to your basest impulses, you will run into trouble.

LUTE To play or see someone else play a lute signifies good news, harmony, and a good relationship between man and wife, master and servants, prince and subjects or among friends. You will go into delightful company and you will have success and happiness.

LUXURY To dream of luxury denotes a late wealthy marriage after many hardships. To the person who is already married it is significant of approaching troubles connected with the home, including poverty, sickness and disappointment.

LYING To tell a lie is a bad omen.

LYNX Several of these animals denote vicious enemies, who will one day do you harm. If only one appears in your dream, you will hear of something which will cause you pain – possibly the secret hatred of someone for you.

LYRE A passionate adventure is in store for you. If the music is out of tune, the adventure will be similarly discordant.

MACE-BEARER Dignities and distinctions will be bestowed on you.

MACHINERY To dream that you are working machinery is a sign that you will not always need to earn your living. It signifies prosperity and wealth. For a girl to dream that she is working a sewing-machine is a sign of happiness in love and an early marriage.

MACKEREL To dream of eating this fish is a sign that you will be disappointed in long-held expectations. To dream of seeing mackerel in clear water signifies success and prosperity; if not fresh, it signifies disappointment in love.

MAD DOG Falsehood will be unmasked and false accusations proved untrue. A contented future is augured.

MADNESS To dream that you are mad and commit ludicrous behaviour in public means that you will live to an old age, and will be well-liked and powerful. All your undertakings, however unpromising or foolish they may at times appear, will in the end bring you success and command admiration from your friends. If you dream you meet with, or are in danger of being waylaid and injured by, a madman it is a sign that you will have a friend calling upon you whom you have not seen for years because he has been travelling abroad. He will offer you help and advice, and behave very kindly to you. If you dream that you see a madman it is a sign that you will become more reconciled to the disappointments in life; they will not have as bad an effect upon you as they had before, but you will have learned how to bear the difficulties of life without undue sorrow.

MAELSTROM Difficulties and bewilderments which will trouble you greatly are your lot, but they will be overcome in the end.

MAGAZINE Dreaming of reading a magazine is a luckier dream than that of writing one. The former means that you will shortly have the opportunity of greatly extending your education, and sphere of influence; the latter indicates that you will experience a run of bad luck.

MAGGOT   To dream of a maggot signifies that there will be a dispute in your home.

MAGIC   To dream that you are under a magic spell is a sure sign that you are making a great mistake in thinking that a certain person is worthy of your regard. This dream warns you to beware of rogues, for you should fear loss.

MAGISTRATE   A magistrate is a warning that, unless you are more careful in the way in which you conduct yourself, people will begin to suspect you of a vice of which you are quite innocent.

MAGNET   Personal success and security in business is indicated by this dream.

MAGNIFYING GLASS   You are apt to 'make mountains out of molehills'. Meet your worries confidently and they will soon be ended.

MAGNOLIA   The magnolia tree is a dream of love, passion and marriage.

MAGPIE   If you see several of these birds congregated together, beware of foolish gossip, otherwise it will lead you into trouble. If only one bird appears in your dream, it is a good omen, foretelling celebration.

MAID   To dream of a girl is a sign of disappointment, but not if the girl works for you.

MALARIA   Difficulties will beset you.

MALICE   It is good to dream of anyone bearing malice towards you because it is a sign that a particular person likes you and would do you a good turn if ever it lay in his or her power.

MALLOWS   To dream of eating mallows signifies freedom from trouble and expedition of business.

MALT   A sign of marriage and much domestic joy.

MAMMOTH   Apparently unsurmountable obstacles confront you, but your best efforts will assuredly overcome them.

MAN   To see a man publicly burned signifies loss of

merchandise or sickness. To dream you see a dead man signifies that you will be subject to the same passions and fortune as the dead man. To dream a man who is alive is dead signifies troubles to come. To dream you see armed men is a good sign. To dream you ruin a man signifies sadness. If an unmarried woman dreams of being a man, she will have a husband or, if without children, have a son – but to a girl it indicates difficulties. For a young woman to dream of talking confidently to a young man is a happy sign in love affairs. It is all the more promising if he is handsome, with soft eyes and a serious expression. For a man to dream of talking to a man foreshadows rivalry in business or in love, perhaps in both. An old man means that you will shortly receive a legacy, the amount of which may be guessed by noticing whether the old man has long or short hair. For a young woman to dream of receiving the attentions of a man she does not know is a good omen for her future happiness. If the man is very old, she will not marry until after experiencing a disappointment in love.

MANACLES To dream that you are held helpless by heavy manacles is a sign that someone will help you to a good position in life.

MANE A horse's mane foretells an important invitation.

MANICURE A marriage with a much older partner will prove successful.

MANSION All luxury dreams are bad omens. The greater the apparent prosperity, the worse your troubles will be.

MANSLAUGHTER This dream foretells family troubles and disagreements, whatever the ultimate issue may be. It is an unfortunate omen, even though you are acquitted and set free.

MANTLE Be warned of treachery on the part of someone whom you trust.

MANURE To dream you manure and cultivate the earth signifies melancholy to those who are usually happy, and to labourers it signifies gain and a plentiful crop.

MAP To dream that you are studying a map of a foreign country foretells a short journey to meet a stranger. If the map is of your own country, you will meet an old acquaintance whom you have not seen for some time.

MARATHON You will be under a lot of pressure to make good an ill-considered action.

MARBLE A dream of marble in any shape or form denotes that you will triumph over your enemies, and also that at some time you will live beyond your income and come very near to financial ruin.

MARCHING To dream of marching quickly predicts advancement and success in business.

MARE If anyone dreams they are mounted on a mare that signifies they will gain reputation, dignity and fame.

MARIGOLD Most flowers owe their power in a dream to their colour. But as a rule, they are fortunate, and will to some extent counteract any bad influences at work against you.

MARINER To dream that you are a sailor is a sign of restlessness and change in your affairs. But to dream that you are in the company of sailors shows news from a distance, the arrival of some friend.

MARKET To dream of being at a market denotes that you will shortly have difficulty in disposing of something you want to sell, but if in your dream you are with other people you will succeed in your attempt after a while.

MARMALADE To dream that you are eating preserves by yourself is a bad sign, though it does not foretell great trouble or worry. To enjoy it with others is a fortunate omen. To dream that you are making marmalade is good for your love affairs.

MARRIAGE To dream you are married signifies sickness or melancholy, misfortune or even death. If a man dreams he is married to an ugly woman, that signifies death or some unhappiness; if to an attractive woman, that denotes joy and profit. To dream you marry your sister signifies danger. To dream you marry a wife signifies loss and sometimes death. For a sick person to dream of marriage is a sign of deterioration. To dream you help at a wedding is the forerunner of good news and great success. To dream of lying with your newly married husband or wife threatens danger or sudden misfortunes, and also that you will lose a part of your property; to the sailor it indicates storms and shipwrecks, with a narrow escape from death. It is extremely unlucky for a young woman to dream that she is married when she is not. She will be crossed in love, and lose all faith in the opposite sex.

MARSH This is another obstacle dream, and its meaning depends upon what happens to you – trouble and difficulties if you find it hard to move along. But if you get out all right onto firm ground, then you will be able to put right most of the misfortune.

MARSHMALLOWS Your heart will be melted by a dark stranger.

MASK To dream of a man in a mask indicates that the word of one of your friends in whom you place implicit confidence is not quite to be relied on.

MASS To dream you go to mass signifies honour and joy to the dreamer.

MASSAGE To dream of being massaged indicates enjoyment but potential loss.

MAST To dream of the mast of a ship is considered to be

a sign of a coming journey of importance.

MASTER If you dream of your employer, it is a favourable omen for your prosperity.

MASTIFF Beware of false suspicions if you see a big dog in your dream. If he bites you, it is a warning of trouble in your love affairs. But if a woman dreams of a mastiff, it is a sign that her lover is faithful to her.

MAT To dream of a mat, either in a room or at the door, is held to indicate trouble.

MATCH It means good luck in love to strike a match in a dream.

MATHEMATICS Even if you cannot solve the mathematical problem in your dream, you will succeed in overcoming your difficulties.

MATTRESS A warning of poverty ahead; guard against it.

MAY An unfortunate dream; disappointment and bad news are indicated.

MAYPOLE Joy and happiness. Sign of festivities.

MAZE Should you find your way out in your dream, your perplexities will be happily solved. If you are unable to get out, beware of being dominated by insincere friends.

MEADOW To dream of being in a meadow is a good sign to farmers and shepherds, but to others it denotes business problems. To walk through a meadow, especially in the evening, is a good omen. It announces the approach of a happy interview which may make a favourable change in your fortunes.

MEAL To dream you are eating a good meal signifies meanness and poverty. Judge the opposite if there is nothing for you to eat.

MEASLES If anyone dreams they have the measles, it denotes they will gain profit and wealth.

MEASURING A warning not to carry carefulness to the point of stinginess or you may lose more than you save.

MEAT To eat roast meat signifies falling into sin. To see the meat you have eaten signifies loss.

MEDALS To dream of wearing medals signifies merry times are to come soon.

MEDICINE To dream you prescribe medicines signifies profit and happiness. To dream you give or take medicine signifies loss of money and living in poverty. Unless you make a change in your present situation you will have to swallow a great deal that is disagreeable, and put up with a great deal that might be resented, if you are to become a success in life. If the medicine is bitter you will overcome your enemies.

MEDITERRANEAN SEA To visit towns on the shores of this sea indicates prosperity in the future.

MEDIUM If you visit a medium in your dream you will learn something which may or may not be to your advantage.

MEDLARS Your enjoyment will cease and trouble ensue.

MELANCHOLY A dream of contrary. All will go well.

MELODY All pleasant music is a fortunate omen. Persevere and success will attend you.

MELON For a sick person to dream of melons is considered by some to be an indication of recovery.

MEMORY Loss of memory in a dream presages a rise in the world shortly.

MENAGERIE To dream that you visit an exhibition of wild animals means peace at home and greater friendship with your acquaintances. Someone you love will want to emigrate and nothing that you say to dissuade them will have any effect.

MENDING To dream of darning clothes portends an inferior and miserable position.

MENDICANT This is a dream of contrary meaning. If you dream that you are reduced to begging in the streets, it shows that your affairs are prospering. To dream that you are accosted in the street by a beggar is a sign of difficulty ahead; if you assist the person, you will overcome your trouble by means of a good friend who will help you.

MERMAID For a married person to dream of seeing a mermaid is a sign that either they or some of their neighbours will have a child that will be quite different from the usual run of children, either for better or for worse.

MERRIMENT All excessive enjoyment in a dream is a bad omen. Expect difficulties in your home life.

MESMERISM To dream you are mesmerised is a sign of betrayed confidences. Make none and you need not fear.

MESSAGE To dream a message is given you means a change to a better position.

METALS To dream of gold indicates trouble ahead, but there will be no immediate change. You will have time to put things right. To dream of silver indicates a disappointment in love that will not prove as unpleasant as you anticipate. To dream of copper coins is an indication of small but vexatious worries.

METEOR After dreaming of a meteor you may expect all sorts of trouble and loss.

MICROSCOPE Increase of family.

MIDWIFE A midwife means secrets and problems will be revealed. It sometimes means death.

MIGNONETTE To see and smell this fragrant little plant is a good sign. Your life for the future will be full of gladness, you will have many good friends, your health will be sound, and you will have plenty of good food; you will also have plenty of holidays.

MILDEW An introduction to an attractive stranger in your own home. Be careful of your private papers.

MILESTONE To dream of a milestone signifies the end of considerable problems.

MILK To dream you are selling milk denotes that you will be crossed in love, and that you will be unsuccessful in business. To dream you are drinking milk is an extraordinarily good sign and the forerunner of good news and great success. If you are giving milk away, it shows you will be successful in love, marry happily, have children and do very well. To see milk flowing from the breasts of a woman denotes success in trade, that you will have many children, and that they will become rich by the hard work of their parents.

It is bad luck to dream of spilling milk, for that indicates scattered fortunes, bankruptcy and on the whole a melancholy and dismal future.

MILK PAILS To dream of carrying full milk pails is a sign of good news concerning a birth.

MILKY WAY You will gain your educational ambitions.

MILL To dream of a mill signifies that you will inherit a fortune.

MILLET To see the land sown with millet signifies vast riches to be easily gained.

MILLIONAIRE For a young woman to dream that she marries a millionaire is a sign that when the wedding does come off it will be a union with a man who has been wealthy, but who has lost his money. He will be intelligent, however, and do well in business.

MILLSTONE To dream of a millstone signifies an increase of family.

MINCE PIES To dream you eat or make them indicates your wedding or that you will go to one.

MINE Your business will increase.

MINISTER It is not a good sign to see a minister in your dream. Expect a serious disappointment.

MINSTREL   You will meet a surprising new companion.

MINT   To the sick, recovery; to those in good health, better spirits.

MIRACLE   Unexpected events will astonish and occupy you for some little while.

MIRAGE   To dream of a mirage in the desert signifies the loss of the one friend in whom you have trusted.

MIRE   To dream you wade in a mire predicts toil and trouble, but your perseverance will avail and you will overcome the obstacles.

MIRROR   For a girl to dream of a mirror is a sign that she is in danger of being too vain and neglecting her intellect. It is ominous of future unhappiness, especially if dreamed on a Sunday. For a young man, dreaming of a mirror means personal appearance will be important to his job.

MISER   To dream of being a miser indicates that you will grow rich if you only confine yourself to one enterprise, and exercise a proper economy and control over that.

MISFORTUNE   This dream indicates prosperity, and a happy life.

MISSIONARY   A change to more interesting work and to truer friends. Do not be made unhappy by the desertion of a fickle companion.

MIST   A warning of difficulties which will beset your path owing to bad trade conditions.

MISTAKE   Avoid conceit and make sure of your information before acting. Take counsel of those who are willing to guide you.

MISTLETOE   Take no chances of any kind. You are not in favour with fortune.

MOAN   Be on your guard against doubtful friends, or dubious actions.

MOCKING   Take care not to be swindled. You will be asked to assist others. Do not neglect your own affairs while trying to settle those of others.

MOLE   To dream of a mole signifies that your work will be in vain. Be careful to whom you tell your secrets, otherwise you will find them broadcast.

MOLLUSC Mysterious happenings will claim your attention. There is usually an explanation of the uncanny. Do not believe too easily all you hear.

MONARCH To dream of your sovereign ruler is a sign of difficulties which can be overcome by hard work. Keep at it, and all will go well.

MONASTERY Worldly affairs will prosper.

MONEY If you dream that you have found gold and do not know where to hide it, or that you have found a purse of money and are afraid of being arrested with it, it means that someone of the opposite sex will cause you to lose money. To dream that you are paying money foretells the birth of a son destined to cut a great figure in life. To dream you pick up loose change from the ground denotes want and hard work, but if a large sum is put into your hands it shows that you will receive some money unexpectedly or will be relieved by a friend. A person who dreams of making a present of a sum of money to a stranger will soon have a valuable find. To see a lot of money and not touch it foretells quarrelling and

deceit. If you dream you lose money, it is a proof you will be deceived in love and be unsuccessful in some favourite pursuit.

MONEY LENDER A dream of a money lender is significant of bad luck.

MONK As with others connected with the church, this is an omen of disappointment and trouble.

MONKEY To an engaged person this animal denotes a speedy marriage. A married person who dreams of seeing a monkey will soon be rejoicing over some domestic event.

MONSTER To dream of monsters signifies the vain hopes of things which will never happen. To dream you see a monster in the sea is not good. But every fish and a great monster seen out of the sea is good.

MONUMENT Any handsome monument is a good omen. Success is coming your way, as a reward of effort.

MOON To dream you see the moon shine signifies that your partner loves you and is healthy; it also denotes that you will come into silver. To dream you see the moon darkened signifies the death or sickness of a female in your family; it can also mean loss of money, or danger on a journey, especially by water; or an illness in the brain or eyes. To dream you see the moon darkened and then grow clear and bright again signifies profit, joy and prosperity; the moon first clear and afterwards clouded indicates the opposite. To dream you see the moon in the form of a full white face signifies speedy marriage or a handsome daughter. Such a dream is prosperous to goldsmiths, merchants, jewellers and bankers. To dream you see the full moon is a good sign except for people who conceal themselves, such as criminals, for they will be discovered. It also signifies death to the sick or to sailors. To dream the moon shines on your bed signifies grace, pardon and deliverance by means of a woman. To dream you see the moon pale is joyfulness. To see the moon fall from the sky signifies sickness. To see the moon decrease signifies the death of a powerful woman. To see the moon dyed with blood signifies travel or a pilgrimage. To see the moon darkened signifies sadness. To see the new moon signifies a business

trip. To see two moons appear is increase of reputation. To see the sun and the moon fall together is a bad sign. To dream of moons battling in the sky signifies divisions among near friends and relatives.

MOONSHINE Happiness in wedded life is indicated. A devoted family will be yours.

MOOR To walk over moorlands signifies prosperity, especially should the way lie uphill.

MOP You will need forethought and carefulness to avoid coming trouble.

MORNING An excellent sign. Your fate is protected from evil. Be confident.

MOSQUE You will become more concerned with your spiritual well-being.

MOSS Take care of your correspondence. Write guardedly; seal and post carefully. Someone has an attraction towards you which will soon be expressed.

MOTH To see a number of moths flying around the flame of a candle, then flying into the flame and falling, is a sign that you had better be on your guard as a deception is about to be practised upon you. A grand scheme for making money will be presented to you, which will be described in glowing terms, but if you look into it you will see that those who float the new company or scheme have an eye to filling their pockets at the expense of dupes. Do not enter into any scheme without careful consideration, or you may buy your own experience at a very high price and become both wiser and poorer.

MOTH-EATEN CLOTHES Someone near to you is in trouble of which you will soon hear, but may not be able to assist.

MOTHER To dream you see your mother is a sign of some agreeable adventure about to happen to you, and that you will hear from a friend abroad. To dream you lie with your mother signifies completion of business. To dream you see your mother living signifies joy. To see her dead signifies misfortune.

MOTHER-IN-LAW You will need to exercise patience and tact when dealing with other people.

MOTHER-OF-PEARL Your happiest times lie in the future.

MOTHER'S MILK For a young woman to see in a dream that she has milk in her breasts signifies that she will conceive and give birth to a child. To an old woman it signifies riches; to a girl, that her marriage is near.

To a poor man it means plenty of money and possessions by which he will help others, but to travellers it signifies sickness.

MOTOR If the motor in your dream is working well, you will make progress, but if it is broken you will have problems ahead.

MOTOR CAR If you are riding in one, new surroundings are portended.

MOTOR CYCLE Do not be careless in your sexual encounters.

MOULTING You would be wise to cut doubtful associations and make fresh ties. A small invitation will give you the opportunity to make worthwhile friendships.

MOUNTAIN To dream you are at the top of a very high mountain signifies honour. To dream you travel over high hills and rocky mountains signifies advancement, obtained with much difficulty. If you meet anyone who directs you the right way, a friend will help you. You are either having, or are going to have, a great struggle, but you will get the better of all your troubles, and your life will become as happy as before it was desolate. To dream of descending a mountain, however, denotes a change in your affairs for the worse.

MOURNER To dream of a mourner denotes the death of a friend.

MOURNING To dream of being dressed in mourning is a lucky omen, as it foreshadows joy and prosperity. To the young it indicates that they will shortly be happily married. The married person who dreams that he or she is dressed in mourning will lead a joyful and prosperous life for some time to come.

MOUSE To dream of a mouse or mice means that someone will try to interfere with your business affairs, and will not be shaken off except by the most vigorous measures. However, you may look forward to hearing some good news which will be to your benefit.

MOUSTACHE Small disagreements are indicated. Do not let them deepen into trouble.

MOUTH If anyone dreams their mouth is wider than usual, their family will become rich. If anyone dreams that their mouth has closed up in such a way that they cannot open it, they are in danger of a sudden death.

MOVING Be careful after dreaming that you are moving from one house to another. It is indicative of enemies who will do their best to cause you some serious loss.

MOWING To dream that you are mowing grass foretells a gain of money, and conveys a warning that someone will try to cheat and rob you of it.

MUD To dream of mud foretells that you will soon be hearing good news which will make a big change in your life for the better.

MUDDLE Look to your footing, especially in high places. Take no risks of a fall. Pleasure from a re-established friendship is indicated.

MUFF To dream of a muff warns you to beware of inconstancy.

MULBERRY The person who dreams of eating this fruit will soon have to undertake a journey which will prove most advantageous to their position.

MULE To dream of a mule signifies bad news of a lawsuit; if you are riding on one it either signifies that you will never be married or that you will be childless.

MULTIPLYING Do not trust acquaintances till time has proved them.

MUMMY Be confident. Success is not far off.

MURDER To dream you murder a man signifies success in business. To dream you kill your father is a bad sign. To dream you see a murder shows poverty and sadness. You will live a long life in spite of many trials and difficulties.

MUSEUM Your social life will be fascinating and your opportunities will expand.

MUSHROOMS To dream of gathering mushrooms foretells that several little surprises await you.

MUSIC To dream you hear beautiful music is a very favourable omen as it indicates happy news from a long-absent friend; to married people it denotes good-tempered children; in love, it shows that your sweetheart is very fond of you, and is good-tempered, sincere and faithful. Rough and discordant music foretells trouble, vexation and disappointment.

MUSIC HALL A good omen for later life. Your circumstances will improve.

MUSICIAN If you dream that you are a musician when this is not the case, it is supposed to show a sudden change in your life. Probably you will move to another district. If you really are a musician, amateur or professional, then the dream is of no importance.

MUSTARD To dream you see or eat mustard seed is a bad sign, unless you are a doctor.

MUTINY Your undertakings will lead you into odd company. Keep your promises, but avoid making rash ones.

MYRTLE To dream of myrtle indicates a love vow.

MYSTERY Some happening that puzzles and disturbs you is really an obstacle dream. Solve the mystery, and all will be well.

MYSTIC Your mind is set on worldly matters. Allow your interests to broaden and you will be happy.

NAGGING To dream of being nagged signifies that you will be the recipient of pleasing information. Be careful in whom you confide it.

NAIL To dream of knocking nails into a wall or some article you are making is a sign that all your life you will have to rely on your own endeavours, and it will be as well if you work hard while you are young so that you have something to fall back on later in life.

If anyone dreams that their nails are longer than usual, that signifies profit, riches, prosperity, success in love, a good industrious husband or wife, with dutiful children; it also foretells that you will suddenly receive a sum of money that will be very useful.

The contrary indicates loss and discontent. If anyone dreams that their fingertips or nails have been cut off, that signifies loss, disgrace and arguments with their relations and friends. If anyone dreams that their nails have been pulled off

they are threatened by all sorts of misery and affliction and are also in danger of death. To dream you bite your nails signifies arguments and annoyance.

NAKEDNESS To dream you see a naked man signifies fear and terror. To dream you see a naked woman signifies honour and joy, provided she is fair, clear skinned and beautiful. But if on the contrary you dream you see a naked woman who is old, wrinkled or ugly, that signifies shame, repentence and bad luck. But if a man dreams he sees a woman painted, the luck will not be as bad. If you see a naked woman painted or in a beautiful statue of marble, gold, silver or brass, that signifies good luck and success in business. If a husband dreams he sees his wife naked, it signifies deceit. If a wife dreams she sees her husband naked, it signifies assurance and success in her enterprises. To dream you see a whore naked signifies peril and danger by the craft and deceit of that woman. To dream you see a friend naked signifies arguments. To dream that a man sees himself naked signifies sickness or poverty, and most commonly shame by means of some other person. To dream you are naked in a bath with a person you fancy signifies joy, pleasure and health. If a woman dreams that she is stark naked in her husband's arms, that indicates sadness to her by bad news. But when the husband has the same dream, it signifies happiness and profit. If you dream you are in bed with someone you do not like, it predicts sickness or dis-content. To dream that a man is naked in bed with a beau-tiful woman signifies deceit; and with a handsome man, pain, trouble, loss, damage and deceit. To dream you are stark naked signifies loss and damage to your property. To dream that you are naked in church is bad. For a girl to dream she sees a naked man shows that she will quickly fall in love, be married, and have many male children who will be great cowards.

NAME If someone calls you by the wrong name in a dream, it is an unfortunate omen for your love affairs.

NAP You will not be short of money.

NAPKIN Some unpleasant news is coming to you soon.

NAPOLEON You will be restless and dissatisfied for some time.

NARCISSUS A happy future is certain for those who dream of these beautiful early flowers. But the luck will be lessened if you dream that they are indoors, in pots, or cut and in a bowl. For the best result they should be growing in a garden.

NARROW Struggling along a narrow path in a dream means that every effort will be required to lead you to success, but that you will attain it when almost despairing.

NAUSEA You will be suspected of theft. Be careful of those who would lie about you.

NAVAL BATTLE To dream that you witness a naval battle is a sign that you will have more than one relative on board a naval vessel. They will prosper in their situations, and be distinguished in the service.

NAVEL If you dream you have a severe pain in your navel you will receive bad news of your father and mother, who will be in danger of death; if you have neither father or mother, you will lose any money you inherited from them or be forced to leave your native country.

NAVIGATION If you dream you are sailing in a boat, you will have comfort and success in your affairs, but if the water is rough it means the opposite. To dream of being in danger of overturning or shipwreck is a sign of danger.

NAVY Dreams of the navy foretell troubles in love.

NECK The neck signifies power, honour, wealth and inheritances. To dream that the neck has become larger than usual but not deformed means you will be well known for good deeds, and grow richer. A slender neck signifies the opposite. To dream that someone is trying to strangle you is a bad sign and the dreamer will be injured in some way by that person. To dream that you have a crick in your neck so that you hold your neck on one side is a sign of misfortune, shame and loss. To dream your neck is swollen signifies sickness. To dream you have three heads on one neck signifies domination, power and reputation.

NECKLACE To dream of wearing an expensive necklace is an unfortunate sign for a woman, denoting that she will probably have more money than happiness. To dream of breaking a necklace is still worse, since it signifies that she may in the end experience poverty and neglect. To dream that you have received a necklace as a present foretells that you will not always be content with your lot; you will aspire to higher things. If you are wearing a necklace and it is particularly gorgeous, be careful you are not led astray by someone who, while protesting great friendship, is really jealous of you.

NEEDLE For a girl to dream of using a needle denotes that she is of an industrious nature, and will reap the rewards of her hard work. Her husband and children will praise her as she will ensure their comfort and success.

NEGATIVE Photographic negatives are good omens of your ability to foresee and avert danger. You will need your powers.

NEIGH The neighing of a horse foretells serious illness for someone dear to you. To a business person it denotes a falling off of business.

NEIGHBOUR To dream you see your neighbours at the street corner gossiping is a sign that you will be the subject of a practical joke, in which you will lose your temper and make yourself more ridiculous than if you took the matter calmly.

NEPHEW Your family will bring you many happy hours.

NERVOUSNESS The solution of a puzzle will occur to you after long thought and bring you great good luck.

NEST To dream of seeing a nest with neither eggs nor young birds in it means that you will marry someone with nothing to recommend them but their industry. A nest full of eggs foretells gain and profit.

NET To dream you see fishing nets signifies rain and change of weather.

NETTLE To dream of stinging yourself on a nettle shows that you will work hard to achieve your ambitions.

NEW YEAR An improvement in circumstances is at hand. You have an unscrupulous rival;

be careful of your confidences.

NEWS Receiving good news in a dream indicates good fortune, but bad news means trouble.

NEWSPAPER To dream of reading a newspaper indicates that an expected letter is sure to arrive, though its content will not be to your liking. You may expect someone to deceive you.

NIB Not a good sign; if you dream of breaking it, misfortune is portended.

NIBBLING Be careful what you write or sign and you will find that all your good times are to come.

NICKNAME To dream either that you are being called by a nickname, or that you yourself are calling someone by theirs, is an educational dream, since it is a lesson that if you are too straightforward you will upset other people. Exercise a little tact.

NIECE Mutual affection and assistance between you and a relation.

NIGHT Dreaming of the approach of night means that you are about to lose something of great value, and not to recover it again for a long time, if ever. If you are walking on a dark night it indicates grief and disappointment as well as financial loss.

NIGHT BIRD   To dream of any kind of night bird, such as the owl, is ominous.

NIGHT WALKS   To dream of walking in the night signifies trouble.

NIGHTCAP   For a girl to dream that she is wearing a nightcap in company is a sign that she will be kissed by a strange gentleman, or that a stranger will fall in love with her.

If a married woman dreams this it foretells that her husband will be jealous of her, and perhaps not without cause.

NIGHTINGALE   This is a bird of good fortune, and to dream of it is a good omen sometimes meaning a successful marriage, at other times a contented home and great prosperity in business.

It is the forerunner of good news, a success in business, plentiful crops and of a sweet-tempered lover. For a married woman to dream of a nightingale shows that she will have children who will be great singers.

NIGHTMARE   To dream of having a nightmare is a sign that you will be domineered over by a fool.

NIGHTSHADE   To dream you eat the fruits of this deadly plant is a favourable dream, meaning new interests and surroundings.

NINEPINS   To dream that you are playing ninepins or skittles is a sign that your affairs are unsettled; you will experience many ups and downs in the next few weeks. There may be a disappointment in love.

NOBLE   To dream you talk with great lords and nobles, or go anywhere with them, signifies honour.

NOISE   To dream you hear strange noises signifies that your position will be influenced by someone who is dying.

NOOSE   Obstacles and competition will come your way; you must hold your own.

NORTH   To dream of a journey towards the north or of being in northern places signifies an uphill struggle for you which will end in a great success.

NOSE   If anyone dreams their nose is larger than

usual, they will become rich and powerful and will be provident and subtle, but to dream of losing their nose signifies the contrary. To dream you have two noses signifies quarrels. If anyone dreams that their nose has grown large and deformed, they will live in prosperity, but never gain the love of people.

If anyone dreams their nose is blocked so that they cannot smell, they are in danger of being deceived by their partner who will commit adultery with one of their friends.

To dream you take hold of your nose signifies fornication. To dream you have a large, attractive nose is good to anyone except a sick person.

NOSE BLEED This is not a good sign. Take good care of yourself.

NOSEGAY Gathering a nosegay, giving or receiving one, are all three favourable dreams and should put the dreamers on good terms with themselves and with the rest of the world. They all point to long-continued happiness and prosperity unless some of the flowers are withered, in which case occasional troubles may be expected.

NOVEL To dream that you are reading a light novel is a sign that you will become a favourite in the company of many of the young people in the neighbourhood where you live. If the novel is a very serious one you will be of a very retiring and sullen character and will not gain many friends.

NUDITY Your love affairs will be passionate.

NUGGET An excellent omen of riches and honour.

NUISANCE Disagreeable news and unhappiness is forecast.

NUMBER To count the number of persons present in your dream foretells power, satisfied ambition, and dignity. Lucky numbers are: 3, 7, 9, 11 and 17.

NUMBNESS To dream that you feel numb is generally a matter of physical health; it is not an omen in itself. Consult a doctor.

NUN These sisters of mercy are always associated with black, which is not a fortunate omen in a dream. Be careful of the motives of the people around you, for you are liable to be deceived.

NURSE To dream that you are a nurse is a sign that you will end your days in peace and happiness at a ripe old age. The girl who dreams she has become a Red Cross nurse and is tending wounded soldiers in the battle line will become famous by some deed of heroism performed in her everyday life.

NURSERY To dream that you spend some time in a nursery means that you will not be fond of children, but will avoid them and only be fit for the company of old people. You will be rather short-tempered and fidgety when the least thing goes wrong with you; you will magnify any problems and a molehill of trouble will be made to look like a mountain.

NURSING To dream you are nursing a sick friend is a sign that you will meet that friend strong and well when you least expect to do so. Should your patient be a stranger, you will experience a great deal of trouble by offending a person of the opposite sex. To dream that your soldier lover has been wounded in battle and that you are nursing him back to health and strength to fight again is a sign that he will be promoted on the field for some deed of bravery, probably for rescuing a comrade or an officer under fire.

NUT If you see clusters of nuts, it denotes riches and happiness; to the lover, success, and a good-tempered sweetheart. If you are gathering them, it is not a good omen, for you will pursue an action that will not turn out to your advantage. If you crack them, your lover will treat you with indifference, and be very unfaithful. To dream of eating nuts is a sign that you will succeed in solving many difficult problems, and become distinguished for wisdom and common sense.

NUT TREE To dream you see a nut tree and that you eat the fruit signifies riches and content, gained through hard work. To find nuts that have been hidden signifies you will find some treasure.

NUTMEG A probable change in your business will lead to travel overland.

NUTSHELLS You will rise to an influential position. If you should dream of stepping on and smashing them, the omen is even luckier.

NYMPH You will experience a strange occurrence out of doors.

OAK To see a stately oak signifies riches, profit and a long life. If in your dream you see an oak felled to the ground it signifies losses.

OAR If you dream of being in a boat and losing one or more of the oars it is a sign of the death of your father, mother or of someone to whom you look for protection; if an engaged young girl or a married woman dreams this it foretells of the death of a lover or husband.

OASIS To dream of wandering in a desert and finding an oasis is a sign of one friend on whose help you can always rely.

OATH A comfortable salary and a good position will be yours.

OATMEAL To dream of either seeing, handling or eating oatmeal means that you will all through life discover that 'economy is the best reve-nue', and that by the exercise of judicious thrift you will attain to a position of respect.

OBELISK You will move from your present surroundings and meet with better luck and new friends elsewhere.

OBESITY Beware of over-indulgence.

OBEYING You have an admirer who is seriously attracted. Do not be depressed by sad tidings from a distance, brighter days are in store.

OBITUARY To dream that you read in the columns of a newspaper an account of the death of a friend is a sign that you will soon read of the wedding of a friend who said they would never marry.

OBLIGATION It is not a good sign to dream that you are under an obligation to someone, or that someone is doing you a good turn.

OBSERVATORY To dream that you visit an observatory to view the stars or for astronomical study is a sign that you will be fond of solitude and retirement and be devoted to a study such as geometry, which will require close application.

OCEAN Should you see a calm ocean in a dream you may infer that your circumstances for the present will continue without change or disturbance, but should the sea be stormy you can expect that your life will shortly become unsettled. It is unlucky to dream you swim, walk on or catch fish in the ocean. But it is nevertheless lucky to dream of the ocean to anyone about to go on a journey.

OCCUPATION To dream of doing work you detest means good fortune in every way.

OCULIST You are being watched; do not be ensnared by people who would like to harm you.

ODOUR Fragrant scents signify contentment; unpleasant odours mean vexation.

OFFENCE To dream you have given offence, or that you have had cause for taking offence, indicates that a friendship will probably grow before long into a warmer attachment.

OFFER It is considered fortunate if someone makes a good offer for your services in your dream. Expect an improvement in your position, but you must work hard.

OFFICE To dream you are turned out of your office foretells loss of property.

OFFICER To dream of an officer signifies anger and authority.

OGRE To dream of imaginary monsters is not a good sign. Difficulties and obstacles will come between you and your dearest wish.

OIL If you dream you perfume your head with oils, it signifies you are vain and conceited. After dreaming of oil look after your money. If you have any investments take steps to see that they are safe and, above all, be careful not to lend any money for some time to come. Whoever borrows from you will have no intention of paying you back.

OINTMENT To dream you make an ointment signifies anxiety and trouble. It is a forewarning of coming trivial illnesses, but nothing serious.

OLD BUILDINGS A dream of old buildings is a forewarning of danger.

OLD CLOTHES A dream of old clothes denotes that someone holds you in contempt.

To dream of wearing old-fashioned clothes signifies dissension in your home life. Be firm, but not angry.

OLD PERSONS Honour awaits the person who dreams that he or she has grown very old.

For a woman to dream that she is being courted by an old man is a fortunate omen; her lover will prove faithful and all that she can desire.

For a man to dream that he is courting, or married to, an old woman is a very fortunate omen for his business enterprises. All will go well. To see old people, without any question of loving them, is fortunate, but in a small and trifling manner. Some unimportant wish will be gratified.

OLD SWEETHEART This presages a return to familiar occupations and surroundings; sometimes a proposal is on its way from someone you knew long ago.

OLIVE and OLIVE TREE If anyone dreams they see or smell an olive, it indicates marriage, children, happiness, prosperity, abundance and success in business. To dream you see an olive tree with olives denotes peace, delight, harmony, freedom, dignity and fulfilment of your desires. To dream of gathering olives off the ground signifies hard work. To dream of eating olives indicates that you will be called upon to undertake a morally distasteful duty.

ONION To dream of this vegetable denotes a mixture of good and bad luck; if you are eating them, you will receive some money, recover something lost or stolen, or discover a hidden treasure; your lover will be faithful, but of a cross temper. You are about to have a quarrel with someone whose influence you need, and it will all begin about nothing. It also denotes attacks of thieves and a failure of crops; it shows that you will be engaged in some disagreeable quarrels, perhaps with your own family. If you are throwing onions away it is the forerunner of quarrels; if you are in love, you will fall out with your sweetheart; if you are in trade, you will quarrel with your customers and employees. If you are gathering onions, it indicates the recovery of a sick person in your family; the receipt of some unexpected good news and a quick removal from your present situation.

ONYX You will change your mind.

OPAL Good luck should follow a dream in which an opal figures. To a person engaged to be married it promises a happy life.

OPERA For an unmarried person to dream that they are at the opera with their lover is a sign that the lover will try to blind them to character faults by flattery and boasting. To a married person the dream is a sign that they will have cause for serious complaint regarding their spouse's attentions to others unless they do more to retain their love.

OPERATION It is an obstacle dream if you imagine that you are undergoing an operation. Success will come to you if no trouble comes in the dream. It is, however, considered a sign of unexpected news if you watch an operation performed on someone else. Neither of these meanings would apply in the case of a nurse or doctor.

OPIUM Worries, bad news from the sea or serious illness of someone dear to you is portended by this dream.

OPTICIAN To dream of buying spectacles means that you have not seen a good chance until it has gone by.

ORANG-UTAN A cruel enemy will seek to destroy you.

ORANGE To dream that you see or eat oranges signifies wounds, grief and anxiety, loss of goods and reputation, burglaries and unfaithful lovers. It indicates jealousy and bad temper to lovers. For people in business it is also a bad dream, meaning losses of various kinds and a serious diminution of profits for the current year. To dream of eating a sour orange, however, is a sign of happiness.

The colour orange indicates that your affairs will not change for some time.

ORANGE BLOSSOM Nothing could be more unlucky than for a single woman to dream of this bridal decoration. It denotes disappointment in love and marriage. To a married person the dream comes as a sign that trouble and sickness will enter the house.

ORATORY To dream of listening to an orator signifies a scolding.

ORCHARD This signifies that you will marry a discreet and beautiful wife and that you will have very attractive children. Although you will have many small cares, no serious trouble will spoil your happiness.

ORCHESTRA To dream that you hear or see an orchestra playing is an omen of bad news already on its way to you.

ORGAN To hear the music of a church organ is a forewarning that you will have a serious illness, which will make you alter your life considerably. To dream that you are playing a church organ, however, is indicative of fair dealing and honesty. Should you see a church organ without hearing any music, you will hear bad news from a friend whom you have recently visited.

ORGY Be more careful of the company you keep.

ORIENT To dream of oriental people or countries is an omen of romantic happiness which will not prove lasting. Do not be too absorbed in it.

ORNAMENT To dream that you see a great number of ornaments is a sign that in spite of all your thrift you will be able to just keep your head above water financially. You will have many debts and financial problems. To dream that you buy a number of ornaments is a sign that you will suffer financial hardship because of your extravagance.

ORPHAN Whoever dreams of an orphan will receive profits and riches from a stranger.

OSTEOPATH Beware of accidents.

OSTRICH To see this bird in your dreams is a sign that you are inclined to be conceited. Unless you think less of yourself and more of others you will have a serious fall socially.

OTTER To dream that you see an otter is a sign that you will be the subject of intense spite of people you have long thought to be your best friends. You will experience not only slighting remarks, but expressions of positive hatred from some of your relatives or those you thought had some affection for you. Your feelings will be hurt, as you never had a bad thought of those friends before.

OTTOMAN This is not considered a good omen for love affairs or domestic life. Troubles are in store in your personal life.

OVEN To dream you see an oven foretells that you are about to be separated from your family by changing your present home; it also shows you an attack by thieves and that your sweetheart is flighty and unlikely to make you happy. To dream of kindling a fire easily in an oven or hearth is a sign of generation, but for it to go out straight after lighting it signifies injury. To dream of cooking in an oven is meant to convey the fact that nothing can be done well without preparation, and to indicate that your affairs will prosper as long as you continue to exercise hard work and intelligence.

OVERALLS To dream of working in overalls signifies that you will be well repaid for a small kindness. To tear them means ill-luck.

OVERBOARD To dream that you have fallen into the water from some boat or vessel is a sign of misfortune. Do not speculate, or you will lose your money. But to the sailor or anyone professionally connected with the water, this becomes a dream of contrary and foretells prosperity.

OVERCOAT To dream of an overcoat is a sign that the time will come when you will suffer great shame and remorse and will try to hide from your friends and relatives. Be prepared for considerable change in your life.

OVERFLOWING An excellent omen of financial success.

OVERTAKING This means advancement in position and the good influence of one whom you have known on or by the sea.

OVERTURNED If you dream you are overturned while riding it is a sign that you will be greatly distressed for a short time.

OVERWORK A difference in your life either in your feelings or your business.

OWL To dream of night birds such as the owl is a bad omen, and those who dream of such birds must undertake no business on that day. This bird denotes poverty and misfortune, although to an unmarried person it also indicates that they will one day marry a clever person who will possibly give them an easy life. For the young it predicts that they are in danger of marrying someone stupid. For the middle-aged and the old it denotes the approach of poverty.

OXEN To dream you have the horns of an ox denotes anger, pride, or violent death by the hand of justice. To dream you feed oxen is a good sign. To see fat oxen signifies a fruitful year. Lean oxen signify scarcity of provisions and famine. To see oxen ploughing in the field signifies gain. To see black oxen signifies danger. To see oxen drinking is a bad sign.

OYSTERS To dream that you are eating oysters is a very favourable omen; if you are married, your wife or husband will be very fond of you, and you will have many children. To an unmarried man it denotes that his future wife will be very fond of him, and they will have many children. If you are in trade your business will increase very fast, and you will become rich; if you are a farmer, you will have plentiful crops. For a girl to dream of eating oysters shows that she will soon be married to a young man who will do well by hard work, and they will have many children. To dream that you have difficulty opening oysters is a sign that by your own endeavours alone you will obtain much enjoyment late in life. To dream that you are eating oysters is an omen of good health.

PACIFIC To dream of this ocean foretells successful investments.

PACKET A disappointment is in front of you – work hard or you will have to face trouble. The bigger the packet that comes to you, the greater the trouble. It is a good sign if you open the packet.

PACKING To dream that you are packing luggage for a journey indicates that you will never see much of the world. You will be a home bird rather than a traveller. To dream that you are packing a present to send to a friend is a sign that you will shortly receive a communication from a person you have not seen for some years.

PADDOCK Do not speculate or you will most likely lose; news of an engagement will surprise you.

PADLOCK The person who dreams of a padlock will never have much valuable property to guard, although

he will probably never be in real financial trouble.

PAGEANT A warning against judging by appearances or paying too much attention to outward things.

PAGODA A journey will be cancelled through sudden news.

PAIL An unfortunate omen; be careful of your new business ventures.

PAIN To dream that your shoulders are painful or swollen signifies trouble and displeasure from relations. If you dream your stomach aches, you will have family problems. If you dream you have a severe pain at your navel you will receive bad news of your father and mother, who will be in danger of death. If you have neither father nor mother, you will lose the money or property they left to you or will be forced to leave your native country. If you dream you have a pain in your heart, it is a sign of some dangerous illness approaching, according to the proportion of the imagined pain.

PAINTING To dream you see your picture painted signifies long life. To see tapestry or pictures signifies treachery and deceit. To dream of painting your house is a sign of sickness in the family, but at the same time thrift and good luck in business. If you see a white house newly painted outside, you will probably have to attend a funeral; to see any other coloured house newly painted indicates that you will hear of the sickness of a friend or relative. Dreaming of beautiful paintings of landscapes, portraits, etc. is an omen of bad luck and poverty.

PALACE If you dream you are in a palace or see one from outside you will experience a shock which will temporarily injure your health. To dream of living in a palace signifies that you are about to experience a change of circumstances for the better.

PALL Probably a legacy and great sadness through bereavement will come to you.

PALLID To dream of seeing the face of anyone you know very pale presages danger, perhaps death, to that person.

PALM To dream you hold or smell a palm means that a woman will have children, a girl will soon be married, or a man will find happiness, prosperity, abundance and success in his business. To dream you are gathering palms denotes plenty, money and success in undertakings, and is a very good omen indeed.

PAN To dream of the god Pan indicates that you should use your sense of humour to overcome problems.

PANCAKE To dream of eating a pancake is a good omen both for business and love. The woman who dreams of cooking pancakes will rule her home and have few troubles to contend with.

PANIC Do not lose your temper over constructive criticism.

PANSY Denotes modesty of spirit. You are too bashful to rise much in life, but you will be happy and stand high in other persons' esteem.

PANTHER An acquaintance will cause you misfortune unless you scare away the animal in your dream.

PANTOMIME Beware of joking with one of your friends who is of a particularly jovial nature. Something you say will be misconstrued, perhaps purposely, and you will be caused much pain and annoyance.

PANTRY If a young woman dreams that she is at work in a pantry it means that she will meet an untidy young man who will want to take her out. He will be lazy, and make a precarious livelihood by getting a job where he can; he will try to borrow money from her, and will con her if she gives him money. She will do well to avoid him, and have nothing to do with him. If a young man dreams that he is in a pantry it is a sign that he will never become wealthy, but always remain poor because he does not look ahead.

PAPER To dream of paper is a good omen; if it is clean you will be successful in your undertakings, marry the person you love, have good children, and be very happy. If it is dirty or scribbled on, then it shows temporary want and an unpleasant argument. If it is plainly written, you will receive good news, make an advantageous bargain, or inherit some money. If it

appears crumpled and carelessly folded up, it shows that some difficulties will occur, which will cause pain. If it is neatly folded, you will obtain whatever you most want. It depends altogether on what sort of paper you dream about. If it is white paper it means that your life for some time will be without incident, colour or importance. To dream, however, of printed paper, especially of seeing countless newspapers, signifies great agitation and uncertainty in all your affairs for some time to come.

PARACHUTE Be careful of all extremes and do not overwork or overplay.

PARADE To see a parade of soldiers drilling means you will do well to add some order to your life.

PARADISE To dream of being in paradise signifies that by the exercise of good principles, you will experience lasting happiness, make large profits and no, or at least only trifling, bad debts in business.

PARALYSIS If you dream that you are paralysed, it is a sign of a broken engagement.

PARAPET Dangers and worries which you will

surmount by your own efforts.

PARASOL To dream that you are walking with your parasol, or your umbrella, open indicates that although you may shortly fall ill, you will quickly recover your health.

PARCEL The person who dreams of carrying a parcel will shortly be guarding a secret of vital interest to their own and other people's happiness. There is something coming to you in the shape of a fortune, but whether good or bad depends on the appearance of the parcel. A neat parcel means prosperity, an untidy one troubles. Brown paper wrapping signifies that the gift will come from an unexpected source, and white means that the fortune is exactly both what you deserve and what you might naturally expect.

PARCHED A voyage to a hot country is indicated.

PARCHMENT Legal affairs will trouble you.

PARENT For a young person to dream of their parents is a good or bad dream, according to the circumstances. To dream that

you see both your parents in comfortable circumstances is a sign that you will live to an old age and never need money. To dream of quarrelling with your parents indicates that you will one day be guilty of a serious crime. If your parents are dead and you dream you receive a visit from them, it means that you are about to undertake a new calling or speculation and that you must be careful or give up your new project. If you have been guilty of any act of indiscretion and you see your parents in a dream it is meant as a rebuke, and if your actions have made other people suffer you must try to make some reparation to them for it. If a young woman is about to be married and her parents appear to her smiling she can be sure that her marriage will be a happy one, but if they appear to be frowning it means that it will be best to break off the engagement for nothing but bad will come of it.

PARK This dream of a fine open space is a favourable one. If you are accompanied by one other person, it shows a happy love affair. But if several people are with you, then expect difficulties for a time.

PARLIAMENT To dream that you are a Member of

Parliament means advancement; if you are a visitor, quarrels.

PARROT To dream of a parrot means that if you are wise you will keep your own secrets, because several you have lately told have been published abroad by those in whose reticence you reposed confidence.

PARSLEY Like most green things, this is an omen of success that has been achieved by hard work.

PARSNIP Subjection to a master is denoted.

PARTRIDGE To dream of a partridge foretells entanglements with women who are devoid of conscience and are ungrateful and hard.

PARTY To dream you have received an invitation to a party is a sign that you will soon hear of a wedding. To dream that you are present at an evening party denotes that you will move to a new neighbourhood before very long and have to make new friends. To dream of giving a large and sumptuous party to your friends is a sign of losses and poverty.

PASSAGE This is really an obstacle dream. The longer the passage, the greater the difficulties you will have to overcome.

PASSION It is a warning of trouble, generally domestic, to lose your temper in a dream.

PASSION FLOWER To dream of this flower signifies sacrifice and sorrow.

PASSPORT Travel abroad will be financially rewarding.

PASTE To dream of imitation jewellery is a sign of inferior friends.

PASTING Loss of a friend, but success to your plans.

PASTRY To dream of pastry signifies that you are about to fall ill and will endure great pain.

PATCH To dream of a patch on your garments betokens inherited wealth.

PATCHWORK An excellent dream; money will come to you in an unexpected way.

PATH To dream you are walking in a good broad path denotes health.

PATIO You will be invited to a party where you will meet artistic and influential people.

PATTERN Small vexations of home life are indicated, but your greater worries will be overcome.

PAVEMENT A rough pavement indicates envy of others.

PAWNBROKER To dream that you have been forced to pay a visit to a pawnbroker foretells first success and afterwards reverses – the latter brought about by your own foolishness. Be careful not to waste, and you may possibly steer clear of the unpleasant part of this prediction.

PAY It is not fortunate to see yourself paying away money in a dream, even if you are settling a debt.

PEA To dream of peas is a sign of prosperity. You will have many children, who in their youth will be a cause of care and anxiety but later on in life will be both a credit and a comfort to you. To dream you gather peas shows great happiness and content. Peas dried for seed denote wealth. To dream of eating peas denotes success in business.

PEACH To dream of peaches in season denotes content, health and pleasure. But if you seem to eat them out of season, they signify vain hopes and failure in business.

PEACOCK To dream of seeing this beautiful bird is a very good omen. It denotes success in trade, attractive although perhaps conceited lovers and prosperity by sea.

PEANUT You will receive an invitation.

PEAR To see or eat ripe pears signifies joy or pleasure, elevation in life, accumulation of riches, success in business and constancy in love. If a pregnant woman dreams of them she will have a girl. To dream of pears means that an opportunity for advancement will shortly present itself, of which you should unhesitatingly avail yourself; should you let it slip the rest of your career will be comparatively unimportant. Well-baked pears signify great success.

PEARL To dream of pearls is a bad omen. You will hear of the illness and subsequent death of a dear friend; and should you be wearing pearls, the shock of the news will cause a breakdown in your own health unless you remember the warning and steel yourself for the worst.

PEASANT For a townsman to dream of a peasant is a good sign of business plans which will prosper.

PEBBLE Jealousy and competition will trouble you.

PEDESTRIAN It is generally far more fortunate in a dream to be walking, instead of riding.

PEDLAR To dream of a pedlar signifies deceitful companions.

PELICAN A wealthy acquaintance will invite you to dinner.

PEN To dream of a pen means that you will shortly receive or send a proposal of marriage from someone who lives at a distance, and with whom you cannot meet at present.

PENANCE Be reserved with strangers; a dangerous influence is near you when travelling.

PENCIL Take note of the friend who gave it to you in the dream, as a parting from that person is indicated.

PENDULUM A sudden message will cause you to take a long journey.

PENSION To dream that you have a pension from a friend or a company for which you used to work is a sign that you will hear many degrading expressions and much conversation that will be offensive to you, because of your being dependent on other people who will be overbearing towards you.

PEONY Not a good flower to dream about; it denotes anxiety and annoyance.

PEOPLE To dream of seeing a great crowd of people means affliction in connection with your family. From the age of the chief person in the crowd you can conclude which family member is going to suffer.

PEPPER To dream you grind pepper signifies melancholy.

PEPPERMINT You will be proud of your offspring's attainments, if not your own.

PERAMBULATOR Responsibilities will hamper you.

PERCH A higher position is in store for you if you dream of climbing to a bough or tree top. Do not let it alter your friendships.

PERFORMING To dream of performing signifies too great an attachment to appearances.

PERFUME If you dream you perfume your head with essences or sweet-scented powders it signifies that you have too great an opinion of yourself. If anyone dreams they are presented with sweet perfumes they will receive some welcome news, according to the proportion of the scent in quality and quantity, and will gain profit, advantage and honour among their acquaintances. If a person dreams they make perfumes and gives them to their friends, they will be the messenger of good news which will prove advantageous to themselves and their friends.

PERIL It is an obstacle omen if you find yourself in peril in your dream. If you come off successfully, then all will go well.

PERJURY A bad dream, for you will deserve the misfortune that will befall you.

PERSIAN To dream of Eastern materials signifies an addiction to laziness which would not be for your good if you were able to indulge it.

PERSPIRATION Great efforts will be required of you and duly rewarded.

PESTS To dream of house or garden pests is a token of prosperity beyond your hopes.

PETALS Pulling petals from a flower indicates broken friendships or dying love affairs.

PETROL Danger of fires and disputes; guard against either.

PETTICOAT A dream of warning against conceit and dissipation; keep to moderate ways and feelings.

PEWTER Contentment and joy will be yours but not wealth.

PHANTOM Disappointment is in store for you. For lovers, a ghost dream shows a successful rival, or the fickleness of the one you love. Be careful to avoid quarrels with your friends, or fate is against you. Do not travel, and avoid lending money or giving extra credit in business.

PHEASANT To dream of a pheasant signifies that you are about to have some good fortune. If you carry one, you will receive a great honour.

PHILOSOPHER To dream you argue with philosophers signifies profit and gain.

PHOTOGRAPH To dream of receiving the photograph of anyone is a sign that there is a danger of your friendship with that particular person coming to a speedy end. When anyone dreams of receiving their sweetheart's photograph, let them be on their guard against rivals and quarrels.

PHYSICIAN This is a very fortunate omen. It is always a good sign to see or speak to a doctor in your dream.

PIANO A dream of playing a piano or an organ is a favourable omen and means the discovery of something of great value in a surprising place.

PICNIC To dream that you go to a picnic and meet with a sweetheart there, who is gaily dressed, full of attention and attractive, is a sign that one who is not considered very intelligent will hanker after you and do their utmost to gain your love. You may do worse than allow yourself to be courted by them.

PICTURE To dream you are looking at a beautiful picture

indicates that you will be allured by false appearances into an unprofitable concern, that you will waste your time on an idle project, and that you will always be in pursuit of happiness without attaining it. In love, it denotes great pleasure in the enjoyment of your lover and promises a handsome wife, a good husband and dutiful children. To dream you see your own picture is a sign of longevity.

PIE To dream of watching someone making pies means that your experience in love is likely to prove disastrous, and that you may come in the end to have as many wounds in your heart as there will be wrinkles on your face. Dreaming of eating pies, whether they are meat pies or fruit, signifies that you will shortly have an opportunity of laughing at something till your head aches.

PIG A pig in a dream denotes idle and lazy people, who love doing nothing and think of nothing except how to prey upon other people's goods so they can live at ease. Pigs also signify envious people who are in no way useful to society. To dream you trade in pigs signifies sickness. To dream of seeing a pig is not good, no matter whether it is alive or dead. It portends a married life spent without comfort, and trade pursued without any satisfactory result.

PIGEON To dream you see a pigeon is a good sign that you will have delight and content at home, and success in affairs abroad. To dream you see pigeons flying denotes unexpected, pleasant news and success in undertakings. They are very favourable to lovers, as they announce constancy in your partner, but also that the person you love will be absent from you for a long while on a journey; if your lover is at sea, they denote that he or she will have a pleasant voyage, continue faithful and will return rich. To dream you see a white pigeon flying signifies consolation, devotion and success in undertakings, provided they are altruistically motivated.

PILGRIM To dream you see a pilgrim or talk with one signifies that you will have a successful future.

PILL A journey abroad is indicated with many pleasures at the end of it.

PILLOW To dream that your pillow is covered with blood means that the head of someone in the family will be injured in an accident. To dream that your pillow is torn means that the reasoning faculties of either yourself or those who are dear to you will become deranged.

But to dream that your pillow is clean and white means prosperity, success and happiness.

PILOT Cheery scenes and good times ahead, but you will be defeated by a rival in the end.

PIN To dream of anyone taking a pin from you signifies that you will soon receive a present, trifling in value, but indicating a growing affection towards you on the part of the giver.

PIN CUSHION For a housewife to dream that she sees a pin cushion with many pins stuck in it is a sign that her house will not be as orderly as it should be.

PINAFORE A great deal of pleasure from a small present; be circumspect in your actions or you will make your position very difficult.

PINE TREE To dream you see a pine tree signifies idleness and forgetfulness.

PINEAPPLE Comfortable domestic surroundings are indicated; invitations and pleasure-seeking.

PINKS These flowers portend gay times and new garments, especially if the dreamer sells them.

PIPE A sign of unusual events resulting in good fortune to the smoker.

PIRATE Exciting times, journeys and financial gains; the deceit of an associate will cause you pain.

PISTOL The report of a pistol heard in a dream foretells the arrival of news of great importance from a distant quarter.

PIT It is a good sign to dream you see a pit full of clear water in a field where there is none at all, since it indicates that you will thrive, marry suddenly and have good and obedient children. If you see a pit whose water overflows the banks, that predicts loss of property or danger to your family. To dream of falling into a deep pit shows that some very unhappy misfortune is about to happen to you, or that your lover is false and prefers someone else; to a sailor it forbodes a sad disaster at the next port. To dream you are in a pit and that you climb easily out of it indicates that you will have many enemies and experience much trouble, but that you will overcome them and surmount your difficulties, marry well and become rich. To a sailor it denotes that he will be hospitably received, fall in love, marry a rich and attractive wife, leave the sea, and live at ease on the shore.

PITY To dream of being pitied means humiliation; of pitying someone else, small vexations.

PLAGUE If you dream you have the plague, your hidden store will be recovered and you will run the risk of losing it.

PLAINS To journey over plains signifies material gain but loss of affection of one you care for.

PLANT To dream of watching plants growing in a garden means that you ought to move from the place you live as you have lived there long enough for any good it is likely to do you.

PLASTER False accusations will be made against you if you dream that the plaster is on you, but if you dream that the plaster is coming off the walls of your house the trouble is for your family.

PLATFORM You will marry where you least expect to; beware of hasty judgements.

PLAY To dream you see a comedy, farce or some other play signifies success in business. To dream you see a tragedy acted signifies hard work, loss of friends and property, with grief and suffering. To dream you play with animals is a good sign. To dream that you are at a play is the forerunner of great good luck; it indicates great happiness in marriage and very great success in business.

PLEADING Take confidence in your own powers; their strength and confidence will soon be proved to you and others.

PLEASURE Always a dream of contrary. The more boisterous your mirth in your dream, the greater your loss or difficulty will be in your business affairs.

PLOT Important correspondence will claim your attention; changes, surprises and a possible engagement will ensue.

PLOUGH To dream of a plough signifies success in life and a good marriage. You will have many children, although perhaps later in life.

PLUM It is a good dream if you are gathering ripe plums. But if they are still green, then your efforts will fail from want of careful planning. If you pick up the fruit after it has fallen to the ground, it is a sign of change of position not entirely for your good. Dried plums – such as prunes – show difficulties.

PLUME Unexpected gain and public honour, especially if the plume is white.

PLUNDER A dangerous mistake; act with candour about it and avoid angry discussion if you would lessen the trouble.

POACHING A very fortunate dream; keep a guard on your speech for a time and everything you undertake will be accomplished.

POETRY To dream of writing verses and having a lover criticise them denotes that you are never likely to marry, even though you fall in love countless times and write poetry about all your lovers.

POISON To dream that you have taken poison is a warning of financial loss through the dishonesty of some person whom you trust. Be careful how you give credit or lend money. Do not speculate or buy shares or stocks. If you recover from the effects of the poison, you will get over your difficulties if you exercise care and tact.

POLICEMAN To dream of being in the custody of a policeman signifies that you may expect to be unjustly blamed by one who wishes you ill, but that in the end the false accusation will do you more good than it ever did harm.

POMEGRANATE If you have gathered pomegranates you will be made rich by a rich person. But if the pomegranates are not ripe, that denotes sickness or anxiety caused by someone wickedly disposed. If anyone dreams that the fruit they have gathered is rotten, that signifies adversity or loss of children.

POND To dream you see a small pond signifies that you will enjoy the love of a beautiful woman or handsome man, and will see your dreams realised. For a married woman to dream of a pond signifies that she will shortly become pregnant; if there are many fish, she will have twins; if the fish are small her next child will be a girl; if large, a boy. To a widow it denotes that she will remarry and be very happy.

POPPY Temptation will come your way. Be on your guard and do not yield.

PORCH Do not be too quick to accept a marriage proposal.

PORCUPINE To dream of a porcupine signifies that you will encounter difficulties in business.

PORK To dream of pork is a good dream for all engaged in money-making. It denotes quick profit, and that customers will as a rule prefer to pay cash rather than take credit.

PORTER Slander and annoyance.

PORTRAIT A warning of danger regarding the person whose portrait or photo is envisioned, especially if it is faded or injured.

POST OFFICE To dream of being in a post office on any

errand signifies that you are in danger from the gossiping tongues of people you think your friends, and that if you want your secrets preserved you had better keep them to yourself.

POSTCARD   You will be accused of unfaithfulness.

POSTMAN   You will receive little correspondence for some time after dreaming that a postman has handed you a letter or letters. If, however, you dream that you see a postman delivering letters at other houses and missing your own, you will hear important news. There is a letter already written to you, and perhaps even posted, and informing you of something of considerable importance.

POT   To dream of watching a pot boiling is a sign of approaching instability, particularly in your love affairs. You will shortly discover that you will have cause for jealousy, and will make the most of it.

POTATO   To dream of planting potatoes means that you are neglecting your opportunities, and that you have a power and ability which only needs to be culti-vated to lead you on to fortune.

POTTER   Others will have a good influence over you.

POUCH   If the dreamer is a man it portends a disclosure much to his advantage.

POULTRY   A very fortunate dream. You will succeed in your endeavours.

POUND   To dream of animals in a pound signifies a rise in salary and a change of scene.

POVERTY   To dream of being poor means that you are on the eve of marrying someone fairly well off, or will receive a legacy.

POWER   The higher your position in your dream the more likely you are to succeed in your business undertakings.

PRAISING   Dreaming of praising someone, or of someone praising you, indicates that you are about to be abandoned by someone to whom you have given your affections, although you should remember that there are 'other fish in the sea'.

PRAYER   To dream you pray devoutly to God signifies joy, comfort and happiness. To dream you make promises and offerings to God signifies love. To dream of prayer or requests for alms or of a poor and miserable beggar denotes anxiety and loss. If you receive alms it is a sign of damage and even death to you or to a close friend. If the beggar enters your house and steals anything or is given anything, it shows adversity.

PREACHER The result of your plans will be satisfactory at last, however worrying at present.

PRECIPICE To fall over a precipice signifies that you will suffer an injury, risk your life, or your property will be in danger from fire. To dream of climbing precipices denotes problems. To be on the brink of a precipice with the danger of falling over is a dream of warning, the meaning of which is that if you are in trade you should look carefully into your accounts, and if in private life that you should consider the character of your present associates.

PREGNANCY Being pregnant in a dream indicates sorrow and sadness to a man, but gifts to a woman.

PRESENT To dream of receiving a present from a friend signifies that the first

advice you receive from anyone on getting up that morning should be followed, because it will have an important effect in securing a result you are at present aiming at.

PRIDE You will rise in the world but others will use your promotion for their own ends, especially one whom you trust.

PRIEST To dream of a priest foretells the settlement of quarrels.

PRINCE A woman dreaming of meeting a prince will gain considerable influence but must guard against jealousy.

PRINCE OF WALES To dream of meeting and speaking with him signifies honours and riches to come; to see him only, a present will be given to you.

PRINCESS A parallel dream for a man, as a prince is for a woman.

PRINTER For most people, to dream of a printer means that their names will soon appear in the newspapers in connection with an event of great importance. To an author, however, it signifies that a period of general disturbance will soon arrive, resulting mostly from his or her own fault.

PRISON To dream of being confined in prison means that you will make money and succeed in life, but it will be by pursuing things against your will.

PRISONER To dream of seeing a prisoner executed is a good dream.

PRIZE This is a 'contrary' dream foreboding loss through sharp dealing. Be on your guard when offered something cheap.

PROCESSION To dream that you are watching a procession foretells steadfast affection from the person you love. The longer it lasts the better, for many years of happiness are foretold.

PROMISE An important decision for you to make. The right answer will lead to happy times for you, so think well.

PROMONTORY This dream predicts an outstanding event which is just round the corner.

PROPOSAL If you dream of receiving one, be careful not to be drawn into another person's schemes. Should

you make one, exciting times are ahead.

PROPERTY This means you will be disappointed in your hopes.

PROSTITUTE To dream you are in the company of a prostitute signifies completion of business.

PROVISIONS To dream that you are hungry and cannot obtain any food foretells business troubles and loss of money. But it is a fortunate omen to have plenty of food on your table, or provisions stored in your larder.

PUBLIC HOUSE To dream you are in a pub with friends indicates happiness and comfort.

PUDDING To dream of eating pudding is an unwelcome omen, meaning that you are about to have an illness and that your complete recovery will be only possible by your following a strict diet.

PUDDLE To be splashed by dirty puddle water indicates an unpleasant experience.

PULPIT Like all omens connected with the interior of a church, this is not a favourable sign.

PUMP To pump clear water is a good sign; your business will prosper. If the water is soiled, however, worries and slander will annoy you.

PUNCH To dream of drinking punch is a warning of unpleasant news to come concerning loss of money and possibly reputation.

PUNISHMENT To dream of being punished signifies an unexpected pleasure at hand.

PUPPY An invitation to a jolly party; laugh with the people you meet there but do not become intimate.

PURGATORY A portent of sickness and travel, but not necessarily to yourself.

PURPLE Happiness, prosperity and esteem; good fortune both in love and at work.

PURSE To dream of finding a purse is a very favourable omen. It denotes great happiness and unlooked-for prosperity; in love, it is a sure token of an early and happy marriage. To dream you lose your purse shows the loss of a friend. In other respects it denotes some unpleasant adventure is about to happen to you by which you will gain. To a sailor it denotes the loss of his sweetheart while at sea. You may be cheated out of a large sum of money, and will not know about it until it is too late to recover it.

PUSH To dream of pushing against a door or other heavy object signifies that some overmastering obstacle will be removed from your path.

PUTTY An omen of hard work and hard times, especially if you dream of using it yourself.

PUZZLE An obstacle dream. If you cannot solve the puzzle, then expect heavy losses in business for trouble is ahead.

PYRAMID A successful future and a high position in the world is assured to you.

PYTHON Hold your ground against those who would try to influence you against your better judgement.

QUACK To dream that you are under the care of quacks is unfortunate and indicates that you should be wary of anyone making false medical claims.

QUAIL To dream of a quail signifies messengers bringing bad news from across the sea.

QUAKER To dream of these simple and quiet living people is always a fortunate omen.

QUARANTINE Unhappiness lies ahead unless you take care of your health.

QUARREL To dream of quarrelling indicates unexpected news. To dream that you are involved in a serious quarrel foretells that you will never lack for friends and will lead a peaceful life.

QUARRY To dream that you fall down a quarry is a sign that some sudden and violent death could take place before many months are over among some of your friends or relatives.

QUARTZ Someone is trying to cheat you.

QUAY To dream that you stand on the quay of a seaport town and see the ships load and unload their goods is a sign that you will shortly receive very costly presents from a relative or friend either in America, Canada or Australia.

QUEEN To dream you see a queen signifies honour, joy and prosperity. If you dream a queen speaks to you, your joy will be short-lived and sorrow will quickly follow.

QUESTION To dream that someone is asking you questions is an obstacle omen. If you can answer properly all will go well.

QUEUE If you dream of waiting in a queue, a re-established friendship will lead to marriage.

QUICKSAND Be especially careful of your health after dreaming of walking on quicksand. On no account go near a house where a person is ill from an infectious disease. To dream that you are sinking in quicksand indicates that you are too easily led astray by flatterers. Try to ignore them.

QUICKSILVER   You will be invited to an enjoyable festivity. Gossip is on foot concerning you.

QUILT   A family reunion is foretold.

QUIVER   Happiness through the joys of home and marriage.

QUIZ   If you answer correctly, you will have good fortune.

QUOITS   To dream that you are watching a game of quoits foretells a holiday in the country. To dream that you play a game of quoits is a sign that you will, unless you are careful, become a gambler, at first for small but then for larger stakes.

RABBIT To dream that you see many rabbits alive is a warning against unknown enemies who will try, by underhand methods, to disgrace you. To dream that you are eating rabbit is a sign that you will be a hard worker all your life and taste few real joys without working hard to attain them. To dream of a rabbit warren signifies expensive enjoyments. To see rabbits signifies an increase in your family.

RABIES You have an unsuspected enemy.

RACE HORSE This denotes that you will lose a sum of money through trying to make money.

RACECOURSE Jolly company but danger or losses through sharp practices are indicated.

RACING To dream you are running a race presages success in life, and that you will soon hear some very happy news. In love, it denotes that you will conquer all your rivals, and be very happy with your partner. To dream you are riding in a race shows disappointments, anger and business problems. To a married person it denotes the loss of your spouse's affections, and that your children will be in trouble.

To win a race is indicative of good fortune at the end of a long and hard struggle for success; to lose a race is a warning that you will experience many disappointments and never climb to the top of the tree.

RACKET This dream betokens loss of leisure which will however be well repaid later by a new friendship.

RADIO Quiet music on a radio foretells a contented home life. Blaring music indicates family discord.

RADISHES To dream of radishes signifies a discovery of hidden secrets and can indicate domestic quarrels.

RAFFLE This dream of risk and chance is a warning to

you that you do not deserve success; mend your ways and be more generous in your treatment of others.

RAFT To dream of being on a raft indicates enforced travel; to see one, a varied life for some time.

RAGS Beware of too much frivolity after dreaming of rags. Try to take life a little more seriously, or you will one day have reason for repentance.

RAILWAY TICKET To dream you have taken a railway ticket to any destination signifies that an unwelcome visitor is about to arrive, and that prudence suggests you should be out of the way. A dream of having lost a railway ticket, on the other hand, means that a journey you are about to take will be prosperous, and that everyone you meet will be good to you.

RAIN Dreams of heavy rain and storms signify problems, troubles, danger, losses and peril. To dream you see it rain signifies great riches. To dream of thunder and rain which do no damage denotes that you have some dangerous enemies, but will overcome them.

To dream of being in a gentle shower of rain denotes great success in your present undertakings; it is particularly favourable to lovers, as it denotes constancy, affection and a sweet temper; to the sailor it promises good fortune at sea. To dream of a sudden shower indicates good luck. It signifies that prosperity is about to smile upon you, but that you must hurry to take advantage of its favours or you will miss your chance.

To see rain falling while the sun is shining is a sign that whatever troubles you may have at that time will soon be swept away and brighter days will arrive.

RAINBOW To dream you see a rainbow in the east is a good omen to the poor and sick, for the former will make money and the latter will recover their health. If you see a rainbow in the west it is a good sign to the rich but a bad sign to the poor. To dream you see the rainbow directly over your head or thereabouts signifies a change of fortune and danger to you and your family.

To dream you see a rainbow in the distance denotes travelling; it also denotes unexpected good news, which you may expect to receive through a stranger. It denotes that your lover is good-tempered and constant, and that you will be very happy in marriage. And you will also be successful in business through foreign trading.

RAISINS To use raisins in cooking means several small gifts. To eat them signifies that you will spend money more easily than you earn it; you must try to economise more.

RAKE It is a fortunate omen to dream that you are going over ground with a rake, signifying that you will be well educated and will use your knowledge for the benefit of others. To dream that you are using a rake in your garden denotes a persevering nature, which should bring you success in some important undertakings.

For a young woman to dream that her lover is a rake, or a wild character, is a sign that she will have comfort and happiness in her courtship. No one will be able to find fault with her lover, because he will be attentive to business, straightforward and honest.

RAM To dream of a ram signifies misfortune for the dreamer.

RAMBLE A wish will be granted after long delay.

RASH A warning against speaking your mind before thinking twice as to the result of your words.

RASCAL To dream of being duped by a rascal in business means increased trade and a comfortable income.

RASPBERRY To dream of raspberries signifies a successful marriage and also that you will receive news from overseas.

RAT To dream of rats means that you may expect to be injured by the interference of someone who thinks he knows your business much better than you do yourself, but by the exercise of courtesy, good humour and common sense you will in all probability soon get rid of them. If you are attacked by rats and get the better of them it means that you will overcome your difficulties. If they bite you and make you run away, then you must expect some serious misfortune.

RAT CATCHER You can rely on having at least one friend in need.

RAVEN If anyone sees a raven, it indicates mischief,

particularly to a husband or wife who will be discontented by their adulterous partner. To hear a raven croak signifies sadness. To see ravens flying signifies complaint and sadness. To see a raven fly over you signifies danger and damage.

RAZOR   Be careful not to interfere in any quarrel among your friends after dreaming of a razor. If you attempt to smooth matters you will find yourself in an awkward predicament, and both parties will be offended by your conduct.

READING   To dream you read romances, comedies or other diverting books signifies joy and comfort. To dream you read serious books signifies wisdom and knowledge. You have a very determined spirit, and although this will sometimes lead you into trouble, it will bring you success in most things you undertake. To dream that you read well signifies that you will go into the country and have goods and honours given to you there, but to read badly signifies the opposite.

REAPING   To dream you are reaping or that you see others engaged in this occupation, cannot be taken as an altogether good omen. Although you will one day know what it is to live in affluence, you will have many trials and experience much sorrow before that time comes. Perhaps you should aim for a simple life in order to be happy.

REBELLION   An inferior who has caused you much trouble will soon cease to annoy you.

RECEIPT   A thrilling time ahead; be on guard with all but the most trusted friends.

RECITING   This portends social popularity and a happy marriage.

RECONCILIATION   This is a favourable sign in a dream.

RED   A warning of quarrels and loss of friends.

REED   Your friends are not all true; try them well before trusting any.

REEL   To wind cotton or silk on a reel signifies delayed success achieved by patience.

REFLECTION   To dream you see yourself mirrored in water signifies serious danger to the dreamer, or some close friend.

REFRESHMENTS To offer them in a dream indicates a happy marriage; to partake of them signifies small vexations.

REFUSAL To dream of a refusal signifies a most certain acceptance.

REGATTA A visit to a strange place will bring you fresh work.

REGIMENT To see a regiment of soldiers marching by means serious disputes in which you will be involved shortly.

REGISTRY OFFICE You stand at the crossroads; decide quickly and do not look back.

REHEARSAL To be present at a rehearsal presages difficulties in the present but honours in the future.

RELATIONS To dream you see or talk with your father, mother, wife, brother, sister, or other of your relations and friends, even though they are dead, signifies you should mind your affairs, and behave yourself.

RELEASE An ill-omened dream if you should be released from a prison, but a sign of troubles soon to end

if you think you are releasing someone else.

RELIGION It is generally a bad sign to be troubled by religion in a dream.

REMOVAL To dream that you are changing your house is a sign that you will soon receive intelligence of someone in a distant town of whom you have long lost sight.

RENT Unexpected gains will be yours following a dream in which you cannot pay rent or any other debt.

REPRIMAND This portends an important offer from a superior, which will surprise and delight you.

REPTILE To dream of any reptile is a sign of a quarrel; you have a subtle enemy of whom you must beware. If you imagine you are bitten it shows that you will come out second best, or badly injured, either physically or by reputation.

RESCUE To be rescued is not a good sign, especially from drowning. Avoid travel on sea.

RESERVOIR To see a reservoir filled with clean water is a good omen of plenty in the future.

RESIGNATION To dream of resigning your work means advancement in the near future, also money gained through legal matters.

REST A 'contrary' dream meaning hard work; good luck in sporting matters.

RESTAURANT To look on at others eating in a restaurant signifies ill-health; should you be eating also, small enjoyments among new friends.

RESURRECTION To dream of the dead reviving signifies troubles and injury. To dream of the dead dying again signifies the death of anyone whose name is called in the dream.

RETIREMENT You may have increased finances but only through hard work.

RETURN To dream you see someone who has been away for a long time is a sign of losses soon to be made good, and renewed prosperity.

REVELRY A 'contrary' dream heralding misfortune unless you dream of looking on at the revelry of others.

REVENGE Anxious times, humiliation, and a quarrel, but the latter will soon be made up.

REVOLUTION All civil disorder in a dream indicates feuds and family discord.

REVOLVER To dream of handling a revolver is a sign of danger by water. Try to avoid travelling by sea or river.

REWARD Failure of your plans through over-confidence. Remember there are things money cannot buy.

RHEUMATISM To dream of suffering from this signifies a new lease of life and happiness.

RHINOCEROS Success in business affairs, but delays and disillusion to those in love.

RHUBARB To dream of rhubarb either growing in the garden or cooked on the table, means that your affection for someone from whom you expected some return is hopeless, and that you would be better to finish the relationship.

RHYMING To dream of writing rhymes betokens worry over business accounts. You are being cheated.

RIB All the ribs or intestines signify wealth if they are healthy or the opposite if they are diseased. For a man to dream his upper ribs are broken shows disagreement between him and his wife in which he will come off the worst. But if his lower ribs are broken it shows arguments with female relatives. If you dream your ribs have grown larger and stronger it shows you will be happily married.

RIBBON For a young woman to dream of ribbons is a sign that she is about to have a new partner but he will soon leave her for someone with more money. To dream that you are purchasing ribbon of a bright colour is a sign that you will shortly have to wear mourning for a valued friend. A girl engaged to be married who dreams of a yellow ribbon should be careful in her dealings with the opposite sex. Her sweetheart is inclined to be jealous, and he will break the engagement for the least cause.

RICE Whoever dreams of rice may rest assured that they will have a large family, but enough money to bring them up comfortably. You will one day possess great wealth.

RICHES To dream that you have inherited a fortune is a bad omen. You will probably lose all your money through the failure of some concern in which you are interested, and feel the loss all your life. To dream that you save a fortune is almost as bad, but in this instance there is a chance for you to retrieve your loss by hard work and patient effort.

RIDDLE An unexpected offer from someone related to you. Be on your guard as there is danger in it.

RIDING To ride a horse is good because the horse signifies a person or even a ship, to guide and govern. If you dream of a horse you will become powerful. To ride a horse through a town is good for anyone who takes a risk or is sick; the first will gain the prize, the other be healed. To ride out of a town is the opposite. To dream you ride a wild horse and can govern it and stay in the saddle signifies rule and dignity, but to fall or be thrown signifies disgrace. To dream you are riding with a woman is very unfortunate: expect to be crossed in love. If you are in trade, your business will fail and you may be brought near to bankruptcy; if you are a sailor, it denotes your lover is unfaithful.

RIGGING To dream you see the rigging of a ship signifies news from debtors.

RING To dream a ring falls off your finger indicates evil and a prison, also the death of a close friend or relation. To a pregnant woman it shows that her child will encounter many difficulties, and may be far from happy. To a girl it is a warning to beware of her present lover, who will use her then abandon her. To dream of losing a ring or rings signifies the loss of someone in charge of your property, such as a husband or wife, tenant or employee; and also your goods, and possessions. To many this dream has foretold the loss of eyesight, because the eyes have an association with the stones in a ring. To dream of a gold ring dropping from your finger shows the loss of a lover or close relation; to put a ring on anyone's finger denotes an early marriage.

To dream of having rings on your fingers denotes honour and dignity. To dream a ring is put on your finger shows success in love but, if taken off, the opposite. To dream of an engagement ring is not a favourable omen

and means that many quarrels are likely to take place between you and your partner and that in the end one disagreement more serious than the rest will separate you forever. The married woman who dreams she is wearing a new ring may expect to receive an invitation to a wedding at an early date. It is a bad omen for a young woman who is engaged to be married to dream that she is wearing a wedding ring. She will not have all the success she might wish for in her love affairs, and if she marries early in life the match will not be a good one. To dream that you receive a ring as a present foretells unexpected news, causing you to take a journey to visit a friend in trouble. To dream that you lose a ring indicates that you will have serious troubles, but will be able to surmount them with the help of someone very dear to you.

RIOT This is a warning of financial failure, especially if you see many rioters fighting.

RIVAL To dream of the discovery of a rival is one of the best omens in love affairs. It means that you will shortly be united with your loved one, and few couples anywhere will be happier than you two.

RIVER To dream you see a flowing river and that the waters are smooth and clear indicates happiness and success in life. To the lover it shows constancy and affection in your partner and that if you marry, you will be very happy and contented, and have many children, mostly girls, who will be very beautiful; to the tradesman and farmer, it shows prosperity and gain; to the sailor, that his sweetheart will be kind and faithful, and that his next voyage will be lucrative and pleasant. If the water appears disturbed and muddy, or has a yellow tinge, then it denotes that you will acquire considerable riches; if you have a lawsuit, such a dream foretells that you will win.

To dream of being in a rough river, and not to escape, signifies danger and sickness. To dream of swimming in a large river signifies future peril and danger. To dream you see a clear river run by your bedroom indicates the arrival of a rich and generous person who will do something to your advantage. But if the water is rough or dirty and seemed to spoil the furniture in the room, that signifies violence, quarrels and chaos caused by enemies. A rich man who dreams he sees a stream of clear water run by his house will be unexpectedly appointed to a position of responsibility that will be financially advantageous and will offer a refuge and asylum to the oppressed. If the river is flowing quietly between its banks, it may be taken as a sign that you will live to a ripe old age and have little to trouble you. If the water is rough, however, you will experience difficulties in life. To dream that you have fallen into a river is a promise of good news.

RIVET To dream of a rivet indicates travel by road or rail.

ROAD To dream that you stand at a spot where several roads meet indicates that you will not always go on in the steady way you are doing now. Several changes will come into your life, and you will not live long in one neighbourhood. To dream that you see a broad and even road stretching before you is lucky, but narrow and crooked roads are bad omens.

ROAR The roar of waters, a traveller will return; of animals, an enemy is watching you.

ROAST MEAT To see or eat roast meat signifies that you will be shortly greeted by one you love.

ROBBER To dream that you are attacked by a robber indicates a calamity in which you will lose some valuable property. To a person in love this dream brings a warning that a rival is in the field striving to gain the affections of your lover.

ROBIN To see a robin denotes that you will make many friends, but that your character and temper are such that you are not likely to form a lasting union with anyone.

ROCK To dream of a rock signifies that you will experience great annoyance. To climb over one signifies that you will overcome the dangers that are before you.

ROCKET Short-lived success is portended. You must build on firmer foundations next time.

ROD To dream you have a rod in your hand signifies jollity. To dream you are whipped with a rod denotes that you will meet with a treacherous friend who will almost ruin you. It also indicates your being shortly at a celebration, where you must be careful of quarrelling; if you do it will be to your disadvantage. If you are in love, it denotes your sweetheart will be fickle and is likely to cause you unhappiness.

ROLL New bread signifies promotion in work; stale rolls mean tedious business.

ROOF To dream you see the roof of a house destroyed by fire denotes loss of goods, lawsuits or friends.

ROOK To dream you see a rook signifies a successful conclusion of business.

ROOM To dream you are in a strange room signifies that you will accomplish your ambitions.

ROOT To dream you eat a root such as a carrot signifies arguments.

ROPE To dream you are tied with a rope denotes happiness, marriage and many children; it also denotes that you will be very angry with someone for a trifling reason. To dream you see many ropes is a very bad sign indeed; it portends some dreadful accident. You may infer from it that you are in danger of being restricted in your actions, willingly no doubt at first, but from which restraints you will soon wish to escape. To the lover it also denotes the loss of the affections of your sweetheart; to the tradesman, poor success in business.

ROSARY To dream that you are telling the beads of your own rosary means reconciliation with a friend. To see someone wearing a rosary signifies bereavement.

ROSE To dream of roses in season is a token of happiness and success. Your marriage will be loving and prosperous; your business affairs will go well. To dream of these, or any flowers out of season, indicates distress, sickness and disappointment. To the tradesman, they forebode bankruptcy and prison; to the married, loss of their spouse and children.

ROSEMARY To dream you smell rosemary signifies hard work, trouble, sadness and weakness to anyone but a doctor, to whom such dreams are propitious.

ROT This signifies the decay of a great family fortune which will affect you indirectly, whether it be rotten fruit or timber, but should the dream be of

rotten cliffs which crumble as you climb them, guard your health most carefully.

ROUGE To dream you are using rouge to make up your face is a very favourable omen, denoting success in life. To the lover it indicates her sweetheart to be faithful, good-tempered and keen to marry. If you are married it denotes children, who will be very happy, become rich and be a great comfort in your later years. To dream you see another person using rouge shows that pretended friends are endeavouring to do you an injury, and that your children will meet with persecution and problems. In love such a dream shows your sweetheart to be fickle and hardly likely to make you happy. To dream that the rouge comes off your face is indicative of loss of property and the affections of the person you love.

ROUSING To dream you rouse a person from sleep is good.

ROWING To dream that you are rowing a boat on a river gives promise that your dearest wish will be fulfilled. To be rowing on the sea denotes a life of trials and misfortunes.

ROYALTY To dream you are a king or emperor indicates death to the sick, but that others will do admirable work and gain a good salary as well as a good reputation. To dream of royalty signifies that you will receive a great honour. To receive an audience with a king signifies gain. To receive a gift from a king signifies great joy.

RUBBING To dream that you are rubbing anything signifies success in marriage or business.

RUBBISH You are about to make a most valuable discovery. Use it, but try not to hurt a friend by doing so.

RUDDER To dream of a broken rudder portends indecision and distress. Do not take a voyage if you can avoid it for some time.

RUE Domestic difficulties.

RUG A luxurious rug means fortune, but a worn one penury.

RUINS It is a fortunate omen to dream that you are wandering amid the ruins of some fine old building. If it is merely a modern house that has tumbled down, that is a bad sign. Beware of speculation.

RUMBLE To hear strange rumbles from below the earth in a dream, such as those which precede an earthquake, is a sign of future trouble which it will take your utmost forethought to avert.

RUNNING To dream you want to run but cannot means that your affairs will be difficult and your ambitions hard to accomplish. To dream of running normally is a good omen. If you dream of running after an enemy, that denotes victory and profit. To dream you are running a race is also usually good, often indicating much success in life, and that you will soon hear some good news.

If you see anybody running quickly along, it could be a sign of hearing of their death soon after. To dream people run into one another signifies wrangling and arguments. If they are little children, that indicates happiness and good weather; nevertheless if those children are armed with sticks or staves, that suggests war and disagreements. To dream that you are running from a relentless pursuer is a warning that you will need to have all your wits about you to withstand some temptation which will be put in your way. To dream that you are running in pursuit of something or somebody indicates that you are too fond of relying on your own judgement. Unless you listen to the advice of your friends when it is offered, you will one day regret your obstinacy.

RUST To dream of rust means approaching sorrow, the decay of health, bad debts in business, separation from friends, loss of popularity, and many other evils which will be hard even for a philosophic mind to bear. A big disappointment is in store for you; probably just when you are looking forward to attaining some long-desired goal, for something will occur to snatch success from your grasp.

RUSTIC This is a fortunate dream, meaning that a busier life will soon be yours, one in which you can be truly successful.

RUSTLING To dream of hearing the rustling of wings is one of the best omens and means that your future will be protected and happy.

RYE Eating rye bread denotes popularity with the opposite sex.

SABLE The colour betokens tidings of loss; the fur is a warning against extravagance.

SACK To dream of a sack foretells an unexpected happening which will cause you much uneasiness.

SACRIFICE A sign of coming festivities.

SADDLE To dream that you are riding a horse without a saddle foretells ill-health through your own carelessness. Revise your plans at once and guard against mistakes.

SADNESS A good omen for your future; lasting joys.

SAGE To dream of sage signifies hard work, trouble, sadness and weakness.

SAILING To dream you are sailing quietly on water denotes a peaceful life, but beware of enemies who will seek to cause trouble between you and your friends. To dream of sailing on a rough sea promises prosperity.

SAILOR To dream that you are talking to a sailor promises news from abroad. The girl who dreams she is engaged to a sailor will marry a shy man and she will have to take charge of things.

SAINT To dream you see a saint signifies consolation, and is a warning to live well and honestly. It also denotes good news and increase of reputation and authority.

SALAD To dream of a salad signifies trouble and difficulty in the management of affairs. To dream you eat a salad signifies evil or sickness.

SALARY If you spend recklessly after receiving a salary increase in a dream, your income will be reduced.

SALMON A dream in which salmon play a prominent part, whether being caught or eaten, denotes that you are likely to see much of the world before finally settling down to marriage.

SALT A bad omen. If you know of any enemies, it will

be better to pacify them rather than arouse their hatred. If you try to harm them, you yourself will suffer.

SAND   Many small vexations.

SANDALS   Comfortable sandals betoken romance.

SAPPHIRE   This is considered a fortunate dream, but it concerns your friends more than yourself.

SASH   To dream of wearing one indicates a happy marriage.

SATIN   To dream you trade in satin signifies loss and misfortune.

SAUCEPAN   An omen of misfortune. Many problems will descend on you together, and you will need a stout heart to battle against them.

SAUSAGE   To dream you see a sausage signifies domestic troubles. If you are making them, it indicates illness.

SAVAGE   Small worries through the dishonesty of another. To dream of many savages signifies rescue by a friend from a trouble of your own making.

SAVINGS   To dream you are accumulating savings foreshadows poverty.

SAWING   To dream of sawing wood foretells that you will do something that you will afterwards regret. If a young fellow dreams this he will probably offend his sweetheart and find it hard work to get her to overlook the disagreement.

SCAB   To dream your arms or elbows are covered in scabs or ulcers signifies annoyance, sadness and failure in business. To dream your legs are scabby signifies fruitless anxiety. If anyone dreams their skin is scabby, they will grow rich proportionately to the number of scabs. You may marry someone rich, or receive a gift of a considerable sum of money.

SCAFFOLD   There will be a dreadful occurrence close to you.

SCALD   A dream of contrary – good fortune will follow after the first difficulties have been overcome.

SCARLET   Quarrels and the loss of friends.

SCHOOL   To dream of attending school means that you are ashamed of your ignorance and will set to work in earnest. A golden opportunity will shortly occur, of which you will only be able to avail yourself if you add to your present stock of knowledge. To dream you go back to school but cannot learn your lessons shows you are about to undertake something you do not understand.

SCIENCE To dream you study the sciences signifies cheerfulness.

SCISSORS To merely see a pair of scissors is a sign of an early marriage. To dream of using scissors is a warning that by dividing your attention between two ambitions you will realise neither. You must make up your mind which of the two you would prefer, and concentrate your energy on attaining it. To see many pairs of scissors together denotes that you will suffer much through unrequited love.

SCRAPBOOK To make a scrapbook signifies that you will be in control of your destiny.

SCRATCH To dream that you have been scratched with nails signifies that you will repay your debts, or that you will be hurt by the people who scratched you. To dream that anyone scratches the soles of their feet indicates loss through flattery.

SCREAMING To dream that you hear screaming is a sign that someone you know will meet with a serious accident. If the screams are prolonged, that person will never really recover from the injuries received. To dream that you are screaming is a sign that you will receive a proposal, which it will be in your interest to accept.

SCREW To dream of a small screw is a good sign and indicates success in all you undertake, but to dream of a large screw indicates trouble brought about by love affairs.

SCULPTURE If you dream of a sculpture, do not meddle in affairs of the heart that are none of your business.

SCYTHE To dream of a scythe foretells injuries from enemies and disappointments in love.

SEA To dream you see the sea blue and gently waving signifies joy, and the successful performance of business. But if the sea is calm, it signifies problems and delays; and when it is tempestuous, it denotes anxiety, losses and adversity. To dream you fall into the water or into the sea, and that you wake suddenly signifies that you will become involved with a married person, and that you will find it hard to disengage yourself from the hands of envious enemies. For a young man to dream that he walks on the sea signifies the love of a delightful woman, but to a woman it foretells a dissolute life. This dream is good also to those who are employed looking after people or in government, for they will receive a good salary and be well regarded.

To dream you are sailing on a smooth sea is a good omen. In love, it foretells that you and your partner will be happy together and live comfortably. To dream you are sailing on a rough sea foretells many difficulties in life, particularly a disappointment in love. To dream you are cast away on a deserted, rocky shore indicates that after many troubles and difficulties you will become rich and happy. To dream that you are surrounded by the sea indicates that someone is nursing a grudge against you, and you must be careful to contradict in no uncertain terms any malicious scandal

you may hear against yourself. To dream that you witness a storm at sea is a sign that a close relative will bring disgrace and disagreement to your family.

SEA BIRD   To see a sea bird such as a cormorant indicates danger to mariners, but not death. To others sea birds signify their supposed friends who are whores, liars or thieves, and if the dreamer loses anything, he or she will never recover it again.

SEAL   Uncertainty regarding a legal matter will vex you, but not for long.

SEASHORE   To dream of sitting by the seashore or of walking on it means that you can shortly expect to take a long voyage. Should you be sitting on a stone, it means many pleasant adventures, but to be seated on grass indicates shipwreck and disaster.

SEAT   To dream that you have fallen off your seat signifies that you will lose your job.

SECRET   To dream of a secret being whispered in your ear means a public dignity to be bestowed on you.

SEE-SAW An unexpected love affair, which may not prove long-lasting.

SENTINEL New business introductions and a journey to the south.

SEPARATION To dream that you are separated from those you love foretells the failure of some cherished plan.

SEPULCHRE Good news concerning a birth, and a letter will lead to great happiness.

SERMON Approaching indisposition.

SERVANT For a woman to dream that she is a servant is an obstacle dream. Persevere and stick close to your job. To dream that you employ several servants is an unfortunate omen.

SEWING For a young woman to dream of sewing is a favourable omen, indicating that she will shortly marry one of the most loving husbands, whose home she will make happy and comfortable by her good sense and industry.

SHABBY New clothes will soon be yours when you dream of going about in shabby ones.

SHADOW To dream that you see a shadow denotes that you will do something of which you will be ashamed.

SHAMROCK News of long past matters will change your affairs.

SHARK This presages a narrow escape from serious trouble or illness.

SHAVING To dream you are shaving or cutting someone's hair signifies profit to the person whose hair is being cut, and bad luck to the dreamer. To dream you are being shaved or that your head has been shaved is a very unfavourable omen. In love, it denotes treachery and disappointment and unfaithfulness and arguments in marriage. To the tradesman it augurs loss of goods and business; to the sailor, an unpleasant and stormy voyage; to the farmer, bad crops and diseases among livestock.

SHAWL If a girl dreams of getting a new shawl it foretells that she will soon have a new boyfriend who will be very attentive and likeable. If she dreams that her lover gives her a shawl, that interesting young man is currently thinking of his next partner, and will soon be involved elsewhere.

SHEARING SHEEP To dream you see sheep shearing is indicative of loss of property, the affections of the person you love and even your liberty; though to dream that you are shearing them yourself shows that you will gain an advantage over someone who meant to harm you.

SHEEP To dream you see or have many sheep signifies wealth, plenty and advancement, especially to those who want to be in government or for those who are already in powerful positions. It is also a good dream for academics and schoolmasters. To dream you see a flock of sheep feeding is a very favourable omen since it denotes success in life. To the lover, it indicates your sweetheart is faithful, good-tempered and inclined to marry you; for those who are married, it denotes children, who will be very happy, become rich, and be great comforts in your later life; to tradesmen, it foretells increase of business and wealth, but also warns that one of his employees is untrustworthy. To the sailor, nothing can be a greater sign of good luck; his next voyage will be pleasant and lucrative, and his sweetheart kind and true. To dream you see sheep running away from you shows that pretended friends are endeavouring to do you an injury, and that your children will meet with persecutions and great troubles. In love, such a dream shows your sweetheart is fickle and unlikely to make you happy.

SHEIK Hard times are in store for you; save while you can.

SHELF Your desires will be thwarted.

SHELL To dream of a shell with the fish alive in it predicts prosperity, but an empty sea-shell is a bad omen.

SHEPHERD To dream of a shepherd is a bad omen.

SHERRY To dream you are drunk on sherry, or another sweet and pleasant wine, is a sign that you will have powerful friends who will help you grow rich.

SHINGLE Advancement in position is indicated.

SHIP To dream you are in a ship and see a clear light a long way off indicates that you will not experience many problems and will achieve your ambitions. If you dream you are walking in a boat or ship and entertaining yourself, you will have comfort and success in your affairs. But if the water is rough it indicates the opposite. To dream of being in a boat or ship in danger of overturning is a sign of danger, unless the dreamer is a prisoner in which case it denotes liberty and freedom. To sail in a ship or see ships sailing is a good sign. To see ships laden with goods signifies prosperity. To see ships endangered by a storm signifies peril. To dream that you are on a ship predicts that you will not take any really long journey by water. To see a ship is a warning not to jump at an offer which will shortly be made to you. It will be to your advantage to reject it.

SHIPWRECK   To dream of a voyage in which you are shipwrecked means that you and a companion will shortly start on a journey liking each other, but you will return hating each other intensely. To dream that you are on a sinking ship denotes false friends. You must be on your guard against confiding any secret for some time.

SHIRT   To dream of putting on a shirt signifies travelling in foreign countries.

Whatever happens you can always keep smiling. No serious troubles will happen to you.

SHIVER   New garments will soon be yours and they will be very much to your liking.

SHOES   To dream you are wearing good shoes signifies financial advantages and a good reputation. The opposite signifies damage, disdain and dishonour. To dream you make shoes or slippers signifies poverty, except to artists. To dream you have new shoes on signifies comfort. To dream you see old shoes signifies loss. To dream of shoes falling off your feet or being old denotes poverty and distress; that you go barefooted signifies you will suffer much pain and affliction. To dream of your shoes being in need of repair is not a good dream, because it signifies that you will often be short of money. The lover who dreams that he or she is wearing new shoes will suffer from fickleness in the opposite sex, and will not marry his or her present sweetheart. Old shoes promise success in marriage. To married people, new shoes warn of coming financial problems, while old ones indicate that a stroke of good luck is coming to the dreamer.

SHOOTING To dream you shoot with a bow signifies comfort; that you fire a gun indicates profit, deceit and grief through anger. To dream you are out shooting is very favourable if you kill plenty of game. But if you dream you kill nothing, then it indicates bad luck and disappointment in love.

SHOOTING STAR To dream of seeing a shooting star means that lovers will be ardent in their affection.

SHOP When a man believes a shop is destroyed by fire, it signifies loss of goods and possessions.

SHORE Decide to see for yourself the person in your thoughts; you will not be disappointed.

SHOULDERS If anyone dreams they have large shoulders which are more brawny than usual, that signifies good luck, strength and prosperity, although such a dream is bad for prisoners as it denotes annoyance and grief, and that they are in danger of enduring much pain. To dream that your shoulders are painful or swollen signifies trouble and displeasure from relations.

SHOWER A light shower signifies gain and profit to labourers, but quite the opposite to businessmen, mechanics or craftsmen to whom it denotes obstruction, loss and damage to their merchandise.

SHROUD News of a wedding is at hand.

SICKNESS To dream of sickness is only fortunate to those in captivity or want. To the young, dreaming of sickness means marriage, although not always happy; the old dreaming of sickness may expect to receive money, often after it has ceased to be of much use to them.

SIEVE Lost opportunities; make up your mind to grasp the next.

SIGH To dream of hearing a sigh denotes trouble and anguish.

SIGHT To dream you have lost your sight indicates that you will violate your word, or else you or some of your children are in danger, or you will never see your friends again. To dream you have good and quick sight is an extraordinarily good dream, and indicates success. But a troubled and weak sight signifies want of money, and failure in business.

SIGNAL Waiting in a station for a train that is signalled is a portent of long delayed wishes that will at last be realised.

SIGNATURE Loyal companions will uphold you at all times.

SIGNPOST If you see a signpost, you must change your business methods or you will lose out. If you are in love, you will never succeed unless you are friendly and honest with your partner's parents.

SILK To dream you trade with a stranger in silk signifies profit and joy. To dream of silk either in pieces or for sewing signifies prosperity. To dream you are dressed in silk foretells that you will become rich. If a girl dreams of it she will soon see her lover.

SILKWORM These insects are good and productive to see in a dream as they indicate that you will emulate their industrious habits.

SILVER If you dream you gather up gold and silver, it signifies deceit and loss. To dream you eat silver signifies anger. If a pregnant woman dreams of silver, it shows she will have a girl and a straightforward delivery, but the child will not be wealthy. To dream of silver shows false friends are around you who will try to ruin you; in love, it denotes falsehood in your sweetheart. To dream you are receiving or packing up pieces of silver or money, if they are of little value, denotes want and a prison. If they are worth slightly more they indicate the receipt of a small sum of money, and the acquisition of some new friends. But if they are coins of value, they denote lack of success in all your undertakings. To dream you are looking at silver means that you are in danger of an attack of illness, only to be warded off by the greatest attention to cleanliness. If the silver is given to you in a dream it denotes sorrow.

SINGING If anyone dreams of singing, it signifies they will have reason to weep. To dream you hear singing signifies consolation in adversity, and recovery of health to those who are sick. To dream you sing a hymn or psalm signifies problems in business which may be eventually overcome.

SINGLE AGAIN For a married man or woman to dream of being single again is a sign of jealousy and gossip which will cause you much worry. Be true and trustful and all will be well.

SINKING Bad news of a friend, and losses in business.

SIPHON A happy time in a pretty frock; many compliments. For a man this dream signifies an invitation to a bachelor party.

SISTER To dream you see your dead brothers and sisters signifies a long life for the dreamer.

SITTING Advancement in the world, especially if sitting on a high stool.

SKATING Generally considered a warning of some coming danger.

SKELETON If you see a skeleton it is a sign of anxiety and domestic troubles.

SKIFF To watch one pass on a smooth river indicates that a valued friend will rise out of your sphere. To see one in difficulties or upset signifies a business failure. To be in one rowing yourself, however, means achievements and gain.

SKIN To dream you see a dark-skinned stranger is a sign of achievement and success.

To dream you have any disease or irritation of the skin signifies wealth and achievement. But to dream you see others with skin diseases signifies anger and worries.

SKULL An engagement is on the horizon.

SKY To see the sky clear and beautiful means that you will be loved and esteemed by everyone, and that even those who envy you will come to like you. If you dream of the sky, you are probably of a calm and affable character. Some eminent authors affirm that to dream of seeing the air clear and free from clouds signifies that something which has been lost or stolen will be discovered, and you will be respected and liked by everyone and make a successful voyage or journey – if you are planning this. But on the contrary, if you dream of a cloudy sky, that signifies sadness, sickness, melancholy and business problems.

SLATE To write on one, new plans; to break one, your plans will fail.

SLAUGHTER To see people sacrificed or killed is good for it is a sign that your business is accomplished or near completion.

SLEDGE Exciting times are in store for you, but do not be too venturesome.

SLEEP To sleep under shady trees with an attractive person means success in love.

SLEET Tedious company will demand your patience and an interesting disclosure will be made to you.

SLEEVE Much travel will be your lot in life.

SLIDING News of a wedding is just around the corner.

SLIPPERS For a bachelor to dream of a pair of slippers portends he will soon marry; for a young woman it signifies that she has recently met the man who in all probability will be her partner for life.

SMALLPOX To dream of smallpox denotes profit and wealth.

SMELLING To dream of sweet-smelling flowers in season signifies joy, pleasure and consolation. To dream of smelling them out of season, if they are white signifies business problems and lack of success; if yellow, the difficulties will not be as severe; if red, the difficulty will be extreme.

To dream of smelling roses in season is a good sign to anyone except those who are sick or criminals as they are in danger of severe illness. Roses out of season indicate the opposite.

To dream that you smell marjoram, hyssop, rosemary, sage or other herbs signifies hard work, trouble, sadness and weakness, except to doctors to whom such dreams are propitious. To dream you smell lilies out of season signifies your hopes and ambitions will be frustrated.

For a woman to smell laurel, olive or palm means she will have children; a girl will soon be married, a man will experience joy, prosperity, abundance and success in his enterprises.

To dream your feet smell bad signifies problems.

SMILING One of the very best of omens, whether you yourself are smiling or whether you see someone else smiling. Good luck will attend you.

SMOKE To dream of smoke signifies that you will meet

with success at an early date but it will be very short lived.

SMUGGLING This betokens a plan that will almost succeed but not quite.

SNAILS A dream of snails signifies intemperance and inconstancy.

SNAKE To dream you see a coiled snake signifies danger and imprisonment; it also denotes sickness and hatred. To dream you see a snake signifies you will be deceived by your lover. To dream you kill a snake is a sign you will overcome your enemies and anyone who envies you. To dream you see a snake that tries to bite your feet signifies envy; and if the creature bites painfully, that signifies sadness and discontent. Your adversaries will hurt you. If the snake hisses, however, they will have no power over you. To dream you see a serpent or seven-headed hydra signifies sin and temptation. To fight with serpents and adders signifies the overthrow of enemies. To dream you see many serpents signifies that you will be deceived by a woman.

To see a large serpent rise up to attack you indicates a powerful female enemy whom it will be very hard to avoid. If it tries to hurt you

but cannot, beware of false praise. If you kill it, you will defeat your adversaries.

SNOW To dream of snow in winter has no particular meaning because your mind is recalling the cold of the preceding day. If it is in another season, however, to dream you see the ground covered with snow, or that it is snowing out of season, is a very favourable dream to farmers, denoting a good harvest; however to businessmen, it signifies problems; and to soldiers, that their intentions will be frustrated. To see snow melting away means that you are in danger of losing money which you have worked hard to make.

SNUFF Pleasant surroundings and a happy time ahead.

SOAP An unexpected encounter will result in a solution of the matters which have puzzled you.

SODA A sign of a contented life despite much labour.

SOIL To dream that the soil is black signifies sorrow, melancholy and lack of intelligence.

SOLD To dream of being sold is a good sign unless you are rich or sick.

SOLDIER To dream of soldiers means that you have a considerable number of enemies, and from their actions in your dream you will be able to conclude whether they are to beat you, or vice versa.

SOLE To dream of soles means misfortune and anxiety.

SON If you dream of your son, you will gain happiness through your own efforts.

SORROW To dream of sorrow and being comforted means accidents and injury to the rich, but aid and assistance to the poor.

SOUP Speculations will turn out well.

SOUTH If you dream of a journey southwards or of being in southern places it is a good sign in love matters, but not in business.

SOWING SEEDS Avoid being involved in any uncertain matters such as speculations or lotteries.

SPADE A new vista of contentment will open before you. Keep to beaten tracks when out alone.

SPANGLES An invitation to a place of amusement will come your way.

SPARROW To dream of sparrows denotes that you will not receive much assistance from others in life, but will have to rely mainly on your own exertions. These however, will enable you to get a full share of what is available.

SPARROW HAWK A dream in which a sparrow hawk predominates is a warning to the dreamer against enemies who are conspiring against them.

SPATS An influential man is attracted to you, but be on your guard. He can help you, but may have an ulterior motive.

SPEAR A good sign of worldly successes and renown to come soon.

SPECTACLES A short change of scene; beware of double-dealing from strangers.

SPECTRE Few dreams are more certain of good luck to the dreamer than to dream of spectres.

SPELLING Success to all your plans will ensue if you dream of spelling.

SPENDING Be careful to economise for a time; money matters will improve after a long while.

SPIDER Should you dream of a spider you can infer that the failure of efforts you recently made must not discourage you because, by continued perseverance, you will in the long run be sure to succeed. If you dream that the spiders are crawling over you, you may expect to receive a large sum of money before you are much older. If you kill one it foretells future enjoyment for you. To see one spinning is a sign that much money is to come to you.

SPINNING To dream of spinning is good and shows a person to be diligent and industrious.

SPIRE Love and friendship will inspire you.

SPIT To dream you are in a kitchen turning a spit is the forerunner of troubles and misfortunes. Expect to be robbed, to lose your trade or money and that your friends will desert you. If you are in love, it shows your lover is bad-tempered, lazy and doomed to misfortune and poverty.

SPLEEN The spleen denotes the pleasure and content between friends. If anyone dreams his spleen is very healthy, he will be invited to a feast or celebration which will be very enjoyable. If, on the contrary, he imagines his spleen is swollen or diseased, some business or other of great importance will fall into his hands, that will bring him problems and anxiety.

SPONGE A portent of a highly placed admirer in the army or navy.

SPOTS An offer of promotion which you will do well to take.

SPRAIN To dream of a sprain means that you can expect an attempt to be made to borrow money from you under false pretences, and, if you yield, you will experience financial problems.

SPRAY High walls and fine surroundings will come into your view in an interesting manner.

SPRING To dream of spring in winter is an omen of a wedding soon to take place.

SPY Adventure will come your way, but you have a protective influence near you and will meet with no harm.

SQUARE Chequered material or a pattern of squares is a good sign of success.

SQUINT It is fortunate to dream of a man who squints; you have the affections of the one you love. But the reverse is true should the person in your dream be a woman.

SQUIRREL To dream of a squirrel shows that enemies are endeavouring to slander your reputation; to the lover, it shows your sweetheart is bad-tempered and drinks too much; if you have a lawsuit, it will be decided against you; if in trade, con-men will try to defraud you, and you will quarrel with your principal creditor.

STABLE A good companion will be yours for life.

STAG To dream of a stag signifies that your investments will prove profitable. If you chase one it foretells losses in business.

STAIN To dream of stained clothes presages scandal to their wearer.

STAIRS To descend a staircase means that your wish will be granted; to descend or tumble down them means the reverse.

STAMMER Fresh interests will lead to happiness.

STAMP Association with someone in a high official position will cause you some worry but much gain.

STAR To dream you see a clear starry sky signifies prosperity and advantage in a voyage or journey, and good news and profit in everything you do. If the stars are pale, it indicates all kinds of problems. To dream you see the stars disappear signifies loss and great anxiety. Such a dream is only good to criminals who will escape punishment. To dream you see the stars fall on top of your house signifies sickness, or that the house will be empty, or destroyed by fire. If you see the stars shining into the house, it signifies that the chief person of the family will be in danger of death. To dream you see stars with streaming tails signifies future evils by war and famine.

STARCHING To dream you are starching linen shows that you will be married to an industrious person, that you will be successful in life and save money, perhaps also that you are about to receive a letter containing some pleasant news.

STARLING To dream you see a starling signifies a small discontent.

STATIONERY You will be successful in business.

STATUE To dream you make a statue, whether of clay or anything else, is good for teachers and those who look after children. Statues also signify children to those who are married. To dream of seeing a bronze statue moving signifies riches.

STEALING A gift of jewellery will be offered you.

STEAM Doubts and dif-ferences will occur between you and one you love which only you can clear away.

STEEL A true and steadfast marriage partner will be yours unless the dream is of a knife, which means an enemy.

STEEPLE An unfortunate dream unless you think you are climbing one, which means achievement of your greatest wish.

STEPPING-STONES An omen of good fortune in love matters.

STEW A variety of presents will be made to you, including one from a sweetheart.

STILE Walk warily, for an enemy is trying to entrap you.

STILTS Pleasant views concerning children. Do not offend your associates by conceit or you may regret it.

STING To dream of being stung signifies grief and anxiety. To many, stings have signified love and also injuries by wicked people. To dream of being stung by bees is unlucky, for it means that you are about to enter on a succession of difficulties.

STOCKINGS The meaning depends on the stockings. If they are a light colour, it indicates sorrow; a dark colour indicates pleasure; a hole in one means you will lose something; woollen stockings indicate affluence; silk ones, hardships.

STOMACH If anyone dreams that their stomach is bigger and fatter than usual, their family and property will increase proportionately to the size of their stomach. If you dream that your stomach has grown thin, you will escape a bad accident. If anyone dreams that their stomach is swollen but still empty, they will become poor, though they will be well regarded by many people. To be wounded in the stomach by anyone you know signifies bad news to old women, but to young men and women it indicates good news.

STONE To dream of having a stone thrown at you denotes that you are in danger through your too free use of speech, and is a hint that to call people fools and expect that they will applaud you as intelligent is a mistake.

STOOL To dream of sitting on a stool means honour and achievement through your own merits.

STOOP If you dream of stooping to speak to someone it means a thrilling time followed by a quiet future.

STORK To dream you see storks in flocks in the air foretells the approach of enemies and thieves. In winter it signifies bad weather. To dream you see two storks together signifies marriage and procreation of good children who are helpful to their parents.

STORM To dream of a storm is an omen of dangers and difficulties.

STOUTNESS To dream of growing stout signifies that you are on the way to considerable wealth.

STOVE A burnt-out grate is a sign of hard times to come, but a stove filled with burning coal foretells prosperity.

STRANGE PLACE To dream of being in a strange place denotes a good legacy from a relation while you are in difficult circumstances.

STRANGER If you dream you strike a stranger, it signifies victory, assurance and success in your affairs. To dream you trade with a stranger signifies profit. To dream of a complete stranger indicates the return of a long-absent friend.

STRANGLING To dream of being strangled means that you will experience trouble caused by the one you dream of; to think you are strangling someone means that your wish will come true.

STRAW To dream of straw signifies misfortune and losses.

STRAWBERRIES To dream of strawberries denotes to a pregnant woman a straightforward delivery of a boy. To a girl, it means marriage with a man who will become rich and make her happy, while to a young man they denote that his wife will be sweet-tempered and they will have many children, all boys.

STREET To dream of a street in the heart of a great city is a sign that you will soon move to the country to find more peace and happiness there than is possible for you in the town.

STRIKING To dream you strike someone on the ear with your hand or punch them with your fist signifies peace and love between a man and his wife. If the dreamer is unmarried, it means they will soon meet someone for whom they have great respect, and that they will defeat their enemies.

STRING Strong powers of attraction are yours, which you must use carefully; a voyage is in your near future.

STRIPTEASE You must avoid indiscreet action or pay the price for it.

STRUGGLE To dream of struggling to escape from something or someone means great improvements in your health and strength.

STUMBLING Dreaming of stumbling means that a business in which you are interested is about to sustain severe losses through quite innocent misfortune.

STUMPS To dream of knocking out cricket stumps signifies a new friendship made within high walls and near water.

STUTTERING If you dream of someone stuttering, you will have problems making relations understand your point of view.

SUBMARINE You will need to explain your absence from an important event.

SUFFOCATION Avoid crowds or large groups of people.

SUGAR A dream into which sugar enters, whether eaten or seen only, denotes approaching illness, but not of a severe nature.

SUICIDE A sign of an overstrained mind and a warning to change your surroundings for a time.

SUITCASE You will receive an unwelcome visitor who will remain for some time.

SULK To dream of being sulky forebodes poverty; of a sulky friend, a fickle sweetheart.

SUMMER 'Dream of times out of season; hear of things out of reason.' If the dream comes in winter, the above holds good, but it is not a sign of good fortune at any other time.

SUMMERHOUSE Pleasant prospects for the future are indicated.

SUMMONS Adverse criticism and scandal will vex you.

SUMS If you cannot get them right, a dangerous friendship is portended which would be better broken.

SUN The sun represents unity, truth, light, fruitfulness, heat, abundance and wealth. To dream you see the sun rise above the horizon signifies good news and success in your designs. To dream you see the sun set signifies the opposite. To dream you see the sun signifies completion of business and revelation of secret things; to the sick it indicates recovery, to the prisoner liberty, and a cure to anyone with an eye problem.

To dream you see the sun clouded, red or hot, signifies obstruction in business, or danger to yourself and your family, but such a dream is good to criminals. To dream that the sun descends upon your house signifies danger from fire.

To dream the sun shines in your bedroom signifies gain, profit and happiness, and a son to married people.

To dream you see the sun obscured, or disappear, is a very bad sign, except to a criminal, for to others it can signify death or at least loss of sight through an accident or illness. To see the sun shine around your head signifies pardon to criminals and good reputation to others. To dream you enter a house where the sun shines signifies acquiring property.

To see the sun clear signifies that you will achieve your ambitions. To dream you see the sun in a cloud signifies danger. To see the sun and moon fall together is a bad sign. To dream the sun rises or sets in a clear sky is a very good augury to those who are just going to law. To dream of the sun rising and setting in a cloudy sky is bad.

Should the sun go behind a cloud and then emerge again, you may take it that even if you experience some problems all will come good in the end. If you are in love and dream that you see the sun shining brilliantly, your lover will make you a good partner in life. For a married person, the dream promises an improvement in domestic and business affairs.

SUNBEAM To dream you see sunbeams come into your bed signifies a fever.

SUNDAY For a young woman to dream of it being Sunday means that she is about to form an alliance with a clergyman, and the happiness or discontent of that alliance may be gathered from the brightness or otherwise of the day seen in the dream.

SUNDIAL Coming events in your immediate circle include a marriage and a death.

SUNFLOWER Carrying a sunflower indicates that you should try to be more modest in your behaviour.

SUNRISE To dream of seeing the sun rise denotes that you are about to take a step up in the world, perhaps by being offered a

partnership in a company in which you are at present only an employee.

SUNSET To dream that you are watching a particularly fine sunset is an omen of lingering illness.

SUNSTROKE You will be much envied and with good reason.

SUPPER To dream of this meal foretells news of a birth.

SURF You will need all your tact to avoid the attentions of an unwelcome admirer.

SURGEON The slight illness of a friend will cause a deeper relationship between you.

SURPLICE Contentment to the married and marriage to the single are indicated.

SUSPENDERS Anxiety caused through your own careless words; a broken suspender means an apology to be made.

SWALLOW To dream of a swallow signifies good news and good luck to those in whose houses they build their nests. To dream you see a swallow flying away is a sign that you will be forced by unforeseen circumstances to undertake a long journey. If several of these birds appear you will return much richer than you were when you started out.

SWAMP Bad luck in money matters or family arguments.

SWAN To dream of seeing swans denotes a happy marriage and many children, who will do well and become rich, and fill your old age with joy and happiness. To the lover, they denote constancy and affection in your sweetheart. In trade they show success but much anxiety from the disclosure of secrets.

SWARM A swarm of bees means prosperity in the family.

SWEARING To dream that you hear violent arguments and swearing is a sign that you will go down in the world, and be short of money.

SWEAT If you dream of sweating, you will work hard but gain satisfactory rewards.

SWEEPING To dream of sweeping means that the death of a relative, though at first a sorrow, will eventually prove of advantage in improving your worldly

position. The unmarried woman who dreams that she is sweeping will one day be wealthy and have everything she wants. To a married woman the dream promises a dutiful family, who will more than repay her for her care and attention.

SWEETS To dream you taste sweets signifies subtlety.

SWEETHEART To dream that your lover is beautiful and pleasing to you is a good omen. But be cautious if you dream that he or she is fickle and changeable.

SWELLING To dream that your face is swollen shows that you will accumulate wealth; or if in love, that your sweetheart will marry you.

SWIMMING To dream of swimming denotes much hard work, sadness and sickness. To dream of swimming in a large river signifies future peril and danger. To dream you are swimming with your head above the water denotes great success in your undertakings, whether they are in love, trade, sea or farming. To dream of swimming with your head under water shows that you will experience a great trouble, and hear some very unpleasant news from a person with whom you had lost contact. In trade it shows loss of business, and that you may be imprisoned for debt; in love it denotes disappointment.

SWING   A change of plan will prove very successful in the long run. A gift of flowers will soon be made to you.

SWOON   To dream you see a person swoon is unfortunate to the unmarried. To the married it is a sign they will become rich and prosperous.

SWORD   If you dream you have been stabbed with a sword, you will receive an extraordinary kindness from the person who attacked you. If blood is not drawn, the advantage and delight will be the less. If you dream that you are mortally wounded with a sword, it is a sign that you will receive several good

turns from whoever wounded you, according to the proportion, number and size of the wounds. If you dream that your friend strikes you over the breast with a sword, it signifies bad news to the old, but friendship to the young. To dream of having a sword is a sign of poverty; if you dream you see a man flourish a sword it indicates that you will make a loss.

SWORDFISH   If you are fishing for a swordfish, the object you are working towards is not worth the effort.

SYNAGOGUE   Progress in business or academic achievement.

SYRUP   You enjoy the company of young people and can advance their careers or their love-life.

TABLE A dream in which a table is the most prominent object means that your life is to be calm and methodical, without startling events, and almost entirely destitute of ups and downs.

TABLEAU If a young lady dreams that she is appearing in a tableau it is a sign that her future husband will be fond of showy dress, and not very intelligent.

TABLECLOTH To dream of a dirty tablecloth foretells that you will have plenty to eat.

TACK Your quick speech and sharp wit make you feared; be kind, unless you do not mind a lonely future.

TACKING COTTON To dream of using quantities of tacking cotton presages new clothes for a joyful occasion.

TAFFETA To dream of taffeta signifies that you will have wealth but that it will bring you no satisfaction.

TAIL To dream you have a tail indicates that you will have to apologise for someone else's actions.

TAILOR If a young girl dreams that her boyfriend is a tailor and she likes him it is a sign that she will marry an easy-going chap, who will allow her to be both master and mistress after marriage. The married woman who dreams of a tailor will do well to give less thought to dress than before. Vanity is causing her to be talked about and snubbed.

TALISMAN To see a talisman or charm warns the dreamer of danger on land. Walk carefully in crowded places.

TALKING To dream you talk idly at church and are in a daydream signifies envy and sin. To talk with your brother signifies anxiety. Talking with powerful men signifies honour, profit and gain. To dream you talk with an enemy signifies you must beware of him. To talk with your son signifies damage. To dream you see many people in debate shows some design against you, and that you will argue with relations.

TALON If a creature with talons should scratch you in a dream an enemy will triumph over you. But should it run away or fly, your enemies are powerless to hurt you.

TAMARIND TREE To dream of tamarinds shows much anxiety and uneasiness caused by a woman; failure in trade; also, a rainy season, and bad news from abroad.

TAMBOURINE A dream of a tambourine forebodes inconstancy in husband or sweetheart; be watchful or a rival will supplant you.

TAMING To dream you tame wild beasts signifies damage.

TANDEM To dream of driving horses in this manner signifies two lovers who will cause you difficulty through jealousy.

TANGLE To dream of a tangled skein of wool means difficult people to contend with; patience, however, will be well rewarded.

TANTRUM If you see someone having a tantrum, you will be at a loss to know how to deal with a situation.

TAP To dream of a water tap is a sign of a good income, especially if water is running freely from it.

TAPER If you dream of carrying a lighted taper, it is the only burden you will ever carry – for wisdom and good fortune will protect your path.

TAPESTRY Great enjoyment will come to you from small causes.

TAPIOCA To cook tapioca is a sign of luck in some small speculation; to eat it in dreams is a warning of small losses.

TAR To see a barrel of tar merely presages travel; if it is on your clothes, it means much vexation through gossip.

TARANTULA Ill-health and a nasty experience.

TARGET Architectural plans will claim your attention. A change of residence is indicated.

TART To dream you make tarts signifies joy and profit.

TASSEL Cheerful company will visit you; many small gifts will please you.

TATTOO   You will hear gossip which should not be repeated.

TAX   You will make money.

TAXI   Hasty news will be sent to you; be on guard against false information.

TEA   After dreaming that you have received an invitation to tea with a friend, be wary of new friends. You will probably meet someone it would be well to avoid. To dream you are drinking tea is a sign that, although many joys will come to you during life, they will be interspersed with troubles, which will give you rather more than your share of worries. To dream of sitting drinking tea means that gossip will soon be busy with your reputation, and that you will in consequence be caused a great deal of annoyance.

TEACHER   If the dreamer is teaching, an invitation to a solemn occasion is portended; if being taught, anger about a trifling slight will vex you.

TEAM   To dream of a team can denote the death of a relative, a bad-tempered lover or lack of success in undertakings.

TEAPOT   To dream of a teapot signifies that you will soon form new friendships.

TEARS   To dream of tears has the opposite meaning. You will have joy and pleasure on the day following your dream.

TEASE   Your secret hopes will be discovered and much discussed, yet you will gain them in the end.

TEETH   The teeth are taken for the closest relations and best friends; the front teeth are applied to children, brother and other close relations, the upper teeth signify the males, and the lower the females. If anyone dreams they have lost or damaged one of their teeth, that indicates injury or death to a relation. But if you dream that your teeth are more attractive and whiter than usual that signifies joy, prosperity, good news and friendship among relations. If a person dreams that one of their teeth has grown longer than the rest, they will be in trouble with some of their relations. The upper eye-tooth signifies the father and the lower the mother. If you dream that one of your front teeth is loose, or turned black, or that it is painful, one of your friends or relations will be sick, or in trouble. If you dream your teeth have grown more attractive, white and firm than usual, you will enjoy happiness and profit from your relations and friends. If anyone imagines they are cleaning their teeth they will give money to their relations or friends. If some of the teeth are larger than the rest, so that the dreamer is hindered from speaking and eating, that signifies arguments among relations. To dream you pull out your teeth is not a good omen for you. To dream your teeth are taken out or fall out denotes serious troubles for your children or some relations.

TELEGRAM   Sending a telegram is a sign that before long you will be giving serious news to your friends. To receive a telegram indicates that you will be concerned at the silence of a friend from whom you have heard regularly.

TELEPHONE   To dream of receiving or making a telephone call signifies that you are on the eve of making a considerable sum by a lucky invention.

TELESCOPE   A young man dreaming of looking through a telescope learns from it that his lover has another admirer of whom he should beware. If the telescope is seen pointing to the right it is an indication that at present your lover cares nothing for the rival.

TELEVISION   To view an important event on television indicates commercial activity crowned with success.

TEMPER   For a lover to dream of being in a violent temper denotes that you will have many formidable rivals who, after causing you a great deal of anxiety and uneasiness, you will triumph over. It also indicates that you will receive good news from a long-absent friend abroad who will have overcome many hardships and extreme difficulties.

TEMPEST   To dream you are in a storm or a tempest shows that you will, after many difficulties, be very happy, that you will become extremely rich, and marry exceedingly well.

TEMPLE   A foreign temple is a portent of curious experiences to be yours before long. Discretion will bring you a big reward.

TEMPTATION   If you dream you are tempted to do some

foolish action it means that you will experience much unrest through being the object of unjust suspicions.

TENNIS Social advancement is indicated by seeing or playing tennis in a dream.

TENT You will find great pleasure in helping the love affairs of some youthful friends of yours.

TERRACE A rise in income will be yours.

TERRIER All dreams of dogs signify friends, except when they snarl or bite – which forebodes quarrels.

TERROR Be wary of others who may cheat you of what is your due.

THAW A former adversary will become your friend shortly.

THEATRE To dream that you are in a theatre is a sign that you will shed many tears of repentance for some action which cannot be undone.

THEFT To dream that you steal is only good to someone who is trying to deceive another.

THERMOMETER Be more

attentive to your appearance or you will be ridiculed.

THIEF To dream of thieves denotes loss and trouble.

THIGH The thighs represent the relations. If you dream that both your thighs are broken, or beaten black and blue, you will die in a foreign country alone, without the assistance of your relations. If you dream that your thighs have grown bigger and stronger than usual, your relations will be promoted to an important position which will prove advantageous. If you dream that you have been wounded on the thigh, you will not accomplish your desires, but be annoyed by your relations. To dream you see the fair and white thighs of a woman signifies health and joy. If a man dreams he has well-proportioned thighs it signifies a happy voyage.

THIMBLE The girl who dreams that she has received a present of a thimble will never marry. To dream that you lose your thimble promises continued happiness in your home.

THINNESS If a girl dreams that she has grown thin, it predicts tears for a lost lover.

THIRST If you dream your thirst is quenched with clear,

fresh water, you will live happily and become very wealthy; if the water was luke warm or dirty, you will end your days ill and unhappy. To dream you are thirsty and cannot find a drink is a bad omen and a sign that the dreamer will not finish their business.

THISTLE Quarrels can be avoided if you are tactful.

THORN In dreams, thorns signify problems. To dream that you have a thorn in your foot indicates that you will move to another district, and will not like the people with whom you will have to associate.

THOUGHTS To dream that you are unsettled in your thoughts signifies joy.

THREAD To wind thread denotes wealth gained by thrifty ways; to break it, hard times, to unravel knotted thread, a mystery solved.

THREE To see three birds flying, or ships sailing, is a sign of a perilous journey to be taken, which you will, however, come safely through.

THRASHING It is not a fortunate omen when you find yourself being thrashed in a dream, but it is a good sign if you thrash someone else.

THRESHING Should you dream that you are threshing corn you will rise to an important position, and will have the satisfaction of knowing that you have achieved the success solely by your own efforts.

THRIFT To dream of being thrifty is a dream of contrary. You must avoid extravagance.

THROAT If you dream that your throat is cut with a knife, you will be injured by someone. If you dream you cut the throat of an acquaintance you will do them an injury; if you do not know the person, you will injure a stranger. To dream your throat is cut and you are not dead signifies hope and success in business. To dream that you have anything wrong with your throat may generally be taken to mean that you will have a good voice or be a good public speaker, if only you will take the trouble to develop your talents.

THRONE After seeing an empty throne you must be prepared to hear that the head of your family has met with an accident.

THUMB To dream that you have injured your thumb indicates that you will shortly be in a serious quandary. You will have to choose between giving offence to someone, whom it would pay you to please, and making yourself look ridiculous in the eyes of your acquaintances.

THUNDER To dream you hear thunder and see lightning is a very good omen; it denotes success in trade, good crops to the farmer, and a speedy and happy marriage to the lover. If you are looking for a job you will get it; if you have a lawsuit, it will go in your favour. It also indicates news from a distant country, intimating that a close relative has obtained a very lucrative situation, in which he will have an opportunity of doing his friends a great deal of good.

THUNDERBOLT To dream you see a thunderbolt fall near you without a storm signifies that the dreamer will be forced to run away and live elsewhere. To dream that a thunderbolt falls on your head or on your house signifies some serious loss or damage to you or your property.

THYME Almost all herbs are a sign of good fortune, especially if they seem to be growing strongly or are in flower.

TIARA Should a girl dream of wearing a sparkling diadem, it is a warning that her ambition is beyond her reach.

TICKET Good tidings long expected will come at last.

TICKLE A misunderstanding will be cleared up. If the tickle is in the nose or throat, so that the dreamer sneezes, they will surely be asked to lend money.

TIDE To dream of seeing a strong tide flowing in is a sign of favourable circumstances soon to happen.

TIGER If you dream that you escape from a tiger it is a good omen but it signifies great danger if you are caught by one.

TILE Be careful of accidents with tools, especially should the tile fall and break.

TILL To dream of a shop till filled with coins betokens wealth and affluence; an empty till is a warning of dishonest employees.

TIMBER To fell timber is a presage of a long engagement

ending in a happy marriage, unless the timber seems to be old and rotten – in which case the engagement will be broken.

TIME To dream of anyone playing music out of time indicates that if you persevere you will become a musician, perhaps even a professional one.

TIN A dream signifying that counterfeit friendship will be taken for true. Test your friends before you trust them.

TINKER Do not meddle in a friend's affairs after you have dreamed of a tinker, or you will do more harm than good.

TIPTOE A slight tiff will part you from one you love if you do not take care to make up a quarrel before nightfall.

TIREDNESS Take no risks with your business affairs. You are in danger of losses.

TOAD To dream of fighting with a toad indicates success.

TOADSTOOL Eating a toadstool signifies a risk not worth taking.

TOAST This is a favourable sign presaging true friends and homely joys in the family circle.

TOBACCO To dream of smoking indicates waste, though it is not exactly an omen of poverty, though waste always precedes shortages. If you dream of seeing large piles of tobacco it is a sign of bad luck and loss in speculation. To dream you take snuff is a bad omen in love affairs. But if you dream you sneeze when you take it, it is a sign of long life.

TOBOGGAN You will soon be involved in someone else's affairs so deeply that it will be difficult to extricate yourself. Be careful of every step.

TOMATO A portent of comfortable circumstances which you will attain by your own efforts.

TOMB To dream you see a tomb is in general a good dream, but fallen and ill-kept graves are the opposite. To dream of wandering among tombs denotes that you will shortly receive money through the death of a relation. To dream that you are erecting a tomb signifies marriages, weddings and the birth of children. But if the dreamer imagines that he sees the tomb fall to ruin, that signifies sickness and problems to him and his family.

TONGUE If you dream of having a sore on your tongue it is a sign that you have either spoken slander or will be tempted to do so.

TOOL Dreaming of tools portends increased financial reward.

TOOTHACHE You will have much to be grateful for in a letter from a distant friend.

TOP To dream that you play with a spinning top signifies pain and travel which will lead to some advantage.

TORCH If you see a torch put out, it signifies sadness, sickness and financial problems. If you hold a burning torch it is a good sign, especially to the young, for it signifies that they will enjoy their lives, achieve their ambitions, overcome their enemies and be respected and liked. To see someone else hold a torch is bad news to anyone who wants to conceal a secret.

TORNADO A dream warning you against strife in your home or in business. It will surely bring disaster in either.

TORPEDO A presage of love at first sight, which will completely alter your life.

TORRENT Do not rush at things too violently; power is not the only good thing in the world. If you cross the torrent in your dream, you will accomplish your aims.

TORTOISE To dream of seeing a tortoise crawling along, especially if crawling up a hill, means that you will reach a high position in life through hard work and perseverance. This animal also signifies long life and success.

TORTURE To dream of being tortured signifies domestic bliss.

TOTEM POLE An impending love affair.

TOURNAMENT Excellent news and a healed quarrel are denoted.

TOWEL You will undergo a brief illness, but will recover very quickly.

TOWER To dream that you are ascending a tower signifies that you will experience reverses in the fortune of your affairs.

TOWN For a country dweller to dream of a large town is a warning against dangerous ambitions. But for a townsman, increased business and gain is signified.

TOWN CLERK   To dream of being a town clerk signifies that you will do someone else's work with difficulty and without payment.

TOY   This dream indicates that your family will be very clever and successful.

TRADING   To dream you are trading in wool with a stranger signifies profit; in iron, loss and misfortune; in silk, satin, velvet and other fine fabrics, profit and joy.

TRAFFIC   Many friends and some public dignity are promised.

TRAGEDY   To dream you see a tragedy acted signifies hard work, loss of friends and money, together with grief and anxiety.

TRAIN   To dream that you carry a young bride's train is a sign that you will meet a young man at a wedding who will fall in love with you. He will ask to see more of you, and even hint that he would like to marry you, but his motives are dubious.

After dreaming that you see a train travelling quickly be careful not to undertake a long journey for at least a week. You will be in danger of losing your life if you ignore the warning.

TRAMP   An absent friend is thinking of you. A letter from that friend is on its way.

TRANSFIGURATION   To dream that you are changed from small to large and then even larger is a good sign signifying increase of business and goods, but to be much larger than a man signifies a crisis. For a man to dream he is a woman means that you will find a woman to love, or that your work will become easier. If a woman dreams that she is an unmarried man, she will find a husband, or, if she has no children, she will have a son. But if she is both married and has a son, she may become a widow. To dream that you are made of gold means you will become very rich. To the sick, however, it means worsening health. To dream that you are made of brass indicates success. To dream that you are made of iron foretells infinite miseries. To dream that you are made of earth is not a good omen, except to potters or anyone who earns their living through the earth. To be made of stone is a sign you will receive injuries and wounds. If you dream that you have been changed into a beast the significance depends on the animal in question.

TRANSFORMATION To dream you see yourself transformed into a tree signifies joy and profit.

TRAP To dream of traps and anything used to catch animals is a bad omen, unless you are looking for employees.

TRAP DOOR A surprising and unpleasant letter, together with the loss of an important key, will worry you. Look for the latter in a wooden hiding place.

TRAPEZE Being an acrobat on a trapeze signifies passionate affairs. But if you fall, be cautious.

TRAVELLING If you travel through a wood and catch yourself on the briars and bushes, it means that you will encounter many troubles and hindrances. To travel over high hills and rocky places signifies advancement.

TREACHERY Beware of hypocritical friends.

TREACLE You will hear pleasant words, which will certainly stick in your memory.

TREASURE To dream you find a treasure shows you will be betrayed by your closest friend. You have placed your confidence in someone unworthy of your regard. To dream you are seeking treasure is a sign that you will travel abroad and perhaps settle in a foreign country.

TREAT Financial affairs will prosper for you owing to the good influence of one much above you.

TREE To dream you see all sorts of green or blossoming trees is a sign of comfort and enjoyment. But if you dream they are dry, or without leaves, uprooted, burned or struck by lightning, that denotes annoyance, fear, displeasure and grief. If you dream you have gathered the fruit of an old tree, that indicates you will be heir to an elderly person. To dream you fell trees signifies loss. To see trees or climb them signifies future honour. To see withered trees signifies deceit. To see trees bearing fruit signifies gain and profit. To see trees without blossom signifies completion of business. To dream you see trees in blossom denotes a happy marriage with your present lover and many children who will all do extremely well in life. To the tradesman it denotes success in business. To the sailor, pleasant and lucrative voyages. To dream that you are planting trees foretells that, although at present there may seem little promise of your ever reaching a high position, your affairs will gradually improve until you will have nothing to worry you. To dream of seeing a tree growing means that though comparatively unimportant now, you will in the end be the most important person where you live. Should the tree seen in your dream be in leaf, it signifies that you will be happy in your children when you have them, and that some of them at least will rise to distinction.

TRELLIS A firm friendship will prove the foundation of your success in life.

TRENCH An evil influence is near you; do not be entrapped.

TRESPASSING To dream you are on forbidden premises presages a very strong attraction towards one who is already married. There is the utmost danger in this friendship and your dream is the warning sent to you.

TRIAL You have an admirer whose merits you have not hitherto valued. You would be wise to study and develop this friendship.

TRIANGLE You will have to choose between two lovers.

TRIDENT The girl who dreams of a trident will most certainly be loved by a sailor.

TRIGGER You will receive compliments upon your abilities and these may shortly lead to advancement.

TRINKET Your loved one is vain and fickle. Do not wear your heart upon your sleeve.

TRIPE A rival in business is trying to steal your position. Be watchful and attentive to your own interests.

TRIPLETS You are very unlikely to have such an occurrence in your life or family if you dream of them. Instead, you will have cause to regret your lack of home ties.

TROUBLE A change of residence is indicated.

TROUSERS This dream signifies flirtations to the married, and quarrels to the single dreamer.

TROUT To dream of trout signifies that your troubles will vanish.

TRUMPET To dream you play or hear trumpets played signifies trouble and arguments. To the tradesman it indicates the loss of business; to the farmer, bad crops; to the lover, insincerity in his lover. Sickness and death will cause you to shed many tears during the following year. To dream of playing the trumpet is good for anyone who fights, but it indicates the revealing of secrets, and means death to the sick.

TRUNCHEON To dream of wielding this is a warning against thieves.

TRUNK A traveller will return from abroad. A wish will be granted in connection with a home.

TRYST A reconciliation or a re-established friendship will end romantically.

TUB Hard times, if empty, but better days to come if full.

TUG Merry company and a wedding between middle-aged lovers is indicated.

TULIP A short engagement and a secret marriage will be the fate of the girl who dreams of tulips.

TUMBLER To dream that you drink from a clean tumbler denotes health and activity, but from a dirty one the reverse.

TUMOUR To dream you have a tumour in your shoulder signifies trouble and displeasure from relations.

TUNNEL To dream that you are in a tunnel and experience fear is a sign that you will shortly make a wrong decision in a matter of some importance. To anyone in love it foretells that you will have reason to mistrust your sweetheart. If, however, you can see light at the end of the tunnel, your lover will reform and make a good companion if you reason with them. To dream of going through a tunnel with a light at the end is a good dream for the depressed, for it signifies that if their lives are now dull and gloomy they will brighten up in the long run into peace and joy.

TURKEY This bird brings a warning of sickness. Take good care of your health, or you will have a serious breakdown. To dream you see a turkey strutting about is a sign you will overcome your enemies. To dream of dead turkeys denotes that you will encounter trouble.

TURNIP   To dream of being in a turnip field denotes the acquisition of money, and if you marry you will be happy and thrive in the world.

TURTLE   A promise of wishes to be fulfilled. The lover who dreams of eating a turtle will marry into a good family.

TURTLE DOVE   To dream of a turtle dove signifies that much affection will be given to the dreamer.

TWINS   To dream that you see twins is a sign that you will have to work for your own upkeep to the end of your life.

TYPEWRITER   As long as the machine is working well, this indicates success at work.

UGLY The girl who dreams that she has received a proposal of marriage from an ugly man will marry a handsome one.

ULCER To dream you have ulcers on your arms signifies annoyance, sadness and failure in business. If anyone dreams that their flesh is swollen by an ulcer, that indicates money. If a parent dreams that one of their children is troubled with mouth ulcers, it is a good sign that the child will be eloquent.

UMBRELLA To dream that you lose your umbrella is a sure sign that you will receive a gift from an unexpected quarter. To dream that you break or tear your umbrella indicates that you will be blamed for a misdeed which you have not committed, and will find it difficult to prove your innocence.

UMPIRE Family content-ment or arguments are indi-cated, appropriate to whe-ther your umpiring decisions are accepted or questioned.

UNDERTAKER To dream of an undertaker is a promising omen. You will enjoy good health for some time to come.

UNDRESSED If you dream of being in public not fully dressed, be cautious of word and act, or gossip will distress you.

UNFAITHFULNESS A dream of contrary. All will go well with your future, if you dream that your lover, husband, or wife is unfaithful.

UNFORTUNATE To dream that you are unfortunate foretells that your hard work will bring you success.

UNHAPPINESS A dream of contrary. The more miserable you are in your dream, the better for you in real life.

UNICORN To dream of fabulous creatures presages anxiety caused by falsehoods.

UNIFORM This dream signifies a chance of promotion which will bring you the utmost good fortune in love as well as a better position.

UNION JACK   This is an excellent dream denoting a chance to go abroad with a faithful marriage partner.

UNIVERSITY   A sign that you are fortunate in your talents and in your friends.

UNKINDNESS   To dream of the unkindness of one you love means the reverse. Your affection is as deeply returned.

UNLOCKING   A discovery will be made in your home; do not try to keep a secret from those who love you.

UNMARRIED   For married people to dream of being single again is a sign of danger from jealousy and gossip. Be true, and trust each other and all will be well.

UPROAR   To dream of scenes of confusion and uproar signifies a decision which will be arrived at soon after long delay; it will be as you wish.

URN   This portends news of very young relations who will achieve great distinction much to your pride and delight.

VACCINATION You are in danger of giving more affection than its recipient is worth; keep a guard on your heart and obey your head.

VALENTINE This predicts news of an old sweetheart who still thinks much of you.

VALLEY To dream of a valley signifies a temporary sickness.

VAMPIRE A bad omen; you will marry for money and find it a bad bargain.

VAN Do not act on the impulse of the moment; all things come to one who waits.

VASE You are apt to give too much thought to appearances; try to value useful qualities in one who loves you.

VAT To dream of a full vat indicates that you will always have a fund of wisdom and wealth at your disposal; an empty vat signifies your need for both in the near future.

VAULT To dream of being in a hollow vault, a deep cellar or the bottom of a deep pit signifies a marriage for a widow; her husband will work hard and never understand her.

VEAL Dreaming of veal foretells good luck.

VEGETABLE To dream of any vegetable is an indication of unrewarded work; to gather vegetables signifies quarrels, and to eat them indicates loss in business.

VEIL To dream you are wearing a veil predicts that you will have reason to hide from someone who seeks you for revenge. For a young woman to dream that she sees a bridal veil is a sign that someone will soon fall ill and die in her house. To dream that she sees a bride wearing a veil means that a female cousin of hers will be engaged to a young man, but when everything is ready for the wedding her lover will elope with another woman he knew before. A black veil foretells a separation.

VEIN   Cutting a vein foretells bad news from a close friend.

VELVET   To dream you trade with a stranger in velvet signifies profit and joy. You will talk with a powerful person after dreaming of velvet. To dream you are wearing a velvet dress promises wealth and enjoyment. To dream of buying, wearing or looking at velvet indicates that you will shortly make a considerable profit. If the velvet is black, it will be in a business transaction; if it is red, it will be a personal gain.

VENISON   To dream about venison denotes change in affairs. To dream you eat it signifies misfortune.

VENTRILOQUIST   Someone you do not like will spread false and disparaging rumours about you.

VERDICT   This dream indicates hasty preparations for a land journey caused by the good fortune of a friend.

VERMIN   To dream of vermin indicates that you will soon be entertaining a person who, while pretending to do you a favour, will do his or her best to make trouble between you and your partner.

VERSES   This means that you will not succeed if you work alone; take a partner.

VERTIGO   Your lover may be taking advantage of your credulity.

VEST   There is hostility around you; guard your actions and conceal your suspicions if you would overcome it.

VET   You will suffer a slight accident.

VEXATION   Foretells prosperity.

VICAR   To dream that the vicar of the parish calls upon you is a sign that you will shortly call upon him, to ask him to officiate at a wedding, baptism or funeral.

VICTORIA CROSS   To dream you are presented with this honour is a sign that you will win your good fortune by merit alone.

VICTORY   This is an omen of failure through strife; do not take sides in other people's quarrels.

VICTUALS   To help others to food denotes social pleasures; to eat in dreams signifies loss of business.

VIEW To dream of a beautiful and sunlit scene presages a most fortunate future.

VIGIL To dream of keeping a long vigil is a sign of hope deferred, but sure to be fulfilled in the end.

VILLA To dream of buying a villa denotes a marriage as soon as you have saved enough. Selling a villa in a dream is unfortunate and indicates losses.

VILLAGE This dream promises an offer of a change which will prove most important to your future.

VILLAIN To dream of a ruffian or villain denotes a letter or present from one you love.

VINE To dream you see a vine signifies abundance, riches and fertility. It is an especially good omen. A dream of a vine is a sure indication that things will go well with you. Your dearest wish will be fulfilled, and you will not suffer any problems for some time to come.

VINEGAR To dream that you drink vinegar signifies sickness, treachery and deceit. Anyone in love will find that their sweetheart is unfaithful.

VINTAGE This dream foretells successful business operations and affection rewarded.

VIOLENCE If you are violently attacked it portends better things for you; to see violence to others means festivities among cheerful friends.

VIOLET The violet is an omen of good. You have no enemies, and your love is fully returned. To dream of violets when they are out of season signifies a newly awakened affection.

VIOLIN To dream you see someone else play a violin signifies good news, harmony and a good relationship between man and wife, employer and employee. To dream that you hear the music of a violin is a sign that you will receive an invitation to join in a celebration, probably a wedding. To dream that you are playing the instrument promises a rapid rise to a life of ease.

VIRGIN If you see a virgin talking in your dream, it shows that your life will be happy and contented.
    A virgin dreaming that she has lost her virginity signifies great danger.

VIRGIN MARY To dream that you hear the Holy Virgin Mary speaking signifies consolation, recovery of health, and all good fortune. To dream you talk with the Virgin Mary signifies joy.

VIRGINAL To dream you play or see someone else play the virginal signifies the death of relations.

VISION Danger is in store to the person who appears to you.

VISIT To dream of receiving a visit means that you ought to cultivate the art of being friendly with everyone you meet, because a stranger will shortly be introduced to you who will have it in his power to make your fortune. Dreaming of paying a visit indicates that before long you will see the need to leave your present locality and try a new one, which will be a great change for the better.

VISITOR To dream you receive an unexpected visitor indicates that you will soon hear of a birth, probably in your family.

VOICE To dream you hear a voice, but cannot see who is speaking shows that you will be deluded by a con-man. If in your dream you hear voices it is a very significant dream. If they are angelic voices, a friend who is ill may die. If you hear voices of horror or dismay one or more of your friends or relatives will meet with an accident, either on the railway or at sea. If you hear voices of harmony you will have peace and joy in all your relationships.

VOLCANO If anyone dreams of a volcano that signifies that someone powerful will oppress and destroy good men.

VOLUNTEER If you dream you are a volunteer, you will be a soldier and could lose your life in battle.

VOMITING To dream of vomiting signifies profit to the poor; or problems to the rich.

VOODOO Do not be afraid to trust your own judgement.

VOTING You must be more confident if you wish to fulfil your hopes; you are favoured but too diffident.

VOW To dream of a broken vow is a bad omen.

VOYAGE A message from a distance is soon to be received.

VULTURE   A vulture signifies a dangerous enemy. If you kill one it foretells conquest or misfortune. To see one eating its prey means that your troubles will cease and you will be fortunate.

WADDING To see or use quantities of wadding in a dream is a sign that health troubles will cause you to become very thin. Your business, however, will prosper.

WADDLING To see birds that usually swim waddling on land signifies that uncertain matters will be satisfactorily concluded.

WADING If a girl dreams of wading in clear water it is a sign that she will soon marry happily. If the water is muddy it foretells that she will only be happy for a short time, then will experience problems. If a man dreams of wading it denotes that he will be engaged in an intrigue which will land him in the law courts.

WAFTED To dream of moving in the air without wings is a sign of small vexations.

WAGER This portends losses. Act cautiously.

WAGES To receive them,

danger of small thefts; to pay them, money from a legacy.

WAGON A bad omen. Your life will be shadowed by trouble and you will never improve your position.

WAILING To dream you hear wailing and weeping from unseen voices is a bad sign of loss of someone dear to you.

WAINSCOT To dream that you hear a mouse in the wainscotting of a house portends a good friend in humble circumstances.

WAIST To dream of putting a belt around your waist is an omen of unexpected money; to fasten anything round the waist of another, you will be able to assist that person before long.

WAITER To dream of being at a table where you are waited upon is a sign of an invalid whom you will have to nurse shortly.

WALKING To dream of walking in the dirt or among

thorns signifies sickness. To dream you walk in rushing water signifies adversity and grief. To dream you walk at night signifies trouble and melancholy. To dream you walk in a forest signifies trouble. To walk in a garden signifies joy. To walk on holy ground is a good sign. Walking on thorns signifies the destruction of enemies. To walk when your feet are sore signifies lack of food. To walk with four-footed animals signifies sickness. To dream that you are walking a long distance is a sign that you will one day find it difficult to get a job. To dream of walking first with friends then alone signifies that in pursuit of what you think your duty you will give offence to many, but that everything will come right in the end with your unfriendly critics coming to see that you were, in fact, in the right and they in the wrong.

WALKING STICK   You will be given assistance in a great difficulty.

WALL   To dream of walls signifies dangerous enterprises and lack of success; if you climb them and the ascent is easy it foretells success in business.

WALLET   This portends important news from an unexpected source.

WALLFLOWER   To see and smell these flowers is a sign that you will be sought after, especially if you see them growing in a wall.

WALNUTS   To dream you see and eat walnuts signifies difficulty and trouble.

WALTZ   An admirer is concealing his affection from you. Be kind.

WANDERING   Dreaming of wandering aimlessly is a sign of approaching trouble, sometimes about a love affair of the heart but more often about money. To judge whether the problem is to be of long or short duration, try to remember if it was broad daylight or in the dark. If dark, the trouble will be long-lasting.

WAR   To dream of war signifies trouble and anger to everyone except to captains and soldiers. You will become the object of unjust suspicion and suffer much from the sneers of your so-called friends. To dream of fighting and winning shows danger avoided.

WARBLING   To hear birds

warbling is a sign of
happiness in love.

WARDER To dream of a
prison warder is a 'contrary'
dream, signifying a happy
holiday soon to come.

WAREHOUSE A dream of
good omen. You will be
successful in business and
married life.

WART To dream you have
warts signifies you will
become rich.

WASHING To dream of
washing in a fountain, pond
or brook of running water, or
in a clean stream, denotes
happiness and joy. But to
dream you wash or bathe in
your clothes is evil and
indicates sickness and great
danger. To wash your feet
signifies disturbance. To wash
your hands signifies disquiet
and anxiety. To wash your
head signifies avoidance of
danger. To wash yourself in
the sea signifies loss and
damage. To dream of
washing clothes signifies that
you will sustain or escape an
injury. To dream of washing
your face signifies that you
will settle a quarrel to your
advantage.

WASP To dream you are
stung by a wasp, signifies
anxiety and trouble caused
by envious people, and a
warning of strife to come.

WASTING If you dream you
have grown thin and wasted,
you will suffer problems of
one kind or another, either
illness or loss of money. If
you dream that your tongue
has grown small and wasted,
it signifies you will show
wisdom, prudence and
discretion for which you will
be respected by everyone.

WATCH To dream that your
watch has stopped can
indicate death, but to a
young man this means that
his love will end in nothing.

WATCHDOG To dream of a
dog signifies farms, servants
and possessions to come.

WATCHMAN You are
protected by silent love and
friendship near you.

WATER To dream that you
see a clear, calm river
indicates good. To dream you
see a rough river signifies
that you will be threatened
by someone powerful. To
dream of being in a rushing
river signifies the danger of
sickness or other problems.
To dream of swimming in a
large river signifies future
peril and danger. To dream
you see a clear river run by
your bedroom indicates the

arrival of a rich and generous person, who will do something to your advantage. But if the water is troubled, and spoils the furniture of the room, that signifies violence, quarrels and disorder in the family. To see a stream of clear water running by your house, you will be unexpectedly offered a promotion which will be financially advantageous, and in which post you will be able to help the oppressed. To dream you see a rough stream signifies loss and damage by fire, lawsuits and enemies.

It is a good sign to dream you see a pond full of clear water in a field because it signifies that you will thrive, and soon be married, if you are not so already, and will have good and obedient children. To dream you see a pond whose water overflows the banks predicts loss of money and death of relatives or loss of money. To dream that you see a small pond signifies that you will enjoy the love of a beautiful woman or a handsome man.

To dream that you are in a boat on a river, lake or pond of clear water is very good, and signifies joy, prosperity and success. If a sick person dreams that he sees a river or fountain of clear running water, that indicates his

recovery (but if the water is rough and muddy, it signifies the opposite).

If a young man dreams that he draws water out of a clear well, it signifies he will soon be married to an attractive girl; if the water is troubled, he will not be happily married and will fall ill. If he seems to give others clear well-water to drink he will enrich others, or afflict them if the water is troubled.

If anyone dreams that his river, pond or fountain is dried up, that signifies poverty or even death. If anyone dreams that he sees water flow from a place where it could not possibly come, that signifies problems. If he imagines that he has taken up some of that water, the mischief will be of a longer duration, according to the quantity he has drawn; if the water dries up, the problem will be solved.

To drink warm water means that someone who has been offended by your behaviour will try to harm you.

To see a bath signifies affliction or grief. If a person dreams he gets into a bath which is too hot or too cold, he will be troubled by his family; the problems will be greater if the water is very hot. To undress without getting into the bath indicates a minor problem. If the water is comfortably warm it is a good dream, indicating prosperity, pleasure, joy and health.

To carry water in a garment, broken vessel, cloth, or anything else which could not hold water denotes loss and damage, and that you will be deceived by people to whom you have trusted your money or property. If the water in these impossible vessels is not spilt, then you will keep your property, though with much difficulty. But if the water is spilt, you will lose it. If you think you have hidden the vessel and water underground, you will experience severe problems, be in danger of being made a public spectacle, and of dying a shameful death.

For a man to dream someone gives him a glass full of water, that signifies he will soon marry and have children. If the glass seems to be broken but the water unspilt, that signifies the death of his wife, but that his child will live, and vice versa.

If a minister dreams he gives his people clear water to drink, it signifies that he will teach them the word of God faithfully, and will be instrumental in their salvation; if the water is troubled, he will teach them heretical and false doctrine. If anyone dreams that he has spilt water in his house, that denotes care and problems according to the quantity of water.

To dream you are drinking water denotes great trouble and adversity; in trade, loss of business and being arrested; to the lover it shows your sweet-heart is false, prefers another, and will never marry you.

WATER CARRIER To dream of a water carrier signifies increases in money.

WATER LILY Your wish is out of reach; do not try to gain it in case you suffer further loss.

WATER WHEEL To see a water wheel working indicates additional work will bring you new friends and more money.

WATERCRESS Danger in love affairs, especially if you pick the plants from the water.

WATERFALL An invitation to a place of amusement. You are observed and gossiped about.

WATERMILL To dream of being in a watermill is a favourable omen. To the tradesman it denotes great increase of business; to the farmer, abundant crops; in love, success and a rich sweetheart and a happy marriage.

WAVE To dream of waves foretells that you must be prepared to fight as luck will not come your way. You will succeed only by your own efforts.

WAYFARER To dream of meeting a wayfarer on a lonely path is a sign of a new friend.

WAX Neither borrow nor lend money. You will have occasion to do both shortly. Try to avoid it.

WEASEL To dream of a weasel means you must beware of those who would appear to befriend you without reason.

WEATHER VANE An excellent omen for trade, but not for love affairs.

WEATHERCOCK Change, uncertainty and vexations are on the horizon.

WEAVING A wedding dress will soon be made for you. Good news will be received in a letter.

WEB Travel and gratified wishes. A sign of wealth.

WEDDING If a man dreams he is married to an ugly woman, that signifies great discontent; if to a handsome woman, that denotes joy and profit. For the sick to dream they are married or celebrate their wedding is not a good omen.

To dream of being married, or of a wedding, is a very unfavourable dream especially for lovers. It denotes the death of a near friend or relation, or loss of property and severe disappointments. It is unlucky for a girl to dream of a wedding. She will remain single for most of her life, and will have reason to distrust the male sex. To a married person the dream gives warning of sickness.

WEDDING RING For a woman to dream that she has lost her wedding ring signifies that she does not have much love for her husband. But if she dreams that she has found it again, it is a sign that her love is not wholly lost.

WEED To dream that you are weeding a garden is a sign that your children will cause you much trouble and anxiety. However fond of ease you may be, you must become wise enough to face continual exertion cheerfully because your work will never be completed. To see weeds growing in profusion is indicative of blighted hopes.

WEEPING To dream you weep and grieve whether for a lost friend or for any reason signifies joy for a good action you will perform. You are on the eve of hearing something which will excite in you the deepest joy.

WEIGHING To dream of weighing anything in scales denotes that you will soon experience the truth of the remark that it is better to have a grain of fortune than a pound of wisdom.

WELL If a young man dreams he draws water out of a clear well, it signifies he will soon be married to a beautiful girl; if the water is troubled, he will be disturbed by her and suddenly fall sick. If he seems to give others clear well-water to drink, he will enrich others by this girl's means or if the water is troubled he will harm them. To dream you cleanse a well or fall into it signifies injury.

The person who dreams of a well will either be renowned for learning and wisdom or will marry someone who will gain fame through the same acquirements.

WEST To dream of places in the far west, or on the west side, signifies a coming journey.

WHALE Misunderstandings will be cleared up in time. A delayed wedding is indicated.

WHARF Separation from loved ones.

WHEAT To dream you see the land sown with wheat signifies money and profit with difficulty and hard work. To dream you see or are walking in a field of wheat is a very favourable omen, and denotes great prosperity and riches; in love, it predicts a completion of your dearest wishes, and foretells much happiness with fine children, when you marry; if you have a lawsuit you will gain it, and you will be successful in all your undertakings.

WHEEL To dream you see a wheel come off a carriage, or coming off, is a warning that if you have arranged for a railway journey you ought to postpone it, for to you, at least, it will result in mishap.

WHEELBARROW A dream of pushing a wheelbarrow means that you will marry soon and have a considerable family, and that you will gladly work long hours for the sake of your children.

WHIPPING To dream that you whip someone is good. To dream you are whipped by the gods or the dead is not good. It is always good to be whipped with rods, or with the hand, for it signifies profit. But with leather, reeds or cudgels. It indicates evil.

If you dream that your hips are black and blue with whipping, that indicates a serious situation for you in a short time – or at least that you will hate your spouse and have several grievances.

WHIRLPOOL Advice will be given to you which is well worth following. An inheritance may be yours in the future.

WHIRLWIND A dream in which a whirlwind appears warns you to beware of dangerous reports.

WHISKY This is a foreboding of bad times; it signifies severe difficulties.

WHISPERING To hear whispering in a dream means that many people are talking ill of you, and that on consideration of your conduct you will find that they are not doing so quite without reason.

WHIST To dream of playing the game means a better position in life.

WHISTLE To hear a whistle indicates that scandal is being spread about you; to dream that you are whistling merrily indicates sad news coming.

WHITE Always a favourable colour, especially in matters concerning other people – such as public affairs.

WHITEWASH Introductions in gay company.

WIDOW To dream that you are a widow is a sign that there is a rival striving to gain your affections. The single man who dreams that he has married a widow will receive more than one disappointment in love.

WIDOWER The girl who dreams that she has married, or is about to marry a widower will give her love to the wrong man, and only find out her mistake when it is too late. If a man dreams that he is a widower it is a sign that his wife will outlive him by many years. A man dreaming of a widower may safely infer that he is about – if a husband – to be deserted by his wife, and if single, that the young woman he is going out with is going to play him false.

WIFE To dream you hear your wife scold signifies great torment. You will be separated from her by death or quarrelling and live to regret the day you met. If a man dreams he sees his wife married to another, it denotes change of affairs or condition.

WIG Two proposals soon to come. The darker man loves you best.

WIGWAM You will receive a costly gift.

WILDERNESS A festive occasion in your home. Keep to old friends.

WILL To dream of making a will is one of the most reliable indications that you are destined to have a long, contented and prosperous life. For a pregnant woman to dream that she has made her will is unfortunate as it denotes a difficult labour.

WILLOW Do not trust a new acquaintance. Good news will soon arrive of someone dear to you.

WINCH A disappointment, but unexpected good news will follow.

WIND To dream that you are out in a strong breeze is a sign that you will have a hard battle to fight in life. But providing you can endure and conquer, ease and happiness will follow. When the wind blows high it signifies that you have to encounter several perils, but that you are destined to emerge safely from them all.

WIND INSTRUMENT To dream of any instrument you can blow signifies trouble, with the exception of the bagpipe and reed.

WINDMILL Gives promise of a short holiday in a strange district or a change of home.

WINDOW To dream you see the windows at the front of the house destroyed by fire signifies the death of brothers; if they are those at the back of the house, it means the death of a sister. To dream of looking out of a window means that you will shortly travel through many foreign countries, get acquainted with many strange faces, and return home without having contracted even the ghost of an attachment for anyone.

WINE To dream that you are drinking wine means that you are about to suffer in health from too eagerly pursuing your duty, but that the injury will not be permanent.

WINGS A bad dream; you will lose money.

WINK To wink at someone of the opposite sex indicates that your love affairs will be disastrous unless you respect your partner's wishes.

WINTER To dream of a wintry scene with snow on the ground is an omen of prosperity, but to dream of summer in winter is the reverse.

WIRELESS Unexpected good news about money will come soon.

WISHING WELL Two admirers are seeking your company. Choose carefully.

WITCH To dream of a witch foretells that you will leave your home and live among strangers; if the witch attempts to injure you it denotes that you will be dependent upon strangers for your support.

WITNESS To dream of being a witness in court is a warning to be on your guard against false accusations which will be made against you.

WIZARD Family prosperity and contentment.

WOLF The wolf signifies an avaricious, cruel and disloyal person. If you dream you have overcome a wolf, you will conquer an enemy with the same qualities. And on the contrary, if you are bitten by the wolf, you will be injured in some way by a cruel and disloyal enemy. To dream you have the head of a wolf is a good sign as it means you will achieve your ambitions. To dream you see many wolves signifies that you will be robbed.

WOMAN A dream in which an old woman figures largely is good. It means safety, prosperity and comfort. To dream of a young woman means much the same thing, but these good features will be combined with not a few worries and distractions. Should a man dream of parting from a young woman it signifies that he will fall in love.

WOOD To dream you are cutting or chopping wood shows that you will be happy in your family, and become rich and respectable in life. To dream you are carrying wood on your back shows that you will rise to affluence by your hard work, but that your partner will be bad tempered and your children unloving. If you dream you are walking in an extensive wood, it denotes that you will be married several times. To dream of travelling through a wood and striking the briars and the bushes as you pass is an evil sign for it means many troubles and hindrances in important affairs.

WOOD PIGEONS To dream of these birds signifies the dreamer keeps company with wild and dissolute women.

WOODCUTTER Your efforts will not result in much profit.

WOOL To dream you are buying and selling wool denotes prosperity and great affluence by means of industry and trade.

WORKING To dream of being hard at work anywhere or at anything means that you are in danger of losing your present job and you should take the utmost care to please your employer, for his attitude towards you is just now none of the best.

WORKMAN To dream of a workman signifies that your enterprises will bring great profit.

WORKSHOP To dream of a workshop signifies good fortune.

WORMS To dream of earthworms signifies enemies that try to ruin you. To dream that you vomit long worms or see them on your feet signifies that you will discover your enemies and will overcome them. Little worms signify care and anger and often displeasure which you will have because of your wife or family.

WORRY To dream you are worried and unsettled in your thoughts signifies joy.

WORSHIP To dream you worship God signifies joy.

WOUND If anyone dreams that he has been stabbed with a sword in the front of his body and draws blood, the injured person will receive an extraordinary kindness from the attacker; if blood is not spilled, the advantage will be less. If anyone dreams that he is fatally wounded with a sword, that is a sign that he will receive several courtesies and good turns from the person who wounded him. If anyone has a wound which he dreams is healed, he will boast of his valour and gain honour by it in public opinion. To dream of being wounded in the palm of the right hand signifies debt or war. To dream of wounds in the stomach foretells joy to young people.

WREATH To dream of a wreath foretells a wedding and much happiness for the dreamer.

WRECK Trouble is threatened to your home or business.

WREN To dream of this pretty bird denotes great happiness and content through life; to the lover it is particularly favourable; it shows your sweetheart is kind and amiable, much attached to you, and one who will make you very happy.

WRESTLING To dream you wrestle with a stranger signifies danger of sickness. To wrestle with a child and throw him on the ground signifies that you will lose a child by death, while to be beaten by the child foretells mockery and sickness. To dream you see a little child wrestle with a man is good, for the child will do greater things than you imagine. But if you wrestle or fight with a champion, this is not good. To dream you wrestle with death indicates sickness. A woman who dreams she wrestles with her husband will bring sorrow into the family. Wrestling in a dream with death denotes a long sickness and lawsuits.

WRINKLES Compliments and social pleasures will soon come.

WRISTS To dream that your wrists are broken is very good. It foretells that you will marry your present lover and be happy.

WRITING To dream you write to your friends signifies good news. To dream you write on paper signifies accusation. To dream of writing with the left hand if you are right-handed means you will disgrace someone through a secret deceit. To dream of writing a letter means that a friend from whom you have been separated for a long time, and whose whereabouts you do not know, is about to call on you and to bring good news about himself.

WRY NECK To dream your neck is turned so that you look backwards warns you not to go out of the country or engage in new business in case they turn out badly. Anyone in a distant country will return home.

X-RAY A mysterious occurrence will cause you to change a decision.

XYLOPHONE Hearing a xylophone foretells accidents in the home.

YACHT The person who dreams of sailing on a yacht will bring trouble on his or her own head through being too much inclined to put business before pleasure. To dream of watching a yacht sailing is a dream of change in which there will be a considerable element of risk.

YANKEE You will renew a friendship with one from whom you have been long parted.

YARD News of an engagement among your friends will soon be heard. The wedding will bring you a new admirer.

YARN Brings promise of a busy but happy life. The girl who dreams she is using yarn will marry a working class man who will prove to be a much better husband than many far above him in the social scale. To dream of yarn, of whatever type, is a good omen, meaning that you will have a long life and that your experience will be mainly pleasant, even if somewhat monotonous.

YAWN To dream that you yawn is a sign that you will one day grow tired of your present occupation and go abroad to seek your fortune. You will have to show more energy in order to succeed.

YEARNING To dream of a strong feeling of longing means that you will be indifferent where you would like to be kind.

YEAST Money which has been accumulated by thrift will be left to you under strange conditions.

YELL To dream of hideous yells and noises is a sign of peace after strife. An introduction will alter your plans.

YELLOW You should not expect any changes in your affairs for some time to come.

YEW To have a yew tree as a prominent feature in a dream points to the approaching loss of friends, and also to the probable loss of money.

YIELDING To dream of yielding to persuasive words is a warning against pride; do not believe flatterers.

YODEL To hear yodelling indicates happy marriage. To yodel yourself means that you may be too free with your sexual favours.

YOKE To dream of a yoke is unfavourable, unless it is broken, then it denotes a rising above your present situation. For a young woman to dream of seeing a yoke of oxen ploughing is a sign that she will marry a young man who, though poor, will make her a good husband. However circumstances will require her to work at some daily employment that they may together better their condition.

YOLK To beat egg yolks in a dream is a good sign of money gained in a speculation or a lottery.

YORKSHIRE PUDDING To dream of eating Yorkshire pudding means that, though at present you are much taken up with the idea of good living, you will shortly meet one who will alter the current of your thoughts and convince you that it is love after all that makes for the happiness of life.

YOUNG To dream that you have become young again is a favourable omen, but the change for the better will not last long.

YUCCA Fruitful love affairs.

YULE LOG Good friends and contentment.

YULE TIDE A hasty wooing from a new admirer will end happily; business and health matters will improve around you.

ZEBRA To dream of a zebra is a sign that you will strive for a long time to gain something on which you have set your heart, and will be disappointed when you finally reach your goal.

ZEPPELIN A dream signifying an ambition far beyond your reach.

ZIG-ZAG This means many changes of mind and mood. Do not hesitate too long.

ZINC To dream that you see a quantity of zinc is a sign that you will emigrate to a foreign country before many years are over. You will have inducements offered to you to join some of your old friends who have emigrated before you.

ZIP If a zip will not close, you will experience an embarrassing circumstance. If it does close, you will maintain your decorum despite provocation.

ZITHER Your friends will bring you peace of mind.

ZOO To dream that you pay a visit to a zoo is a sign of happy, prosperous and eventful times.

ZULU To see Zulu natives surrounding you in a dream is a sign of release from danger that has threatened your health and happiness.